Disorder in the Court

Trials and Sexual Conflict at the Turn of the Century

Edited by

George Robb
Associate Professor of History
William Paterson University
New Jersey

and

Nancy Erber
Associate Professor
LaGuardia Community College
City University of New York

First published 1999 by
MACMILLAN PRESS LTD
Houndmills, Basingstoke, Hampshire RG21 6XS
and London
Companies and representatives
throughout the world

ISBN 0–333–72562–X

A catalogue record for this book is available from the British Library.

This book is printed on paper suitable for recycling and made from fully managed and sustained forest sources.

10 9 8 7 6 5 4 3 2 1
08 07 06 05 04 03 02 01 00 99

Printed and bound in Great Britain by
Antony Rowe Ltd, Chippenham, Wiltshire

Contents

Notes on Contributors

Nicole Albert recently completed her thesis at the University of Paris, IV – Sorbonne on "Sapphism and Decadence in Fin-de-Siècle European Art and Literature." In 1995 she edited the collection *Chemin des dames* for the GKC Press and has published several articles on lesbian history.

Antoinette Burton teaches in the History Department and the Women's Studies Program at Johns Hopkins University. She is the author of *Burdens of History: British Feminists, Indian Women and Imperial Culture, 1865–1915* (1994) and *At the Heart of the Empire: Indians and the Colonial Encounter in Late-Victorian Britain* (1997). She is currently at work on a project about Indian women and the historical imagination.

Julie English Early is Associate Professor of English at the University of Alabama in Huntsville. She has published numerous articles on Victorian ethnography, travel writing, and criminality, including the recent "Technology, Modernity, and 'The Little Man,'" in *Victorian Studies*. She is currently working on a book about the literature and culture of Edwardian London.

Nancy Erber is an Associate Professor of English as a Second Language at LaGuardia Community College, City University of New York. A French literary scholar, she is the author of the recent article "The French Trials of Oscar Wilde," published in *The Journal of the History of Sexuality*. She is currently working on a book about homosexuality and the arts in turn-of-the-century France.

Ginger Frost teaches British history at Samford University in Birmingham, Alabama. She is the author of *Promises Broken: Courtship, Class and Gender in Victorian England* (1995). She is now at work on a study of cohabitation in nineteenth-century England.

Annalee Golz teaches Canadian history at the University of Victoria and has recently completed her dissertation, "The Historical Relationship between Wife Battering and Wife Murder in Ontario, 1830–1920," at Queen's University. Golz has published several articles on the history of domestic violence.

Ann Sumner Holmes is the Assistant Dean of the Honors College at Louisiana State University. A legal scholar, Holmes has published articles on divorce and child custody cases in Victorian England. She is the co-editor, with Claudia Nelson, of the anthology *Maternal Instincts: Visions of Motherhood and Sexuality in Britain, 1875–1925* (Macmillan, 1997).

Morris Kaplan has recently returned to teaching after practicing criminal law in New York City for fifteen years. He is a member of the Philosophy Department at Purchase College – the State University of New York, and his book, *Sexual Justice: Democratic Citizenship and the Politics of Desire*, was published in 1997.

William Peniston is the Librarian of the Newark Museum. He has just completed his dissertation on homosexuality in the French Third Republic at the University of Rochester. His article, "Love and Death in Gay Paris," appears in the collection *Homosexuality in Modern France* (1996).

George Robb teaches British History at William Paterson University in New Jersey. He is the author of *White-Collar Crime in Modern England: Financial Fraud and Business Morality, 1845–1929* (1992). He is presently working on a history of spousal murder in Victorian England.

Gail Savage teaches History at St. Mary's College of Maryland. She is the author of a book on the British Civil Service and social reform, *The Social Construction of Expertise* (1998). She is currently writing a history of the Victorian Divorce Court and divorce law reform.

1 Introduction

Nancy Erber and George Robb

This collection of essays examines the role of the state in regulating sexual morality at the turn of the century in France, England, and the British Empire (India and Canada). It focuses on trials, both well-known and obscure, and explores in detail how the disputes were played out in the courtrooms and newspapers of the time. While the cases range from murder investigations to divorce suits to charges of public indecency, all are rooted in differing ideologies of gender and sexuality and are inflected by the cultural and class-specific particularitics of their participants. The conflicts documented and analyzed in this collection are symptomatic of changing definitions of gender roles, sexual propriety, and deviance. They shed light on often unexpressed fundamental assumptions of the criminal justice system regarding gender, and thus provide a snapshot of critical moments of social contestation during the era that witnessed the emergence of the New Woman, the New Man, and the Third Sex as social constructs.

As we rapidly approach the end of our own century and the beginning of a new millennium, interest in the 1890s and early 1900s has increased in both scholarly and popular discourse.[1] The men and women who saw out the nineteenth century and ushered in the twentieth certainly believed that theirs was a unique and important watershed in human history. While some viewed it as an age of unlimited prosperity and expansion and called it *La Belle Epoque* or the Gilded Age, many others saw instead a dark period of decline and decadence, the *Fin-de-Siècle*. Fears of national and "racial" degeneration preoccupied Western society during the late nineteenth and early twentieth centuries. A flagging industrial sector, falling birthrates, urban poverty and crime, and venereal disease were all seen as obvious manifestations of racial decay.[2] In this climate of economic uncertainty and social malaise, traditional bourgeois values of work, thrift and propriety were offered as the surest antidote to degeneration. The need for social stability, law, order, and normality never seemed greater.

The period 1880–1914 was therefore one in which defining categories such as "normal" and "abnormal" became a central activity and preoccupation in the realms of science and law.[3] In addition, manners and mores that had mainly been regulated by the family, community, or Church were increasingly considered matters for public scrutiny. As Kali Israel argued in a recent article, "throughout the late nineteenth century a series of highly mediated but spectacularly detailed scandals, *causes célèbres*, and exposés permitted diverse constituencies to engage in struggles over the construction of meaningful stories about sexual danger and sexual truths."[4] Among the more notorious cases from England and France, were the "Maiden Tribute of Modern Babylon" scandal, the Cleveland Street Affair, the trials of Oscar Wilde, and divorce cases involving society figures or politicians like Lady Colin Campbell, Lord Russell, Charles Dilke, and Charles Stewart Parnell. There was also the murder trial of Henriette Caillaux, prosecutions of aristocrats like the Count de Germiny and the Baron d'Adelsward-Fersen for homosexual acts, and the trials of Naturalist and Decadent writers for publishing obscene literature.[5] A number of these cases, and others like them, will be treated in this volume.

While historians have discounted Michel Foucault's overly finite dating of the birth of the modern psychological category of the homosexual to this period and have argued convincingly that homosexual behaviors and communities in Western Europe existed in earlier centuries, the turn-of-the-century obsession with sexual normality and perversion is well documented and indisputable. The concern expressed in medical and popular literature over proper masculine and feminine roles makes it clear that the heterosexual/homosexual distinction constitutes one of the "great divides" in the evolution of late nineteenth-century Western European thought.[6] For this reason, the collection includes cases which speak to both sides of this "divide." Many, in fact, attest to the interdependency and indeterminacy of that particular categoric imperative.

As the essays reveal, social and sexual behavior are regulated simultaneously by the state and the community, the one chiefly through legislation and the courts, the other mainly by the force of public opinion. Each of the cases in this collection demonstrates the interplay of the two realms. Contributors have focused on two areas of gendered behavior – the institution of marriage on the one hand and the public expression of deviant (mainly homosexual) identities and behaviors on the other. Essays which treat spousal conflicts include those by Gail Savage, Annalee Golz, Julie Early, Ann Holmes, Ginger Frost, George Robb, and Antoinette Burton. Cases involving homosexual acts and identities are analyzed by William Peniston, Nancy Erber, Nicole Albert, and Morris Kaplan. These once-scandalous cases challenged commonly held views of the sanctity of marriage and the implacability of gender differences – two notions deemed essential to social stability by conservative ideologues and many judges of the time. Nonetheless, the neat mapping of essays into one subject area ("Marital Conflict") or another ("Homosexuality") is in the end a pointless task since each case is rich in multiple contents and contradictions demonstrating, as Kaplan observes, the "strange combination of indeterminacy and overdetermination that attends the use of law to control personal lives."

Legal proceedings have frequently been overlooked in the study of past sexual behavior and attitudes and the shifting social meanings associated with them, but now social and gender historians have recognized that legal documents, police archives and court records are rich sources for broadening our understanding of both the legal regulatory process and the complexities of social/sexual relations. This volume adds to a growing literature concerned with the judicial contestation of sexual matters, including works such as Ed Cohen's *Talk on the Wilde Side*, Ruth Harris's *Murders and Madness*, Joëlle Guillais' *Crimes of Passion*, Karen Dubinsky's *Improper Advances*, and Angus McLaren's *Trials of Masculinity*.[7] Our collection, however, differs in several important respects from these works and others like them. We have not focused on a single famous trial or even a single type of sexual crime/conflict. Rather, the collection examines a number of different trials, some famous, others not, that deal with numerous kinds of sexual issues. Neither does the collection reflect only one scholarly discipline, as the contributors include historians, literary scholars, and philosophers.

In treating cases from France and England, as well as British North America and India, we are purposely departing from the usual practice of geographical isolation that has tended to study the sexual practices and legal traditions of a single nation in isolation. We do not deny important differences in British and French society, but focussing merely on difference obscures the more important sexual assumptions and behaviors that the societies of Western Europe and North America shared at the turn of the century. Both France and England encountered cultural anxieties and fears of degeneration that stemmed in part from similar experiences of industrial and imperial competition with Germany and the United States, and declining birth rates. Both nations also experienced common debates over the "New Woman," common bourgeois criticisms of "decadent" art and literature, and common fears that homosexuality posed a new and serious threat to the social/political order. Non-western societies, however, obviously had different sexual mores and different historical experiences. Yet, in an age of imperialism, there were many opportunities for comparison and conflict.

Antoinette Burton's article on child-marriage in India points out the bitter struggles that often ensued when Western values and laws confronted alien sexual customs.

The individual essays elucidate the differences in French and British law (for example, concerning homosexuality) as well as the very real differences in the operation of each nation's judicial system. In general, the British placed a greater burden of proof on the state for demonstrating guilt, which resulted in lower conviction rates than in France. Some historians would argue that the trial itself in France was a mere formality, following an elaborate and lengthy pre-trial process in which an examining magistrate questioned the accused, interviewed witnesses and assembled evidence. The French legal system was based more on an "inquisitorial" model, the English on an "accusatorial" one.[8]

While some observers have characterized the *fin-de-siècle* as the "Age of Opulence" or "Age of Anxiety," it could just as plausibly be labeled the "Age of the Trial." The trial can clearly be seen as a defining moment of modern culture. It was certainly viewed as pivotal by contemporaries whose bitter tug-of-war over Captain Dreyfus or pillorying of Oscar Wilde put their stamp on an era.[9] Especially sensational trials could keep a nation spellbound for weeks or even months, a phenomenon all too familiar today in the age of Court TV, and the trials of O.J. Simpson, and Louise Woodward. Verdicts might divide a nation then as now, often leading to popular demonstrations and petition drives for and against the accused. Prosecutions of sex crimes especially forced society to clarify the boundaries between normal and deviant behavior, while the issues raised by sexual/marital disputes evoked strong feelings and elicited complicated, often emotional, responses. As might be expected, this often led to high drama.

The complexity of turn-of-the-century trials is illustrated by the Austenesque twists and turns of Emily Hall's suit (often known as the Clitheroe case) analyzed by Ginger Frost, whose essay documents the waning influence of coverture and the notion of wife as property while exploring the promises and disappointments of middle-class marriage and the subtle class gradations of the English provinces. Ann Holmes's essay, centered on a spouse's accusation of homosexual infidelity, explores the many ramifications of Lady Russell's determined pursuit of a divorce, which resulted in related suits for libel and bigamy and pitted her and Earl Russell against the matrimonial laws of the 1890s as well as the unwritten social codes of the Edwardian aristocratic establishment. Nicole Albert examines attempts at literary censorship of lesbian-themed novels in *belle époque* France and a parallel effusion of lesbian imagery in popular culture. As she points out, these trials were paradoxically initiated not to make lesbianism publicly anathema but to make it publicly invisible. George Robb and Julie Early view the Victorian sexual double standard through the lens of two famous poisoning cases and uncover not only the extraordinary latitude given judges in their oral summations and instructions to juries, but also the power of public intervention to influence investigations and trials.

Without a doubt, police and court records offer a valuable means to probe and reconstruct the often obscure and conflictual dimensions of gender and sexuality in an age of bourgeois reticence. Sherlock Holmes, the great fictional detective of the *fin-de-siècle*, speculates in "A Case of Identity" that if one could "gently remove the roofs, and peep in at the queer things that are going on . . . it would make all fiction . . . stale and unprofitable."[10] The criminal cases presented in this book provide just such a vantage point. William Peniston's essay gives a glimpse into the world of covert homosexual encounters, police harassment, and repression in France's Third Republic. Likewise, the testimony of John Saul, whom Morris Kaplan sees as a modern homosexual, recovers a sense of the everyday life of a turn-of-the-century male sex worker in London. Annalee Golz assesses the links between domestic violence and spousal murder in Ontario and documents widely disparate sentencing patterns and conviction rates for male and female offenders. Gail Savage's essay examines the transcript testimony of several cases of matrimonial assault in 1890s England, while Nancy Erber's essay explores the public expressions of distaste, denial, and glee which greeted the police raid on a homosexual aristocrat's artistic salon in Paris in 1903. Clearly, the courtroom dramas of sex trials made seemingly private worlds – of the Victorian home, the *belle époque* drawing room and boudoir, the concierge's lodge or workers' quarters – shockingly public.

Since all too frequently court and police archives remain one of the few arenas in which the voices and experiences of working-class men and women are consistently present, the importance of bringing such records to light is demonstrated by several essays in this collection. One such as Savage's, provides a close reading of accounts of working-class marital conflicts, given in spouses' and neighbors' testimony in England's magistrate courts. The lower-class affiliation of plaintiff, defendant, or victim provides an important analytic dimension in several other essays as well, including those by Golz, Early, Peniston, and Kaplan.

The collection's focus on investigative and judicial procedures exposes the roles of ordinary and special police forces in big cities at the turn of the century, such as Paris's *brigade des moeurs* (Peniston), and explores the significance of para-judicial mechanisms such as coroners' inquests (Golz), local magistrates' courts (Savage), and the British House of Lords (Holmes). The emergence of "scientific" methods of criminology and the importance of expert, chiefly medical, testimony are documented in the poisoning trial of Florence Maybrick, known as the "English Dreyfus Case," (Robb) and the morals charges in the "Satanic Masses Affair" (Erber).[11]

Along with the catchy sobriquets they invented, editorial writers and advocates on all sides often attributed national and racial significance to these cases. For instance, the case analyzed by Burton played a key role in the contemporary debate over Indian child marriage. Memorialized in a poem by Rudyard Kipling, the refusal of the child-bride Rukhmabai to cohabit with her husband, and the subsequent debates by opponents and advocates in the English and Indian press point to larger social questions of race, empire, and "the woman question." Golz examines the temperance issue in Canada and the rhetorical association of male intemperance with loss of masculinity and the decline of national vigor, and she demonstrates how murder trials were constructed as "temperance lectures" or temperance dramas. Erber examines the association of theories of national decline and racial degeneration in France with expectations of appropriately gendered behavior. Robb and Early highlight the anti-Americanism which became part of the public agitation around two separate murder trials in England.

In addition to trial records, the essays in this volume examine the public perception of the event through contemporary newspaper coverage and popular literature. This period in modern history is marked by significant technological improvements in paper-making and printing and the relaxation of many legal restrictions (in France) on printing, publication, and the daily press. As a result, the second half of the nineteenth century saw the rise of mass circulation newspapers which competed for readership by focusing on sensational stories of crime, scandal, and sex.[12] Reportage of criminal trials, especially those involving sexual indiscretions, shocked, titillated, and entertained the public. In addition to catering to mass voyeurism, newspapers gave a larger audience than ever before possible a sense of active participation in scandalous trials through letters-to-the-editor columns. Correspondents could play the role of prosecutor, fulminating against the accused and the vices that threatened society, or they could act as armchair detectives, offering their own ingenious theories and interpretations of evidence.

Some criticized the press for its zeal in publicizing vice and giving currency to the sexual peccadilloes of high society. Newspapers' excesses in covering sexual matters were often excused by their editors, who cited the overriding hygienic value of such public exposure. The coverage reinforced a shared standard of "normal" behavior among its readership by implicitly presenting models of correct behavior for men and women, for spouses, parents and children, contrary to the "bad" examples of those who violated the codes. Crime reports and trial coverage were also motivated by publishers' stakes in competing social agendas and political affiliations. At times, news events were exploited to teach a particular moral or political lesson, to mock the elite or condemn the proletariat. Defendants or their advocates used the press too as an outlet to garner sympathy and tell their side of the story, as the battling spouses considered in Frost's essay and the unwilling bride in Burton's did.

The element of spectacle was undeniably present in trials. In an age of melodrama, newspaper accounts and courtroom behavior often mimicked the language and style of the theater. At times, the very architecture of the courtroom was reminiscent of a theater with its stage and audience, and the accused, witnesses, judge, and lawyers were all given opportunities to enact their version of events from specially constructed, and usually elevated, platforms – "on the bench" or "in the dock."[13] In England tickets were issued for spectators at controversial trials, and demand could be fierce as at Crippen's murder trial in 1910, where four thousand applications for tickets were received for a courtroom that could only "seat" seventy-five.[14] Among many in attendance were Winston Churchill, Sir Arthur Conan Doyle, W.S. Gilbert, and one of the most luminous of the London theater beauties, Phyllis Dare, who because of the overcrowded courtroom was honored with a seat next to the judge on the bench. Although the *Times* sputtered its outrage that "a Criminal Court is not a show room, nor is such a trial of the nature of a matinee," the public continued to regard trials as popular entertainments.[15] Courtroom audiences responded to the action before them as they would to a play: laughing at jokes, gasping at unexpected revelations, and applauding at the end. Like melodramas, sex trials taught moral lessons and presented familiar tableaus of sin, redemption, and punishment.

The self-consciously dramatic structuring of legal proceedings is paralleled by another contemporary phenomenon: the cross-fertilization of literature and criminology. Criminal trials furnished dramatists and novelists with material while doctors, penologists, and other commentators on social issues mined literature for apt examples of their theses.[16] Several of the plaintiffs and defendants in this volume have had their stories retold in ballads or transposed into the plots of novels and plays;

some were reincarnated as the heroes of pornographic literature ("Confessions of a Mary-Anne," "Sinful Ruttings of Baron Jacques"). All of this interest attests to the importance of exposition at the turn of the century, and the many layers and levels of discourse (trial testimony, memoir, confession, speech, letter-to-the-editor, novel, medical report) reveal the enhanced access to public speech by diverse constituencies and disparate readers.

Although narrative competition waxed intense, there remained a strong, and typically Victorian, desire for a single truth or meaning. This phenomenon can even be summarized by the public reception of a celebrated genre painting at the century's end. W.F. Yeames's *Defendant and Counsel* caused a sensation when it was first exhibited at the British Royal Academy's summer show in 1895. Yet another example of the fascination with trials, the painting (reproduced on the cover) depicts a pretty young woman in velvet and furs sitting in a solicitor's office and being questioned by her counsel in wigs and gowns. Their tense expressions and the worried look on her face all suggest a moment of high courtroom drama. *Defendant and Counsel* seems to be telling an exciting story, but no one was quite sure what story. What crime had this lady committed, or been accused of? No doubt it was something sensational, even scandalous. Had she poisoned her faithless lover? Or was she the defendant in a divorce suit, charged with adultery? Yeames received many questioning letters regarding the picture, one female correspondent going so far as to admit that the mystery was keeping her awake at night. Indeed, the picture was so obscure in its narrative implications that *Cassel's Magazine* offered a prize for the best explanation of it, and docents at the Bristol Art Gallery, which later acquired the work, invented stories to satisfy curious patrons.[17] This need "to know the story" likewise filled the courtrooms of England and France, sold millions of newspapers, and fueled debates among jurists, politicians, doctors, and others as to what was appropriate behavior for women and men at the dawn of a new century. These struggles over meaning speak to a "disturbed cultural moment" and rend the façade of bourgeois sexual orthodoxy.

NOTES

1. Popular fascination with this period can be gauged through such diverse media as Broadway plays (*Jeckyl and Hyde*, *Ragtime*), films (*The Age of*

Innocence, *Wings of the Dove*), and best-selling novels like Caleb Carr's *The Alienist*. The serious study of the *fin-de-siècle* began in earnest during the 1980s, with works such as Carl Schorske, *Fin-de-Siècle Vienna: Politics and Culture* (New York: Alfred A. Knopf, 1980) and Eugen Weber, *France: Fin de Siècle* (Cambridge, Mass.: Harvard University Press, 1986), and scholarly publications on this period have continued unabated. For further references, see notes below.

2. The earliest fears of degeneration were expressed by B.A. Morel, *Traité des dégénerescences physiques, intellectuelles et morales* (Paris, 1857), though concern did not become widespread until the 1880s. See, for example, Charles Féré, *Dégénerescence et Criminalité* (Paris, 1888); Max Nordau, *Degeneration* (London and Paris, 1895); Valentin Magnan and Paul-Maurice LeGrain, *Les Dégenérés* (Paris, 1895); Eugene S. Talbot, *Degeneracy: Its Causes, Signs and Results* (London, 1898), and H. Havelock Ellis, *The Problem of Race Regeneration* (London, 1911). Among the considerable recent literature on the history of degenerationist thought, see Robert Nye, *Crime, Madness and Politics in Modern France: The Medical Concept of National Decline* (Princeton: Princeton University Press, 1984); J. Edward Chamberlin and Sander Gilman, eds., *Degeneration: The Dark Side of Progress* (New York: Columbia University Press, 1985), and Daniel Pick, *Faces of Degeneration* (Cambridge: Cambridge University Press, 1989).
3. Attempts to label, categorize, and therefore control "deviant" behavior while simultaneously promoting normality are documented in numerous recent studies, including George L. Mosse, *Nationalism and Sexuality: Respectability and Abnormal Sexuality in Modern Europe* (New York: Fertig, 1985); Carroll Smith-Rosenberg, *Disorderly Conduct: Visions of Gender in Victorian America* (New York: Alfred A. Knopf, 1985); Elaine Showalter, *The Female Malady: Women, Madness, and English Culture, 1830–1980* (New York: Pantheon, 1985); Frank Mort, *Dangerous Sexualities: Medico-Moral Politics in England Since 1830* (London: Routledge and Kegan Paul, 1987); Anneliese Mauge, *L'identité Masculine en Crise au Tournant du Siècle, 1871–1914* (Paris: Rivages, 1987); Cynthia Russett, *Sexual Science: The Victorian Construction of Womanhood* (Cambridge, Mass.: Harvard University Press, 1989); Lawrence Birken, *Consuming Desires: Sexual Science and the Emergence of a Culture of Abundance, 1871–1914* (Ithaca: Cornell University Press, 1989); Lesley A. Hall, *Hidden Anxieties: Male Sexuality, 1900–1950* (London: Polity Press, 1991), and Jonathan Ned Katz, *The Invention of Heterosexuality* (New York: Dutton, 1995).
4. Kali Israel, "French Vices and British Liberties: Gender, Class and Narrative Competition in a Late Victorian Sex Scandal," *Social History* 22 (January 1997), 1.
5. For general discussions of turn-of-the-century sex scandals and sexual narratives, see Judith Walkowitz, *City of Dreadful Delight: Narratives of Sexual Danger in Late-Victorian Britain* (Chicago: University of Chicago Press, 1992); Jeffrey Weeks, *Sex, Politics, and Society: The Regulation of Sexuality Since 1800* (New York: Longman, 1981), and Lucy Bland, *Banishing the Beast: English Feminism and Sexual Morality, 1885–1914* (Penguin Books, 1995). For particular cases not included in this collection,

see G.H. Fleming, *Victorian "Sex Goddess": Lady Colin Campbell and the Sensational Divorce Case of 1886* (Oxford: Oxford University Press, 1990), and Edward Berenson, *The Trial of Madame Caillaux* (Berkeley: University of California Press, 1992). For a discussion of social purity movements and French censorship, see Annie Stora-Lamarre, *L'Enfer de la Troisième République: censeurs et pornographes, 1880–1914* (Paris: Imago, 1990).

6. Among the growing body of literature on the modern construction of the homo/heterosexual, see Michel Foucault, *The History of Sexuality, Vol. 1: An Introduction* (London: Allen Lane, 1979); David F. Greenberg, *The Construction of Homosexuality* (Chicago: University of Chicago Press, 1988); Richard Dellamora, *Masculine Desire: The Sexual Politics of Victorian Aestheticism* (Chapel Hill: University of North Carolina Press, 1990); Michael Roper and John Tosh, eds., *Manful Assertions: Masculinities in Britain Since 1800* (London: Routledge, 1991); Robert Nye, *Masculinity and Male Codes of Honor in Modern France* (New York: Oxford University Press, 1993), and George Chauncey, *Gay New York: Gender, Urban Culture, and the Making of the Gay Male World, 1890–1940* (New York: Basic Books, 1994).
7. Ed Cohen, *A Talk on the Wilde Side: Towards a Geneology of Discourse on Male Sexualities* (New York: Routledge, 1993); Ruth Harris, *Murders and Madness: Medicine, Law and Society in the Fin-de-Siècle* (Oxford: Clarendon Press, 1989); Joëlle Guillais, *Crimes of Passion: Dramas of Private Life in Nineteenth-Century France* (New York: Routledge, 1990); Karen Dubinsky, *Improper Advances: Rape and Heterosexual Conflict in Ontario, 1880–1929* (Chicago: University of Chicago Press, 1993), and Angus McLaren, *The Trials of Masculinity: Policing Sexual Boundaries, 1870–1930* (Chicago: University of Chicago Press, 1997).
8. See especially Benjamin F. Martin, *Crime and Criminal Justice under the Third Republic: The Shame of Marianne* (Baton Rouge: Louisiana State University Press, 1990).
9. See Jean-Denis Bredin, *The Affair: The Case of Alfred Dreyfus* (New York: George Braziller, 1986), and Alan Sinfield, *The Wilde Century: Effeminacy, Oscar Wilde and the Queer Moment* (New York: Columbia University Press, 1994). For a comparative study of the two controversies, see Jacques de Langlade, *La mésentente cordiale: Wilde-Dreyfus* (Paris: Julliard, 1994).
10. Arthur Conan Doyle, "A Case of Identity," *The Annotated Sherlock Holmes*, ed. William S. Baring-Gould. 2 vols. (New York: Potter, 1967), vol. 1, 404.
11. On the role of forensic medicine and psychiatry, see Jan Goldstein, *Console and Classify: The French Psychiatric Profession in the Nineteenth Century* (Cambridge: Cambridge University Press, 1987); M. Crowther and Brenda White, *On Soul and Conscience: The Medical Expert and Crime* (Aberdeen: Aberdeen University Press, 1988); Ian Dowbiggin, *Inheriting Madness: Professionalization and Psychiatric Knowledge in Nineteenth-Century France* (Berkeley: University of California Press, 1991), and Vernon A. Rosario, ed., *Science and Homosexualities* (New York: Routledge, 1997).

12. On the rise of a popular press, see Claude Bellanger, *Histoire générale de la presse française*, 3 vols. (Paris: Presses univeritaires de France, 1976); Stephen Koss, *The Rise and Fall of the Political Press in Britain: The Nineteenth Century* (Chapel Hill: University of North Carolina Press, 1981); Lucy Brown, *Victorian News and Newspapers* (New York: Oxford University Press, 1985), and Micheline Dupuy, *Le Petit Parisien: "Le plus fort tirage des journaux du monde entier"* (Paris: Plon, 1989).
13. For connections between theatre and the courtroom, see Katherine Fischer Taylor, *In the Theater of Criminal Justice: The Palais de Justice in Second Empire Paris* (Princeton: Princeton University Press, 1993). The architecture of the English courtroom differed somewhat from its French counterpart, but had powerful symbolic resonance too.
14. *Daily Graphic*, 19 Oct. 1910.
15. *The Times*, 24 Oct. 1910.
16. For literary obsessions with crime, see Richard Altick, *Victorian Studies in Scarlet* (New York: Norton, 1970); Susanna Barrows, *Distorting Mirrors: Visions of the Crowd in Late Nineteenth-Century France* (New Haven: Yale University Press, 1981), and Thomas Boyle, *Black Swine in the Sewers of Hampstead: Beneath the Surface of Victorian Sensationalism* (New York: Viking, 1989). On the inter-dependency of literary and scientific depictions of criminality, see Marie-Christine Leps, *Apprehending the Criminal: The Production of Deviance in Nineteenth-Century Discourse* (Durham: Duke University Press, 1992). For cases and scientific theories concerning female criminals, see Ann-Louise Shapiro, *Breaking the Codes: Female Criminality in Fin-de-siècle Paris* (Stanford: Stanford University Press, 1996).
17. M.H.S. Smith, *Art and Anecdotes: Recollections of William Frederick Yeames, RA* (London, 1927), 220.

2 A Public Offense against Decency: the Trial of the Count de Germiny and the "Moral Order" of the Third Republic

William Peniston

Throughout the nineteenth century, France was one of the few countries in Europe which did not have a specific law against homosexual behavior. It had abolished its medieval laws against sodomy in 1791 and had established a new criminal code in 1810. Its new laws prohibited sexual activities in public and sexual relations with minors, whether homosexual or heterosexual. As a result, it had a reputation for openness and toleration which contributed to the development of a male homosexual subculture in Paris. Yet despite this reputation, the very vagueness of the laws allowed the police to turn on homosexuals as scapegoats for the political, social, or economic problems of the times.[1] The sensational trial of the Count de Germiny for "a public offense against decency" in 1876 is one such example of the authorities' attack on homosexuality as a means of shoring up the social order.

The police had developed a concept of homosexuality as a crime since at least the eighteenth century. As early as the 1720s, they began to deal with the subculture in a very different manner from the way the authorities had dealt with sodomites during the Renaissance and Reformation. Homosexual behavior was no longer treated as a sin – as an act against God, deserving death, because of its association with witchcraft and heresy.[2] Instead, it became a target of state surveillance, and the police watched the subculture closely and gathered as much information about it as possible. The police produced a new understanding about homosexual behavior, which they interpreted as a disorder – as a taste or a disposition, needing to be controlled, because of its suspected association with the criminal underworld. As Mercier put it in his *Tableau de Paris*:

> The police discover dangerous inclinations in certain souls, which may promptly lead them to misdeeds. Such a character already turns to crime, and it is time to sequester him from society. Although it may be a very delicate judgment to prescribe, nevertheless it is impossible to leave punishment to the traditional forms of ordinary tribunals.[3]

Therefore, throughout the eighteenth century, the police developed several extra-legal means of dealing with members of the subculture, which mainly consisted of surveillance, harassment, interrogation, and detention.[4]

After the codification of the new penal code in 1810, the police continued to monitor the male homosexual subculture, but only at certain times did they exercise the full extent of their powers against it. The 1870s was one of these times. As part of the "Moral Order" of the early years of the Third Republic, the police implemented a series of measures designed to keep track of certain individuals and groups suspected of subversive activities. Their primary goal was to limit the political expression and assembly of these individuals or groups, but they often conflated personal behavior and moral attitudes with political points of view. Not only did they rigorously pursue the *Communards*, but they also targeted other radicals, socialists, and communists, as well as the working-class men and women who supported them. New laws against public intoxication, vagrancy, and recidivism allowed the police to arrest working-class men and women who drank in public, who socialized in the parks, squares, or streets of Paris, who insulted public officials, or who engaged in other dubious public behavior.[5] The members of the male homosexual subculture, whose activities often took place in public, were another group of individuals, who were especially targeted by the police in these years.[6]

The police were able to exercise this kind of power over the subculture, because the society, on the whole, was extremely negative in its attitudes toward homosexuality. In both the official and popular writings of the era, the association of homosexuality with criminality was repeatedly stressed. Balzac, in his character Jacques Collin (alias Vautrin, Carlos Herrera, and several other names), popularized the image of the homosexual criminal, while the murderer, Lacenaire, whose trial caused such a sensation in 1835, seemed to conform perfectly to the stereotype.[7] The memoirs of Vidocq, the criminal-turned-informer who helped establish the detective division in the Prefecture of the Police, and of Canler, who headed this division during the July Monarchy, also helped reinforce this stereotype.[8] As Jennifer Davis has argued more generally in her study of the police in the nineteenth century:

> For the most part, they concentrated their attention on marginal social groups who already fit popular stereotypes of the potential criminals. In the second half of the century, this was the urban casual poor. By operating in this way, the police played a crucial role both in creating and also reinforcing these popular perceptions of criminality.[9]

Another agent for the social stigmatization of homosexuals was the press. Like the police and the novelists, it both reflected and shaped public opinion, especially in the second half of the nineteenth century. The popular press began to develop in France during the Second Empire, when Moïse Millard founded *Le Petit Journal* in 1863. This daily newspaper was designed for the masses as a form of popular entertainment. Instead of focusing on politics, which was frequently censored anyway, Millard developed a new style of coverage based on topical reports, true crime stories, and serialized novels. The topical reports were detailed inquiries into current issues which appealed to the emotions rather than the intellect. The true crime stories dealt with the bizarre or the horrible, expressing both fascination with and fear of criminals, as well as sympathy and support for their victims. The serialized novels often drew their inspiration from these topical reports and crime stories, but they were clearly fictions, reinforcing the emotional appeals of the criminal stories.[10]

Frequently, the subjects of these reports were the private lives of public men, who inhabited a world of wealth and power which was radically different from the ordinary routine of the average newspaper reader. These privileged lives became spectacles to be watched and envied or examined and scorned. When accounts of the elite's intimate lives contradicted their public images, then the reports created a sense of moral superiority in the average newspaper reader, apparently highlighting the hypocrisy of the privileged classes. Consequently, these reports provided a means of accepting one's lot in life, while supplying a titillating tale to overcome the mundane existence of everyday life. In his study of *The Trial of Madame Caillaux*, Edward Berenson explained this psychological effect in the following manner:

> The press devoted considerable attention to the private affairs of France's most public men. By revealing the financial and sexual exploits of famous politicians, journalists opened a window onto worlds of excitement and luxury in which most of their readers could never

> directly indulge. In doing so, the press fulfilled a complex psychological function, for it allowed readers both the thrill of identifying with those who ruled them and the pleasure of venting an anger born of envy against them. And when members of the elite were punished for their scandalous behavior, readers could feel confirmed in the justice of their own straight and narrow lives.[11]

So, too, the press exposure of the secret life of a moral pillar of the Third Republic, the Count de Germiny, had powerful reverberations.

Charles-Eugène Le Bègue de Germiny belonged to a distinguished family with roots in Normandy since the fourteenth century. His grandfather, Henri-Charles, had a distinguished career as a prefect during the Restoration, and his father, Charles-Gabriel, was both a minister and a senator under Napoleon III. Another relative, Adrien, was a regent of the Bank of France and had successfully negotiated a loan from the Bank of England for the Government of National Defense in 1870. He himself was a lawyer at the Court of Appeals and an affiliate of the municipal council of Paris. He served as the president of the Catholic Workers Circle and was a member of the Society of Saint Vincent de Paul.[12]

On the evening of 6 December 1876 Germiny was arrested for public indecency at a urinal near the Champs Elysées. It took four police officers to subdue him, all of whom testified at his trial. As a result of this struggle, he was also charged with resisting arrest.[13] Usually, the press did not report on misdemeanor cases, such as public offenses against decency, since they did not provoke fear or elicit excitement. Nevertheless, due to the Count's social position and a well-placed leak to *Le Gaulois*, his trial caused quite a sensation. Soon the term "Germinism" became synonymous with "pederasty" – the usual term used for homosexuality in nineteenth-century France.[14]

The press used this case to reaffirm one of the most common perceptions of homosexuality in the nineteenth century: that it was a vice of the aristocracy, which was intent upon the corruption of youths from the working classes. Such a portrayal had vital political implications for the nascent Third Republic: the aristocracy was seen as decadent, the proletariat as weak, and the bourgeoisie as the bulwark of public morality. However, a closer examination of the male homosexual subculture of Paris in the nineteenth century reveals that such a portrayal did not conform to the experiences of most of the men who made up this underground world. The experiences of Edmond-Pierre Chouard, the 18-year-old jeweler who was arrested with Germiny, were much more typical of these men than the experiences of Germiny himself. Chouard was a young, working-class man from Paris, who had several encounters with the police. His friends included several "known pederasts" who also came into contact with the police. Clearly, he was an active member of the subculture, not an innocent victim of a decadent aristocrat. Chouard's police record demonstrates that he was a repeated target of police harassment. Germiny's "clean record" suggests that he was a victim of another sort, of the hysterical fears and suspicions of the police, the court, and the press.

The trial of Chouard and Germiny began on 23 December 1876 in the Eighth Chamber of the Correctional Court in the Department of the Seine. It was covered by most of the newspapers, including the populist *Le Petit Journal*, the conservative *Le Figaro*, *Le Temps*, and *La Gazette des Tribunaux*.[15] *Le Petit Journal* gave it more coverage than the others, but all of them summarized the main arguments of the case. Not surprisingly, the anti-aristocratic *Le Petit Journal* emphasized the inequality which these two men encountered in the courtroom. It began by pointing out that "the accused are two in number. One is in detention... The other is at liberty." *Le Temps* also noted that "M. le Comte de Germiny took his place at the bench of the freed defendants. Chouard, who is in a state of detention, came accompanied by a guard."[16]

All of the newspapers emphasized Chouard's youthfulness. According to *La Gazette des Tribunaux*, "he was almost a child, beardless, with a pale complexion and an effeminate face." *Le Figaro* also noticed "his almost infantile countenance." It went on to describe him as "a young and beautiful boy, rather undisciplined... who left his family because he did not bother to work." Furthermore, he was "without profession and without known domicile," with a prior conviction for vagrancy in the summer of 1875. *Le Temps* also noted his prior conviction, calling him "the type of pale street urchin of Paris."[17] Although the press mentioned his prior conviction, it did not dwell on it, preferring instead to concentrate on his youthfulness and impressionability.

The 35-year-old Germiny, on the other hand, was identified as a lawyer attached to the municipal council of Paris. He was also well-known to the lawyers, judges, and journalists, who frequented the Palais de Justice. *Le Petit Journal* described him as "pale, but calm, [with] a light trembling of the hands indicating his only emotion." *Le Figaro* reported that he spoke with "perfect lucidity and tranquility."[18] Thus, the age and class differences of these two defendants were emphasized, reinforcing the stereotype of the attraction of the outwardly upstanding, but inwardly decadent, aristocrat for a young working-class delinquent.

The president of the court, M. Auzony, began the trial by asking Germiny to explain himself. "Monsieur le président," Germiny declared, "I have been unwise, but I am not guilty." He then went on to say that "I was taking a stroll along the Champs Elysées. I had just dined with my wife at my brother-in-law's place." "Upon arriving near the Avenue Gabriel, I saw around the urinal a certain number of individuals with suspicious appearances." They "were the kind of men who infest our neighborhood. I had heard of the troubles that they were causing," and "I remembered the scenes of immorality of which the Champs Elysées is the theater. I have had occasion, in my position as a member of the municipal council, of being concerned with this situation, and I wanted to assure myself of what was happening there."[19] As *Le Petit Journal* recorded his testimony: "The idea came to me that I should conduct a sort of inquiry in regards to the activities of certain habitués of these areas, of which the indecency revolts the residents of the neighborhood."[20]

The activity to which Germiny referred was the public sex which took place in the urinals of Paris. The urinals were part of Haussmann's plan to clean up Paris. Designed to improve sanitation, these urinals quickly became the sites of other activities. These activities included exhibitionism, molestation, masturbation, and a number of other sexual acts. Consequently, the police regularly inspected the urinals, which, in turn, were the locations of several hundred arrests for public offenses against decency in the 1870s alone.[21]

Only a few cases involved exhibitionism by itself. For example, on 13 September 1874 the police arrested Jean-Baptist Calmet, a 48-year-old domestic, for exposing himself in a urinal on the rue Grange Batelière in the Ninth Arrondissement. He was probably hoping that somebody would respond positively to this gesture. In another case, which occurred on 18 May 1876 in the urinal near the Restaurant Laurent on the Champs-Elysées, the police arrested François-Basil Lehugeur, a 35-year-old waiter, for exposing himself and trying to touch other men. He, too, was probably hoping that somebody would touch him back. In this case, the charge of exhibitionism was combined with molestation. In a similar case, on 19 October 1875, the police accused Arthur-Amède Mailly, an 18-year-old waiter, of solicitation for showing off his erect penis to others in the urinal near the Grand Hôtel on the Boulevard des Capucines. In this case, an accusation of exhibitionism was added to one of solicitation.[22]

In several cases, exhibitionism took the form of one or two men masturbating themselves, another man, or each other, in front of a group of spectators. For example, on 4 September 1877, Frédéric Morin, an 18-year-old jeweler, was masturbating himself in front of a group of "curious onlookers" in the urinal near one of the bookstores at the Gare Saint Lazare. On 26 October 1878 Jean Gros, 42, and Théophile Warner, 25, were "holding each other's penises in a group of spectators" on the Boulevard des Italiens.[23] The police charged Morin, Gros, and Warner with public offenses against decency, but they did not arrest or charge the "curious onlookers" and "spectators."

Some of these "onlookers" and "spectators" may have been innocent bystanders who just happened to be in those places at those times, in which case the police frequently considered them victims. However, in most cases, they were clearly *voyeurs*, enjoying the shows or even participating in them. Most of them left the scene of the crime as soon as the police arrived, but the records reveal that sometimes they stayed and attempted to fend off the police. For instance, when the police arrested Louis Doudin, a 44-year-old cook, and Jules Leprestle, a 29-year-old unemployed man, on 1 June 1873 for a public offense against decency at the Café des Ambassadeurs, they also arrested Ibrabin Atas, an 18-year-old boy from Turkey, Joseph Nestor, a 36-year-old florist, and George Peters, another 18-year-old for resisting the arrest of the aforementioned men.[24] In cases, like this one, the men were obviously willing to defend themselves and others from police interference in their activities.

Of all the urinals in Paris, the one near the Café des Ambassadeurs was particularly popular with members of the homosexual subculture. In fact, the Café des Ambassadeurs was in and of itself a fairly popular meeting place. It was a very famous café-concert near the Champs Elysées and the Avenue Gabriel in the Eighth Arrondissement. Initially, the café-concerts were part of a working-class culture, which grew up along the *grands boulevards* in the 1850s and 1860s. By the 1870s they were attracting a mixed crowd as the bourgeoisie began to visit them. They offered their customers cheap alcohol and popular entertainments, which were highly satirical and occasionally subversive. The police, along with many other social commentators, feared that the shows were also obscene.[25]

Contemporary middle-class writers took notice of the café-concerts and recorded their impressions. For example, the Goncourt brothers ventured into the Café de l'Eldorado on the Boulevard de Strasbourg in the 1860s and emerged with a feeling of disdain for these kinds of places. They were appalled by the "tastelessness" of the decor, the "stupidity" of the amusements, and the "vulgarity" of the audience. They confessed that they feared that these café-concerts were destroying the moral and material foundations of Paris, by mixing up the various classes, allowing men, women, and children in the audience, and confusing the private sphere with the public.[26]

Nevertheless, despite the disdain of the Goncourts and others, many members of the bourgeoisie became fascinated with the café-concerts. Edgar Degas, for instance, frequently went to see and hear the singer Thérésa, a very popular entertainer at the Alcazar d'Eté on the Champs Elysées. She had, in his opinion, an amazing way of mocking, insulting, cajoling, and amusing her audience. He painted several pictures of her as well as her entourage and audience. In these paintings, he portrayed the singer's ability to identify with the people around her and to include them in her songs, despite all of the distractions which were occurring off stage. These distractions, which included some of the ordinary (and extra-ordinary) occurrences of everyday life, were equally as important to Degas and others as the antics which Thérésa performed on stage.[27]

One distraction that was taking place outside these popular places of entertainment was the gathering of members of the gay subculture, who began to put on shows for themselves. For instance, on 22 May 1876, Jean Pommaux, a 38-year-old domestic, was masturbating Arthur-Paul Martin, a 34-year-old waiter, outside the Café des Ambassadeurs, in the midst of a group of men, who cheered them on. In this case, the police did not arrest the members of the audience, perhaps because they were not directly involved in the public offense against decency or because they were too numerous. In other cases the spectators clearly had a more participatory role in the event. For example, on 2 September 1878 the police had to break up a veritable orgy at the Café des Ambassadeurs. In this case, Olivier Frand, a 25-year-old room attendant in a *maison de tolérance*, and Stanislas-Vital Prieur, a 45-year-old valet, were amusing a crowd with their mutual masturbation, while Joseph Flament, a 46-year-old domestic, was being masturbated by "a bearded man" who escaped the police.[28]

These cases were the kinds of activities of which the Count de Germiny claimed to have heard in his capacity as a member of the Parisian municipal council. According to his testimony, he conducted his "investigation" of these places and these men by watching them from both the outside and the inside. He admitted to the court that "I entered the urinal where I found my co-defendant ... Other persons also came ... They all had suspicious appearances ... " "I then left and stayed outside a few moments in observation. Several minutes later, I went back into the urinal. It was at this moment that the agents arrived and arrested the two of us."[29]

As far as the charge of resisting arrest was concerned, Germiny claimed that he did not know that the four individuals who attacked him in the urinal were police officers. "They did not wear any insignia. I defended myself, believing that it was a surprise, a trap." He believed that these men were either out to rob him or beat him up. Furthermore, by way of conclusion, he said that "I have not ceased to protest an arrest which was not motivated by any obscene act on my part, and I only regret the fatal imprudence which has exposed me to such cruel consequences."[30]

Germiny's explanation that he feared that he had been set up by criminals exploited the association of homosexuality with crimes like theft, blackmail, assault, and even murder. His testimony attempted to emphasize a common fear of the criminal underworld, which both he and the judicial authorities shared. According to Louis Canler, the chief of the detective division in the Prefecture of the Police during the July Monarchy, the police's major concern as far as the subculture was concerned was the perceived connection between homosexuality and blackmail. He devoted a chapter to the subject in his *Mémoires*. He believed that for many of these men, especially the younger ones, homosexuality had become little more than a means of making a living. They had sexual relations with other men primarily in order to satisfy their greed. The means that they employed were either the direct sale of their bodies, or the small-time thefts from their one-time partners, or the elaborate blackmail schemes which they themselves conjured up. They frequented the commercial arcades, like the Passage des Panoramas, the Passage de l'Opéra, and the Galerie d'Orléans in the Palais Royale, all areas known for their commercial traffic in sex, in search of sexual partners or victims for their criminal designs. Hence, Canler implied that most gay men were prostitutes, thieves, and blackmailers.[31]

The victims of these men, according to Canler, contributed to the successes of these criminals by the shame and embarrassment associated with their sexual habits. In other words, in order to hide their habits from their families and friends, these men frequently got themselves into dangerous situations in which the perpetuation of their secrets became a costly endeavor. In this way, Canler blamed the victims as much as the blackmailers for making these situations possible.[32]

At his trial, Germiny claimed that he was investigating behavior of the sort described by Canler. Unfortunately, this claim was not supported by the police report, Chouard's deposition, or even the statement that Germiny signed at the time of his arrest. The president of the court reviewed these statements by reminding Germiny what the police, Chouard, and Germiny himself had said. According to the police report, as the president summarized it: "You were strolling about with the evident intention of entering into relations with one of those individuals of whom you spoke. Six times you made a trip into the urinal. When you were arrested with Chouard, both of you were engaged in obscene touching one upon the other. It was in an area in which immoral deeds of the same nature take place frequently." To this statement, Germiny replied: "If I went into the urinal six times and if I committed the acts of which I am accused, then I am quite astonished that I was not arrested the first time." With regard to his own deposition, he protested: "Perhaps I used terms which I did not weigh . . . I had spent the night in jail, prey to panic and turmoil . . . thinking of my family, of those whom I love . . . I was under the blow of a profound emotion . . . In this state of dejection, I signed the deposition which was presented to me." He concluded, "I acknowledge having gone to the places indicated in the indictment," but "I went in order to observe. I looked, but the rest is incorrect."[33] The Count defended his actions by characterizing them as motivated by a sort of civic curiosity.

In contrast to Germiny, Chouard said very little during the trial. He mainly restricted himself to short answers to the president's questions. Those questions were based on the deposition which he gave the police on the night of his arrest and which he later denied. According to the deposition, as presented by the president, Chouard said that while enjoying the unusually good weather for December, he was sitting on a bench outside the urinal near the Café des Ambassadeurs, when he decided to enter it. There he first noticed Germiny. After leaving the urinal and sitting down on the bench a second time, Germiny also left the urinal, walked around the bench, and then sat down. Soon thereafter, Chouard reentered the urinal, followed by Germiny, who, "standing next to him," showed him his "state of nudity." Immediately, the two of them were then arrested. However, Chouard insisted that Germiny had been the aggressor and that he had refused all of his advances. In court, however, Chouard called this deposition a lie. He said that Germiny did not speak to him outside of the urinal, nor did he make any obscene propositions to him once inside. "He looked at me, but without provocation." He then stated that he had gone into the urinal in order to take care of "a natural act," and that he had been arrested at the moment when he was buttoning up his trousers. Finally, in order to explain the discrepancy between his deposition to the police and his testimony to the court, Chouard declared that "the police officers forced me to make these statements when they arrested me. They promised me to let me go free, if I consented to charge the person who was arrested with me."[34]

Chouard's statement that he had been threatened by the police cannot be dismissed lightly, since, according to Benjamin Martin, one of the standard methods of the police was to extract a confession from a suspect through a series of promises, threats, and beatings. In the common parlance of the day, this method was known as "cooking" the suspect. "Some cases presented little difficulty," Martin argued. "The man or woman might confess readily, sometimes delaying only until promised a good meal. More often the detectives encountered a stubborn refusal to respond or an absolute denial of guilt. If the subject had no connections, he might be beaten until he admitted every charge, guilty or not."[35] Hence, Chouard's claim that the police officers promised to let him go if he made a statement incriminating Germiny is in line with Martin's description of contemporary police tactics. Nevertheless, since Chouard was obviously associated with other members of the male homosexual subculture, it seems clear that his initial statement, coerced or not, contained elements of truth.[36] Be that as it may, the judges in this case disregarded his accusation of police misconduct.

Following Chouard's testimony, the president of the court called the various police officers involved in the case to the stand. "They were all in uniform," according to *Le Temps*, emphasizing their authority and respectability. Inspector Aubry from the *Service des moeurs* testified that he and three of his colleagues were watching the urinal near the Café des Ambassadeurs on the Champs-Elysées, when they noticed a gentleman (Germiny) going in and out on several different occasions. On one such occasion, this gentleman encountered a young man (Chouard), to whom he "uncovered his nudity." "Glances were exchanged," but nothing occurred inside the urinal on this first occasion. Outside of the urinal, the young man sat down on a bench, around which the gentleman walked until he too sat down. "Undoubtedly they understood each other," since the two of them then proceeded back into the urinal. There "a rapport was established between them," and "M. de Germiny used his right hand to touch the young man on the shoulder." Another inspector, Fasset, said that "the two defendants...smiled at each other...Then they practiced the most shocking familiarities on each other." Inspector Fasset's colleague, Briant, "who testified with a certain vivacity," according to *Le Figaro*, told the court a similar story. He said that "they had the air of understanding each other...They approached each other, they looked at each other, and then they indulged themselves in reciprocal touching." Another inspector, Follet, testified that "the physical situation of the two men did not leave the slightest doubt" as to their actions or intentions.[37]

This last inspector from the *Service des moeurs* added some further details about the arrest itself. He said that "Chouard was captured without effort, but Germiny opposed us with an energetic resistance. He cried, called for help, struggled, threw punches and kicks." Only after a uniformed officer appeared on the scene did Germiny give up his fight. This uniformed officer, Hugot, also testified at the trial, but he added nothing new to the charges against Germiny and Chouard.[38]

After a short recess, the commissioner of the police station near the Champs Elysées, Louis Baud, spoke to the court. He was the officer who filled out the official police report on the morning after the arrest. He restricted his comments mainly to the interview that he had with the principal defendant in the case. According to him, as recorded in *Le Figaro*:

> I gave M. de Germiny a complete reading of the report which was addressed against him. He protested against certain passages which related to the obscene touching with Chouard. I made an observation to him that it did not suffice to deny it, since he would be confronted with the young man. I consigned [to the page] in the most exact way possible not only the sense but also the letter of the explanation which he gave to me, and here is what he said to me: 'I could see the nudity of the individual in the urinal, but I deny the touching.'[39]

According to *Le Petit Journal*, however, Germiny had said to the commissioner: "I looked at the nudity of others and I showed off my own" – a much more damaging statement. In any case, the commissioner insisted that he had recorded Germiny's words exactly, even though the newspapers gave varying versions. He was also certain that Germiny understood the deposition before signing it. "Read and reread this document," Baud claimed to have said to Germiny. "If you find something to add, if you find something to retract, if you find something to modify, modify, retract, add. I give you the time."[40] "I asked him to reflect," Baud continued, "before signing the deposition. He exclaimed: 'My God! I am a lawyer. I know only too well that a situation like this is serious.'" Thereupon, according to Baud, he signed the deposition, adding: "I have nothing [more] to say."[41]

At this point in the trial, Germiny reiterated the denial that he had made earlier in the trial. "This official has misinterpreted my words ...," he stated. "I simply said to [him]: 'It is possible that I could have perceived the nudity of Chouard and that he could have seen my own.' That is all!"[42] The implication was that he had not gone there with any kind of illicit intention.

Having heard the explanations of Germiny and Chouard and the testimonies of the police officers, the president of the court proceeded with the closing remarks of the prosecutor and the two defense attorneys. The prosecutor, M. Bonnet, in his concluding remarks, argued that a crime had been committed and that justice should be done, regardless of the Count's reputation or social position. According to *Le Temps*, Bonnet said: "The defendant brought before your bar is a distinguished lawyer, esteemed until now by colleagues and magistrates ... He is brought before you under a shameful charge. It is a horrible situation, a heartrending [one] of the most sorrowful [kind] for the great judicial family."[43] Nevertheless, despite the professional connections which many of the judges and lawyers in the courthouse may have had with the defendant, it was still their duty to judge him according to the law.

According to *Le Petit Journal*, Germiny's attorney, M. Allou, made "a brilliant and moving plea." He began by reminding the court that the Count was "the father of a family, a lawyer of talent, the master at the head of a great fortune." Furthermore, he was well known for his pursuit of truth and justice, and this pursuit had unfortunately led him to make his own investigation into "the shameful disorders which were discussed recently in the municipal council." Perhaps this investigation was the result of "a rather regrettable curiosity," but "for those who know the analytical and philosophical mind of M. de Germiny, the origin of this curiosity is self-evident."[44]

Having reviewed Germiny's reputation and his explanation of the events, Allou went on to attack the validity of the police officers' statements. He claimed that in the place of arrest "the officers could distinguish nothing in a precise manner." "They saw with their habits, their impressions of every day [life], instead of seeing with their eyes." In addition, referring to the disclosure of the arrest by the sensationalist newspaper, *Le Gaulois*, on the day after it occurred, Allou reminded the court that "only one of the police officers could have committed this action," which was "a strange fact of nature [that should] awaken the distrust of justice in regard to the officers of the [*Service des*] *moeurs*."[45] In other words, the officers obviously made a mistake and persisted in that mistake by tarnishing the Count's reputation in the newspapers before his guilt or innocence could have been proved in a court of law. He suggested that a personal vendetta motivated the officer who leaked the story to the press.

Finally, Allou reminded the court that although Germiny had fled to Brussels on the advice of his family and friends, he had, nevertheless, returned for the trial. "When his family wanted him to leave France, he refused. When the doctors came to examine his mental state, he responded: 'I am neither mad nor guilty. I want to defend myself.'" The Count himself had declared that "if I had been guilty, I would not be here, I would have fled, I would have hidden myself, I would have made myself disappear."[46]

Chouard's attorney, M. Bourdillon, spoke very briefly. He pointed out that Chouard came from an honest hard-working Parisian family, that he had no previous conviction, except for vagrancy the summer before, and that he was obviously tricked into a confession by the police officers, who took advantage of his naiveté. "Chouard is a boy . . . who, in the hope of being released, said everything that the officers wanted him to say. But later . . . he told the truth as he has just said it in this hearing."[47]

In an unusual move, the court postponed its decision for a week. When it reconvened on 31 December, it was apparently not persuaded by either Germiny's or Chouard's testimony. Nor was it impressed by the eloquence of the two defense attorneys. It sided with the prosecution and found them both guilty of a public offense against decency. It sentenced Germiny to a fine of 200 francs and a prison term of two months – a rather harsh sentence for the men usually convicted of this offense. Chouard received a sentence of fifteen days and a fine of sixteen francs – a rather light sentence.[48] *Le Temps*, *Le Petit Journal*, and *Le Figaro* all reprinted the judgment in its entirety. *Le Figaro* added the following comment: "We reproduce it in its entirety, despite the crudity of the terms, not believing that we have the right, in an affair of this importance, to change a line or a word." All three newspapers also noted that Germiny was not present at the time of his sentencing. The populist *Le Petit Journal*, continuing its emphasis on the inequalities in this case, reported that "Chouard alone, led into the hearing between two guards of Paris, heard the reading of this sentence . . . As for the principal [defendant] condemned [in this case], he was absent. They say that he was in flight."[49]

Chouard served out his sentence and then, as the police record shows, again came under the scrutiny of the vice squad, demonstrating that he was certainly not as naive as he and his attorney claimed during the trial. In fact, a police report dated 14 January 1877, only weeks after his involvement with Germiny, named him, along with eleven other men, as part of a group of "vagabonds" who roamed around the theaters during the day and the café-concerts during the night. Several of his companions had prior arrest records for public offenses against decency.[50] For instance, Louis-Joseph Garnier, a 49-year-old cook, was arrested on 30 September 1876 for masturbating in view of a young boy near the Théâtre Guignol. François-Jules-Adolphe Loy, a 34-year-old office clerk, was standing in a urinal near the Alcazar d'Eté, another famous café-concert, on 26 October 1876, when he said to the man standing next to him, "Watch how I jerk off!" Emile-Arthur Pelletier, the 21-year-old pastry cook next to him, not only watched, but eventually joined in, so that both of them were accused of mutual masturbation. Jean Gagey, a 30-year-old domestic, was charge with public masturbation and exhibitionism near the *Cirque* on the Champs Elysées on 31 October 1876. And Jean-Baptiste Desjardins, a 25-year-old master cook, was apprehended for masturbating in front of a group of men outside of the Restaurant Balvi on 12 January 1877.[51] Desjardins' arrest may have provoked the official police report, although the report indicates that the police had been watching these men since at least 4 September 1876.[52]

Nearly six months later, at 2:00 in the morning on 12 June 1877, the police rearrested Chouard on the Champs-Elysées, allegedly for "obscene touching, acts of pederasty, and shameful propositions." This time he again claimed that the other man involved, a valet by the name of Henri Flarant, had been the instigator. Luckily for both of them, the police did not file charges for reasons which are unclear.[53] Still, from his police record, it is clear that Chouard was actively involved in the male homosexual subculture of late nineteenth-century Paris.

The Germiny case was covered extensively in the newspapers and provoked a great deal of public attention. During the trial, as *Le Petit Journal* noted, "a tumultuous crowd fought against the doors of the court ... [and] numerous lawyers who populate the judicial interior discussed the case among themselves, recalling the recent occasion when the words of the member of the bar [who is] accused today rang out in a neighboring chamber ... "[54] Georges Herelle, a lycée professor in Vitry-le-Franc in Champagne who later translated the work of Gabriele d'Annunzio, recalled that many people were discussing the Germiny Affair in 1876–7 and voicing opinions on the subject. For instance, Herelle's friend, Ernest, was convinced that Germiny "had the unhappy vocation of this vice, which nothing could stifle, because one does not remake one's nature." Having made a marriage of convenience, as Ernest understood it, which obviously did not satisfy him sexually, Germiny was caught in an embarrassing situation, because he was not familiar with the homosexual subculture of Paris. According to Ernest, "if he had the habit, the practice of this vice, he would not have committed such an enormous imprudence, because he would have had a thousand ways of satisfying [his desire] in a more complete fashion and in more preferable conditions of security."[55]

Edmond de Goncourt referred to the affair when he complained that the attacks on his novel, *La Fille Elisa*, treated him "as if I had committed an infamous deed." Years later, he commented upon "the strange charm that men like Germiny could find in the danger of being surprised." He went on to say that he had heard that Germiny had been arrested twice before the December 1876 incident, but that he had been set free. It was only on the third occasion that he had been charged with a crime.[56]

By the turn of the century, the word "Germinism" had become a synonym for "pederasty." Hector France in his *Dictionnaire de la langue verte* listed it as a "neologism of recent date, created after the adventure of the Count de Germiny." In his *L'argot au XXe siècle*, Aristide Bruant also included it in his list of terms for "pederasty."[57]

The press seized upon this case, not merely because it was a sensational crime, but because it involved an aristocrat, a distinguished professional, and a heretofore respectable member of society. Journalists in the popular press repeatedly pointed out the advantages that Germiny had over his co-defendant, making the point that all were not equal before the law. For example, he was at liberty both before and during the trial, which allowed him to evade his prison sentence. Chouard, on the other hand, was held in custody before, during, and after the trial. Germiny was also a professional lawyer, able to hire a brilliant attorney and mount an elaborate defense. Chouard's attorney was perfunctory and merely pointed out the young man's working-class background.

In addition to their class differences, the press also emphasized the age differences between these two men. It dwelt heavily upon the youthfulness of Chouard, who was made to seem younger than his eighteen years, while Germiny was simply described as a middle-aged man. Connected to this issue of age was the apparent innocence of Chouard. Even though writers for the Parisian press acknowledged his past conviction for vagrancy, they were willing to forgive him this minor indiscretion, but they maintained that the Count's actions clearly deserved the fullest extent of the law. Ultimately, the press saw his actions and his explanations as sheer hypocrisy.

Although this case was reported in a rather matter-of-fact style, still its treatment in the press subtly reinforced the major contemporary stereotypes of the male homosexual and his partners. The homosexual was perceived to be an aristocratic dandy with effeminate manners and pleasure-seeking ways, who preyed upon the idleness and weakness of younger working-class men. These working-class boys, in turn, were delinquents, who were incapable of supporting themselves by arduous manual labor. Consequently, contacts between the homosexual and his partners were a danger to society because they violated the strict separation of the classes, the obvious differences of the generations, and the proper relationships of the sexes. In other words, the socio-economic, generational, sexual, and gendered orders of society were put at risk by the actions of these morally bankrupted members of the aristocracy and the working classes.

The perpetuation of these stereotypes reinforced the concept of the ideal French citizen as a bourgeois, heterosexual, masculine man with a family, working diligently in one of the liberal professions or reliable trades. He was rational, intelligent, patriotic, and disciplined. He was the product of the new institutions of the school, the army, and the workplace.[58] The prison and the asylum were the places for those individuals, like homosexuals and criminals, who violated the proper orders of society.[59]

Despite this stereotype, Germiny represented only a minority of the kind of men who were arrested or investigated by the police. Chouard, the 18-year-old jeweler, was more typical. Most of them were in their teens, twenties, or thirties, from the provinces, working in unskilled, service, or clerical positions. They were usually independent of their parents or guardians, struggling to make a living in a difficult, even hostile urban environment. In their leisure time, they sought to make friends and acquaintances as well as to find amusements and adventures in their new home – the city of Paris. Occasionally they resorted to prostitution and thievery, but most of them were simply seeking diversions from their daily lives in the pursuit of sexual pleasures. In the process, they created their own community with its own sense of identity.

NOTES

1. Claude Courouve, "1791 Law Reform in France," *Cabirion* 12 (1984): 9–10; Marc Daniel, "Histoire de la législation pénale française concernant l'homosexualité," *Arcadie* 8 (1961): 618–27, and 9 (1962): 10–29; Michael David Sibalis, "The Repression of Male Homosexuality in Napoleonic

France (1799–1815)" in *Homosexuality in Modern France*, eds. Jeffrey Merrick and Bryant T. Ragan (New York: Oxford University Press, 1996), 80–101.

2. For a discussion of the association of homosexuality with witchcraft and heresy, see E. William Monter, "La sodomie à l'époque moderne en Suisse romande," *Annales: economies, sociétés, civilisations* 29 (1974): 1023–33; revised and translated as "Sodomy and Heresy in Early Modern Switzerland," *Journal of Homosexuality* 6 (1980–1): 41–53; Guido Ruggiero, *The Boundaries of Eros: Sex Crime and Sexuality in Renaissance Venice* (New York: Oxford University Press, 1985).
3. Cited in Michel Rey, "Police and Sodomy in Eighteenth Century Paris: From Sin to Disorder," in *The Pursuit of Sodomy: Male Homosexuality in Renaissance and Enlightenment Europe*, eds. Kent Gerard and Gert Hekma (New York: Harrington Park Press, 1989), 145.
4. Michel Rey, *Les Sodomistes Parisiens au XVIIIème siècle*, Maîtrise d'histoire, Université de Paris VIII (Vincennes), 1979–80; idem., "Police et Sodomie à Paris au XVIIIe siècle: du péché au désordre," *Revue d'histoire moderne et contemporaine* 19 (1982): 113–24, translated as "Police and Sodomy in Eighteenth Century Paris: From Sin to Disorder," in *The Pursuit of Sodomy: Male Homosexuality in Renaissance and Enlightenment Europe*, 129–46; idem., "Parisian Homosexuals Create a Lifestyle, 1700–1750: The Police Archives," *Eighteenth-Century Life* 9 (1985): 179–91.
5. Irene Collins, *The Government and the Newspaper Press in France, 1814–1881* (New York: Oxford University Press, 1959); Robert Justin Goldstein, *Censorship of Political Caricature in Nineteenth-Century France* (Kent, Ohio: Kent State University Press, 1989); Susanna Barrows, "'Parliaments of the People': The Political Culture of Cafes in the Early Third Republic," in *Drinking: Behavior and Belief in Modern History*, eds. Susanna Barrows and Robin Room (Berkeley: University of California Press, 1991), 87–97; idem., "After the Commune: Alcoholism, Temperance, and Literature in the Early Third Republic," in *Consciousness and Class Experience in Nineteenth-Century Europe*, ed. John M. Merriman (New York: Holmes & Meier, 1979), 205–18; W. Scott Haines, *The World of the Paris Café: Sociability among the French Working Class, 1789–1914* (Baltimore: Johns Hopkins University Press, 1996); Gay L. Gullickson, "*La Pétroleuse*: Representing Revolution," *Feminist Studies* 17 (1991): 240–65.
6. For the link between homosexuality and criminality, see Pierre Hahn, *Nos ancêtres les pervers: la vie des homosexuels sous le Deuxième Empire* (Paris: Olivier Orban, 1979); Antony Copley, *Sexual Moralities in France, 1780–1980: New Ideas on the Family, Divorce, and Homosexuality: An Essay on Moral Change* (New York: Routledge, 1989); Guy Hocquenghem, *Le Désir homosexuel* (Paris, 1972), translated by Daniella Dangoor as *Homosexual Desire* (Durham, NC: Duke University Press, 1993).
7. Jacques Collin appears in *Le Père Goriot* (1835), *Un Grand homme de province à Paris* (1839), *Splendeurs et misères des courtisanes* (1844), and *Le Député d'Arcis* (1853). On Balzac's attitudes towards homosexuality, see Gerald H. Storzer, "The Homosexual Paradigm in Balzac, Gide, and Genet," in *Homosexualities and French Literature: Cultural Contexts/Critical*

Texts, eds. George Stambolian and Elaine Marks (Ithaca: Cornell University Press, 1979), 186–209; Philippe Berthier, "Balzac du côté de Sodom," *L'Année Balzacienne* (1979): 147–77; Victoria Thompson, "Creating Boundaries: Homosexuality and the Changing Social Order in France, 1830–1870," in *Homosexuality in Modern France*, 102–27. On Lacenaire, see Louis Canler, *Mémoires de Canler, Ancien Chef de Service de Sûreté* (Bruxelles: A. La Croix, 1862), reprinted as *Mémoires de Canler* (Paris: Mecure de France, 1968); H.B. Irving, *Studies of French Criminals of the Nineteenth Century* (London, 1901), ch. 1; Antony Copley, *Sexual Moralities in France*, 99–107.

8. François-Eugène Vidocq, *Mémoires* (Paris, 1828).
9. Jennifer Davis, "Urban Policing and its Objects: Comparative Themes in England and France in the Second Half of the Nineteenth Century," in *Policing Western Europe: Politics, Professionalism, and Public Order, 1850–1940*, eds. Clive Emsley and Barbara Weinberger (New York: Greenwood Press, 1991), 1–17.
10. Edward Berenson, *The Trial of Madame Caillaux* (Berkeley: University of California Press, 1992), 208–39; Theodore Zeldin, *France, 1848–1945: Taste and Corruption* (New York: Oxford University Press, 1980), 144–225; Judith R. Walkowitz, *City of Dreadful Delight: Narratives of Sexual Danger in Late-Victorian London* (Chicago: The University of Chicago Press, 1992), 81–134.
11. Berenson, *Trial of Madame Caillaux*, 216.
12. *Dictionnaire des biographies français*, v. 15, 1337–40.
13. Archives de la Préfecture de la Police, *Pédérastes et divers*, BB6, no. 1028–9. Hereafter cited as A.P.P., BB6.
14. *Le Figaro*, 22 Dec., 24 Dec., and 31 Dec. 1876; *Gazette des Tribunaux*, 24 Dec. and 31 Dec. 1876; *Le Petit Journal*, 24 Dec., 25 Dec. 1876, and 1 Jan. 1877; *Le Temps*, 24 Dec., 25 Dec., and 31 Dec. 1876. Claude Courouve, *Vocabulaire de l'homosexualité masculine* (Paris: Payot, 1985), 117–18.
15. *Le Figaro* was a conservative newspaper, catering to the elites; *Gazette des Tribunaux* was a legalistic court reporter; *Le Petit Journal* was a popular paper with a republican orientation; and *Le Temps* was a politically moderate newspaper.
16. *Le Petit Journal*, 25 Dec. 1876, and *Le Temps*, 24 Dec. 1876.
17. *La Gazette des Tribunaux*, 24 Dec. 1876; *Le Figaro*, 24 Dec. 1876, and *Le Temps*, 24 Dec. 1876.
18. *Le Petit Journal*, 25 Dec. 1876, and *Le Figaro*, 24 Dec. 1876.
19. *Le Petit Journal*, 25 Dec. 1876; *Le Figaro*, 24 Dec. 1876, and *La Gazette des Tribunaux*, 24 Dec. 1876.
20. *Le Petit Journal*, 25 Dec. 1876. *Le Temps* (24 Dec. 1876) used the following words: "My intention was to take into account what happens in these areas and to note whether the complaints that I had received were founded. It was my duty as one charged with public functions."
21. A.P.P., BB6, no. 1210–11; and *Pédérastes, 1820–1882 (Services des moeurs)*, DA 230 (6): 395–6.
22. A.P.P., BB6, no. 330, no. 848, and no. 682.
23. Ibid., no. 1301, and no. 1745–6.
24. Ibid., no. 39–43.

25. T.J. Clark, *The Painting of Modern Life: Paris in the Art of Manet and his Followers* (Princeton: Princeton University Press, 1984), 205–58.
26. Ibid., 33–5, 207–8.
27. Ibid., 220–4. Some of the titles of Degas' paintings on this subject are: "Les Musiciens à l'orchestre," 1872; "Cabaret," *c*. 1875–7; "Le Café-concert des Ambassadeurs," *c*. 1875–7; "Au café-concert, le chanson du chien," *c*. 1875–7; "La Chanteuse au gant," 1878; and "Le Café-concert," 1882.
28. A.P.P., BB6, no. 850–1, and no. 1602–4. One of these men, Prieur, had a history of arrests for public offenses against decency. On 18 March 1873 the police arrested him for obscenities on one of the streets of Paris, and on 20 June 1877 they arrested him for masturbating in front of other men in a urinal near the Bourse. Despite his marriage, he seemed to enjoy participating in the various sexual activities of the male homosexual subculture. The first case is not in the police ledger, but it is mentioned in the court records. See Archives de Paris, *Registres du Tribunal de Grandes instances de la Seine*, D1U6, 18 March 1873. The second case is A.P.P., BB6, no. 1223.
29. *Le Petit Journal*, 25 Dec. 1876, and *Le Figaro*, 24 Dec. 1876.
30. *Le Petit Journal*, 25 Dec. 1876, and *Le Figaro*, 24 Dec. 1876.
31. Canler, *Mémoires*, 269.
32. Ibid., 288–9.
33. *Le Petit Journal*, 25 Dec. 1876, and *Le Temps*, 24 Dec. 1876.
34. *Le Petit Journal*, 25 Dec. 1876; *Le Temps*, 24 Dec. 1876; *La Gazette des Tribunaux*, 24 Dec. 1876, and *Le Figaro*, 24 Dec. 1876.
35. Benjamin F. Martin, *Crime and Criminal Justice Under the Third Republic: The Shame of Marianne* (Baton Rouge: Louisiana State University Press, 1990), 78.
36. A.P.P., BB6, no. 1210–11; and DA 230 (6): 395–6.
37. *Le Temps*, 24 Dec. 1876; *La Gazette des Tribunaux*, 24 Dec. 1876; *Le Petit Journal*, 25 Dec. 1876, and *Le Figaro*, 24 Dec. 1876.
38. *Le Petit Journal*, 25 Dec. 1876; *Le Figaro*, 24 Dec. 1876.
39. *Le Figaro*, 24 Dec. 1876.
40. *Le Petit Journal*, 25 Dec. 1876.
41. *Le Figaro*, 24 Dec. 1876; *Le Temps*, 24 Dec. 1876.
42. *Le Figaro*, 24 Dec. 1876.
43. *Le Temps*, 25 Dec. 1876.
44. *Le Petit Journal*, 25 Dec. 1876; *Le Figaro*, 24 Dec. 1876; *Le Temps*, 25 Dec. 1876, and *La Gazette des Tribunaux*, 24 Dec. 1876.
45. *Le Figaro*, 24 Dec. 1876, and *Le Temps*, 25 Dec. 1876.
46. *Le Temp*, 25 Dec. 1876; *Le Figaro*, 24 Dec. 1876, and *Le Petit Journal*, 25 Dec. 1876.
47. *Le Figaro*, 24 Dec. 1876.
48. An analysis of 373 convictions for public offenses against decency between 1873 and 1879 demonstrates that the most common penalties were a prison term of three to eight months and a fine of 16 francs. A.P.P., BB6.
49. *Le Figaro*, 31 Dec. 1876, and *Le Petit Journal*, 1 Jan. 1877. According to the *Dictionnaire des biographies françaises*, he had exiled himself to Buenos

Aires, although Claude Courouve has written that he had fled to Brazil. See Courouve, *Vocabulaire*, 117–18.

50. A.P.P., DA 230 (6): 395–6. His friends were: Armand Burbette, 18; Jean-Baptiste Desjardin, 54; Louis Desmettre, 34; Pierre Dinot, 26; Jean Gagey, 30; Louis-Joseph Garnier, 49; Jean Lalanne, 36; Jules-Adolphe Loy, 34; Léon-Armand Villemard, 18; Jacques Visbecq, 52; and Henri-Pierre Wilmet, 29.
51. A.P.P., BB6, no. 966, no. 1003–4, no. 1005, and no. 1049.
52. A.P.P., DA 230 (6): 395–6.
53. A.P.P., BB6, no. 1210–11.
54. *Le Petit Journal*, 25 Dec. 1876.
55. Georges Herelle, "Anecdotes contemporains. Ex diariis. 1858–1889," Ms. 3395–3396, Bibliothèque Municipale de Troyes, Troyes, France.
56. Edmond et Jules de Goncourt, *Journal: mémoires de la vie littèraire* (Paris: R. Laffont, 1989), 13 Dec. 1876, 2 Aug. 1877, 28 Jan. 1890.
57. Courouve, *Vocabulaire*, 117–18.
58. Eugen Weber, *Peasants into Frenchmen: The Modernization of Rural France, 1870–1914* (Stanford: Stanford University Press, 1976).
59. Michel Foucault, *The Birth of the Clinic: An Archaeology of Medical Perception*, translated by A.M. Sheridan Smith (New York: Vintage Books, 1975); Foucault, *Discipline and Punish: The Birth of the Prison*, translated by Alan Sheridan (New York: Vintage Books, 1979); Foucault, *The History of Sexuality: An Introduction*, translated by Robert Hurley (New York: Vintage Books, 1990).

3 Conjugality on Trial: the Rukhmabai Case and the Debate on Indian Child-Marriage in Late-Victorian Britain

Antoinette Burton

By now it is practically axiomatic that knowledge about the East – and in particular, about India – circulated throughout European cultures from the eighteenth century onward.[1] What passes for a truism in the wake of Edward Said and his critics has yet, however, to be fleshed out in historically specific detail. British newspapers' coverage of the trial of Rukhmabai, a child-bride who contested her husband's claims to conjugal rights in the Bombay High Court in the mid-1880s, is one discrete example of the extent colonial knowledge was available to western metropolitan audiences at home, as well as how constitutive ostensibly domestic matters – in this case, one Hindu woman's conjugality – were to the performance and preservation of colonial rule. This essay argues that the late-Victorian metropolitan press, with some help from Rudyard Kipling, "made public" the body of an Indian woman as evidence of the necessity of British imperial rule at the exact moment that Indian nationalism emerged. Implicit in this display was the argument that by virtue of their incapacity to protect – or manage – recalcitrant wives, Indian men were as yet unfit for self-government. By publicizing the trial, the British press contributed to the reordering of Victorian "domestic" space for the consumption of imperial spectacle, a characteristically *fin-de-siècle* phenomenon in Britain.[2]

Historians of nineteenth-century Indian culture and society have read Rukhmabai's trial as one of the precursors to the Age of Consent Act of 1891 – legislation which raised the age of consent for girls in India from 10 to 12 years of age, making sexual intercourse illegal with a girl below the stipulated age.[3] The Act's most vociferous advocate was

Behramji Malabari, a Parsee reformer and Bombay journalist whose "Notes on Infant Marriage and Enforced Widowhood" were published in 1884 and who championed Rukhmabai's cause not just in Bombay but in Britain as well. Malabari contended that British claims to be a civilizing power were hollow, and its government in India a "sleeping giant," if legislation to ameliorate the fate of child-brides were not enacted. Although a Parsee, he claimed to be as critical of Hindu social and especially "domestic" practices as the British, and though he tried to align himself with the British civilizing mission, his arguments for the Age of Consent Act were nonetheless a challenge to the legitimacy of British rule.[4] Opposition to the Act was just as vociferous and, because it came primarily from reformers defending Hindu tradition, it was equally (if differently) critical of the Raj. For instance, B.G. Tilak led the agitation against the Act in western India on the grounds that it violated Britain's post-Mutiny pledge of non-interference in religious customs – a campaign which coincided with his emergence as a nationalist leader and with the rise of Hindu militancy in that region. Opposition was also fierce in Bengal, where the mobilization against the Age of Consent Act "played an important part in radicalizing the nationalist movement in Bengal."[5] The trial of Rhukhmabai and the social reform movements that were galvanized in its wake are thus inextricably bound up with the history of Indian nationalism, though not necessarily in any self-evident way. In keeping with presumptions about Hindu conjugality articulated by male reformers supportive of the abolition of *sati* (the practice of widow-burning) in 1829 and the Hindu Widow Remarriage Act (1856), those nationalist leaders who endorsed the 1891 legislation had their own agendas with regard to the bodies of Indian women – rooting the notion of marital "consent," for example, in biological imperatives (age of puberty) rather than in considerations of choice or compatibility.[6] It is in this context that Tanika Sarkar urges us to consider how Rukhmabai's actions "violently foregrounded the sexual double standard" at the heart of Hindu conjugality and "prised opened the imagined community [of Hindus] along the lines of caste and gender." In this respect, the trial helped to reveal the illegitimacy of male Hindu reformers' claims to speak in one voice against British rule and on behalf of "the Indian woman."[7]

While the trial became the stuff of debates over nationalist and social reform in India, it also participated in and helped to reshape longstanding arguments in the imperial metropole about Indian women's education and the readiness of Indian men for self-government. Rukhmabai's defiance of her husband's claims on her person and her willingness to contest those claims in Bombay High Court – not to mention in the court of public opinion – was turned by the press in Britain into a spectacle of why Indian religious custom represented all that was wrong with and redeemable about Indian society. Whether conservative, progressive, or even radical in contemporary Victorian terms, newspapers across the United Kingdom all used Rukhmabai's plight to debate the virtues and limits of the official policy of cultural non-intervention in "native" beliefs and practices, as well as to produce their own versions of what constituted "the Indian woman." If, as Vinay Lal has argued, the trial in the colonial context was itself a form of knowledge where the micropolitics of imperial power might be played out, the publicity given to Rukhmabai's trial in the United Kingdom helped to foreground for imperially-minded Britons the ways in which the regulation of Hindu sexual morality was a "vital political topic," crucial to the stability of British rule in India.[8] Rukhmabai herself was an important contributor to this debate, and not just in India. Nor was she the only Indian woman to take a position on such questions. For instance, Anandibai Joshee, a Maharashtrian woman who became the first Indian female medical doctor, was an outspoken critic of child marriage as early as 1880, and an advocate of interference by the colonial state fully ten years before the passage of the 1891 Act.[9] Yet Indian women were not consulted when the government canvassed the provincial leaders for evaluations of the effects of child-marriage in their localities. But in Bombay presidency (an administrative division of British India) women made a cogent and impassioned case for government intervention in child-marriage in their magazines and social reform organizations in the wake of the High Court's decision, with Rukhmabai and her countrywoman Pandita Ramabai among the most prominent participants.[10] As she did in Bombay, Rukhmabai used the press in Britain to author her own explanations of what her case signified, what was flawed about the Hindu marriage system, and what should be done to secure socio-economic emancipation for Indian women. The gendered critique of both imperial rule and indigenous patriarchy that she produced for the English reading public meant that in this debate about the fate of empires and civilizations at least, the speech of an Indian woman had to be reckoned with.

Rukhmabai's case thus became a political football, with the stories told about it being mobilized by a variety of historical actors in both Britain and India. That her trial was turned into a story about female virtue suggests that contests over the morality of the public realm were not limited to "domestic" British politics, but were threaded through the complex domains of imperial culture and the middle-class colonial imagination as well.[11] While this phenomenon affirms scholars' recent claims that history cannot be told as a single story, it also suggests that no story can be contained inside a single geopolitical space.[12] My argument here is not so much that the nation must be enlarged to recognize the frame of imperial relations which constituted it, but rather that debates over questions like Rukhmabai's trial require us to ask whether the nation remains a useful category of historical analysis at all for understanding the relationships between empire and "home."[13]

* * *

In March of 1884 Dadaji Bhikaji petitioned the Bombay High Court to direct that his wife, Rukhmabai, move into his house and live with him. Rukhmabai (b. 1864), a Hindu woman who married Dadaji in 1876 when she was eleven and he nineteen, had resided for over a decade with her stepfather, the noted Bombay physician Dr. Sakharam Arjun, her mother, and several siblings.[14] Although Dadaji was a distant relative of the doctor's and had visited the house on occasion, their marriage had never been consummated. When Dadaji requested her to live with him, she refused. He filed a case for the "restitution of conjugal rights" and thereby initiated one of the most publicized court cases in Bombay and indeed, in India, in the nineteenth century.[15]

At first it looked as if Dadaji's suit would be in vain. Mr. Justice Pinhey dismissed the case in the fall of 1885 on the grounds that it was not maintainable – first because restitution could not be claimed where no conjugal relations had occurred and second, because such claims had no foundation in Hindu law.[16] As Sudhir Chandra has noted, Pinhey so doubted the legality of Dadaji's claim that the counsel for the defense was not even called upon at this juncture. After trying unsuccessfully to recover costs, Dadaji appealed Pinhey's judgment, and in March of 1886 two appellate judges ordered that the suit be remanded for a decision. The case was heard this time before Justice Farran. He determined in March of 1887 in favor of the plaintiff, Dadaji, persuaded in part by the argument that while Hindu law did not order restitution, neither did it forbid it. Rukhmabai was ordered to go and live with her husband within a month, or else submit to the court's directive – which was six months' imprisonment. Farran's judgment created a sensation among "native" newspapers in India and reached the highest echelons of the British government there, in part because the Matrimonial Causes Act had removed such penal provisions for English spouses in 1884.[17]

Even the Viceroy followed the proceedings, cabling A.R. Scoble, the Law Member, with this admonition: "I hope you are keeping your eye on the Rukhmabai case. It would never do to allow her to be put into prison."[18] An appeal was filed against Farran's judgment and there was talk of Rukhmabai presenting her case to the Privy Council in England. In one last attempt by Dadaji to recover costs from Rukhmabai and her family, he agreed to relinquish his claims in July of 1888 for a payment of 2,000 rupees. Through the influence of Edith Pechey-Phipson, a British medical doctor practicing in India, and with the patronage of some English feminists in London, Rukhmabai traveled to Britain shortly thereafter, where she trained at the London School of Medicine for Women and qualified as a medical doctor in 1893. She was appointed the head of a woman's dispensary at Surat and was eventually hailed as one of India's "pioneering medical women."[19]

The Calcutta correspondent to the London *Times* had introduced Rukhmabai to the English public in March of 1886, when her case was brought before the appellate judges. As James Hammerton has illustrated, the Victorian period was an age when "the drama of sexual antagonism in marriage" was a crucial constituent of cultural discourse, as well as the object of relentless public scrutiny.[20] The 1880s was a particularly highly charged moment in this respect, when Britons may well have had the Dilke divorce trial, the "Maiden Tribute of Modern Babylon" scandal, and the passage of the Criminal Law Amendment Act (which raised the age of consent for girls from thirteen to sixteen and broadened police power over prostitutes) still fresh in their minds.[21] Readers were referred to Rukhmabai's letters to the *Times of India*, which had been written under the byline "A Hindoo Lady" and excerpted in the London *Times* the previous year under the same pseudonym. The *Times* correspondent described the letters, which condemned early marriage and the conditions in which child-widows often found themselves, as "striking," "forcible," and "remarkable." Even more remarkable in his view was the sight of Rukhmabai herself. She "has come again prominently before the public," he reported, "as herself affording an example of her own pathetic description of the unhappy lot of her sex in India." From the start, Rukhmabai-the-child-bride was imagined as performing not just the whole condition of Indian women, but their pathetic destiny as well. While narrating the basic facts of the case (their ages at marriage, her upbringing), the *Times* reporter represented the issue as one of marital incompatibility: Rukhmabai was "well educated . . . a lady of high intelligence" while Dadaji was "said to be little better than a coolie, ignorant, uncultivated, and unable to earn more than ten rupees a month."

If class and status were at issue here, so were Rukhmabai's "lady-like" sensibilities. "The idea of going to live with such a man, was utterly repulsive to her." When the correspondent updated the status of the case some three weeks later, he resumed this theme of the "gifted" lady and the unworthy suitor. After recapping the background details of the court case, he wrote that Rukhmabai refused to live with her husband when he "demanded" it "on the grounds that she had no voice in the marriage, that he was personally repugnant to her, that his character was bad, that his health was indifferent." Where Dadaji was a person of questionable character, Judge Pinhey was, conversely, noble and just, with the best interests of Rukhmabai at heart. He dismissed the suit without calling the defendant because, it was reported, he believed that "it would be a barbarous, cruel and revolting thing to compel her to cohabit under the circumstances... neither law nor the practice of the Courts justified him in making such an order."[22] For all that Rukhmabai was at the center of this case, Dadaji and Pinhey ended up framing this narrative, as the colonial native and the English judge who faced each other off over the body of the Indian woman.

It is worth emphasizing that the debate about child-marriage set in motion by the London *Times* did not arise simply out of the opportunity provided by Rukhmabai's case. Discussions of the good Hindu wife and her "unconquered purity" were crucial to the wide variety of revivalist and reformist debates about politics, religion, and the parameters of colonial rule in nineteenth-century India. Indeed, in Tanika Sarkar's estimation, not only was the Hindu woman's body "molded from her infancy by the Shastric regimen of non-consensual, indissoluble infant marriage," but her "subjectivity and agency... [were] exhausted by this embodiment."[23] Hindu nationalists, for whom conjugality was the centerpiece of nationalist discourse in the nineteenth century, critiqued the Hindu marriage system (early marriage and compulsory widowhood) even as they placed it at the heart of their socio-cultural struggle against western values and influences. It was at the urging of I.C. Vidyasagar that the Government had included an age of consent provision in the Penal Code of 1860, making sexual intercourse with a girl under the age of ten qualify as rape. Mahadev Govind Ranade, a prominent theist and reformer, published an article in an 1878 issue of the journal of the Poona Sarvajanik Sabha (a local reform organization) suggesting connections between the problem of child-marriage and that of overpopulation. He later exhorted the people of Poona to pledge to raise the age of marriage and he also helped Malabari prepare his "Notes" and present them to Lord Ripon in 1884.[24] We know too that Hindu women subjected the Hindu home and its institutional idioms to critical scrutiny from the 1860s onwards. Rather than extolling the pleasures of early marriage they emphasized its traumas, including separation from the family home and especially the lack of access to knowledge through education. For instance, Rassundari Devi recalled in 1870 that although she took some solace in her mother's injunction that leaving home was divine will, as a child-bride she felt "very much like the sacrificial goat being dragged to the altar, the same hopeless situation, the same agonized screams." Kailashbashini Debi was more frank about what a girl bride might face: "conjugal love," she wrote in 1863, "has all but disappeared from our country."[25]

In Britain it was *sati* (which had technically been abolished by the Governor-General in 1829) that tended to preoccupy those interested in reforming Hindu society. It served as an exemplar of the pathologies of Hindu tradition and backwardness into the 1880s and beyond. Such presumptions were aided equally by missionary, official/government, and feminist discourses, each of which equated women with tradition and identified traditional gender prescriptions as the chief object of the civilizing mission.[26] The practice of *purdah* (seclusion) and the existence of the *zenana* (women's quarters) also played their part in locating women and heterosexual relations at the heart of colonial rule – and in structuring challenges to it by orthodox and progressive reformers in India alike. But by the end of the 1860s child-marriage had also become an important issue in domestic social reform circles, due in large measure to the influence of Mary Carpenter, who chronicled the first of four trips to India in 1866 in a sensational and celebrated two-volume account, *Six Months in India*. Part travelogue and part policy statement, the book publicized the plight of Indian women and delivered a polemic on the need for Englishwomen to take up the burden of Indian women's education so that they might in turn rescue India from decay and primitivism. For Carpenter as for many Englishwomen who would take up her call in the later Victorian period, child-marriage appeared to be basic to what was wrong with Indian society. As Carpenter saw it, early marriage fixed Indian women's mental and emotional capacities in childhood, preventing them not just from developing their faculties but more importantly, from nurturing their children – part of the "citizenry," the workforce, and the future livelihood of the British empire.[27]

Carpenter in fact gleaned much of what she knew about the status of Indian women from "progressive" male Indian reformers who she met in Britain before her trip to India and during her stay there. Thus knowledge about child-marriage, like that about India more generally, did not originate either "at home" or in the empire, but was made available by exchanges and transactions occasioned by movement back and forth and back again.[28] In part because of these influences, Carpenter established the National Indian Association in Bristol in 1870. It moved to London under the capable direction of E.A. Manning after Carpenter's death in 1877, where it functioned as a clearing-house for ideas and practical schemes for Indian reform until the First World War. The NIA fostered a sense of community among reformers and philanthropists interested in India, and its journal, the *Indian Magazine and Review*, provided subscribers with news and information through its several branches in India and, most significant for our purposes, kept questions of early marriage and enforced widowhood alive as two of the critical indicators of British claims to progress and "civilization" in India.

The *Times* reporter set the terms of this national debate when he remarked that "the sympathies of the Court were entirely with the lady" but that "the question they had to try was not one of sentiment, but of law." He predicted that the appellate judges would find against Rukhmabai and when they did, the *Times* picked up the story again. In March of 1887, after Farran rendered his decision, the *Times* reported that the case was "on the point of reaching a crisis." Rukhmabai was described in this report as the same "refined and highly cultivated lady" she had been when the trial started and Dadaji was still "a mere coolie." But now, the English public learned, he was not only "utterly ignorant and uneducated" but "consumptive" as well. Clearly, all kinds of characterizations were shifting in the wake of Farran's order. Significantly, in its report of Farran's decision, the *Times* cast all the judges as helpless cogs in the wheel of British justice. Farran became "the Court" and the Court "had no option save to pass an order that [Rukhmabai] should join her husband within a month." Even her counsel "could only repeat" his earlier arguments, that "his client had never consented to the marriage, and never regarded the man as her husband." Rukhmabai's punishment was also described in mechanistic terms: "should she fail to do so she would be liable to six months' imprisonment." This claim of reluctance to enact colonial law did more than echo the theme of empire's unwelcome burden. It worked to all but erase both Rukhmabai's agency in contesting Dadaji's claims on her *and* her determination to resist the claims of the colonial state once she was sentenced – for as her lawyers had made it clear, she anticipated that prison might be the consequence, and she went to court anyway.[29]

What followed was a host of letters to the editor explaining the workings of the law, debating Rukhmabai's sentence, and often articulating, whether implicitly or explicitly, a connection between the body of the Hindu woman and the stability of British rule in India. Someone signing himself "Judge," who wrote from the East India Club, St. James's Square, London, had evidently been a magistrate in India, where he claimed to have "had to decide a great number of these cases" and to "have tried all sorts of devices to set the girls free." In most of those, "the difficulty had arisen from a preferred lover, and not from difference of education or position." His experience had shown him that "in Eastern climates girls are precocious, and, unless early settled in her future home, the girl is almost certain to disgrace her family, and the result of such an event is either her murder or such loss of honour to the family that they will never be able to hold their heads up again." Early marriage was, in other words, the right and proper solution to oriental female sexual promiscuity – a solution which he believed the British courts should rightly enforce. According to "Judge," "the real mistake" in Rukhmabai's case "was educating her so as to make her unfit company for her husband, or rather in so educating her as to make her think only of her own comfort and not recognize her great mission to spread education and information among her humbler sisters." If these two arguments appear to be somewhat at odds, they resonated with a critique of female education in Britain which was prominent during this period – that is, that too much learning alienated women from their wifely/domestic duties, making them selfish and self-serving.[30]

"Judge's" was not the only legal opinion proffered in letters to the editor, though it may certainly be counted as among the least sympathetic to Rukhmabai. In fact, much of the correspondence to the *Times* was concerned with interpreting the relationship between Hindu law and English law as a means of explaining what had happened in the various phases of the trial.[31] F.L. Latham, advocate-general of Bombay and one of Rukhmabai's defense lawyers, insisted that while Hindu law "enjoins infant marriage, and, like other primitive laws, declares the absolute subjection of the wife to her husband," at the same time it provided "no legal process by which a wife could be compelled to return to her husband's society if unwilling." Though the possibility of conjugal rape is alluded to here, it is never directly addressed. If anything, it is the law which intrudes where it is not welcome – acting, as Upendra Baxi has argued, not just as the state's representative but as its phallic emissary as well.[32] It was Latham's contention that "unfortunately for [Rukhmabai], English law stepped in" – that is to say, the English judges had relied on precedents set by the "old Ecclesiastical Courts," precedents which enforced "the duties resulting from the marriage ties as matters of conscience subject to the supervision of the Church." His outrage was thus reserved for the administrators of the Indian courts, who seemed incapable of modernizing the law quickly enough so that it could protect an Indian woman from her husband's unwelcome society."[33]

Max Muller, a German professor of Sanskrit at Oxford who was well-known for his orientalist admiration for India's "golden" (Vedic) age, agreed. For him too, the law was the offending party, capable of doing the kind of violence to the body of the Hindu woman that could not be named, but which circulated nonetheless throughout discussions of Rukhmabai's case. He argued on April 25, 1887 that "the case of Rukhmabai has really very little to do with Indian law," but his was more of a defense of English law than a criticism of its extended purview, as Latham's letter had been.

> Let the Indian law be what it is, let public opinion in India sanction the sale and so-called marriage of children of three or four years of age, let those who, like Rukhmabai and others revolt against this degrading slavery submit to being boycotted or outcasted, but what had English law to do with such abomination? The Hindoos themselves protest against foreign tribunals interfering with their sacred customs of marriage. Why, then should English law offer to aid in the restitution of conjugal rights, supposing that conjugal rights exist?... Whatever the High Court may have decided, the sooner English judges wash their hands of such iniquities the better for the good repute of English law.[34]

Muller, like Latham, was unwilling to admit that although marriage was based on contract, the state, through its laws, was in fact the enforcer of marital relations. Neither man was prepared to confront the role of the colonial state in the "abomination" to which Rukhmabai was subjected. To do so would require them to admit not just the failure of the bourgeois colonial project but its violation of the very notion of contract relations as well.

Muller, for his part, objected to the very concept "restitution of conjugal rights," on the grounds that it was an idiomatic expression of "English legal language." According to him it was "a phrase utterly unknown in Hindoo law" and "quite inapplicable" to Rukhmabai's case. In another letter to the *Times* in August of 1887, he contended that Rukhmabai's troubles had been aggravated by English law. "Formerly, a woman who committed this so-called breach of contract was under the ban of society. She was *patita*, fallen, but she was not exposed to violence, and the idea of sending her to prison, like a common criminal, never entered the minds of native law-givers."[35]

Muller wrote four letters in all to the *Times* during the period of Rukhmabai's trial, and these in turn generated several replies. But if he defended Hindu law in this instance, it was only in order to support his conviction that legal recourse was not the ultimate solution to the problems raised by Rukhmabai's case. Education was what was called for, and Rukhmabai was proof of its success. For it was exposure to western learning that had made her capable, in Muller's view, of becoming "the best judge... herself" of her own marriage choice.[36] Muller thereby vindicated the bourgeois civilizing mission (which since Macaulay had aimed at the internalization through education of English values by brown-skinned subjects) and made the person of Rukhmabai into "evidence" in the case against too-rapid change by government intervention. Most of the letter-writers were staunchly against government interference through legislation, with one J. Scott stating unequivocally that "the Indian people cannot be made moral by an Act of Parliament."[37] Others saw in the Rukhmabai case an opportunity to move the discussion away from legislation to philanthropy and in so doing, to advance specific schemes for the improvement of Indian women's condition. Muller quoted Pandita Ramabai as well as a Hindu pundit with whom he was in correspondence on the plight of Hindu widows and suggested that money be raised through charitable organizations in Britain to establish widows' homes in India.[38] Letters came in to support this idea, especially after Ramabai wrote the *Times* herself on September 27, 1887 explaining in great detail her own scheme for a child-widows' home and calling for donations to be directed to E.A. Manning's address, the site of the NIA offices in London.[39] Ramabai emphasized the plight of child widows, thus linking her particular cause with Rukhmabai's in the public mind – a cause which she had already publicized in her book, *The High Caste Hindu Woman*. The debate which followed in the wake of Rukhmabai's trial thus took off in a variety of directions, moving public attention beyond the question of child-marriage *per se* to "the problem of Indian women" and its relationship – both practical and symbolic – to the projects of empire.

The *Times*' influence was considerable in shaping how news of the trial was reported in Britain, since other newspapers and periodicals depended on it almost exclusively for information about the Rukhmabai case. The *Pall Mall Gazette*, for example, followed the trial in its "Occasional Notes" section until Dadaji settled his suit in the summer of 1888. But it tended to rely on the *Times*' Indian correspondent and often reprinted *in toto* his accounts of the marriage law agitation or of the trial. It editorialized little about the trial itself, except when it expressed the rather hackneyed conviction that "the case will deal a deathblow to the pernicious system of infant marriage, and mark an important step in the progress of social reform in India."[40] But its coverage prompted at least one letter-to-the-editor from someone who signed himself "a Disgusted Hindoo" and who apparently had enclosed a set of newspaper clippings from Bombay in his letter. "From the accompanying papers you will see that in Bombay, in the name of justice, a fearful amount of injustice and atrocity will be committed upon the person of a poor, almost defenseless Hindoo girl." In contrast to the correspondents to the *Times*, this writer thought that "the legal position of the present judgment [Pinhey's] does not appear to be at all sound or logical, either according to Hindoo law or English law."[41]

Women's magazines also covered Rukhmabai's case, again relying heavily on the accounts of the *Times* correspondent. Sudhir Chandra has analyzed the way the *Queen* blamed both Dadaji and the orthodox Hindu community for Rukhmabai's troubles, but not without chastising the more progressive "natives" for bowing to the pressure of public meetings and agitations as well. Although the *Queen* admitted that interference could not be countenanced at this time, the magazine assured its readers that change in India could not but occur "with ever-accelerating velocity, and . . . the time may not be too far distant when such outrage on human liberty, as evidenced in the case of Rukhmabai, may be forever at an end." The *Queen*'s account put less emphasis on the role of English law in the case in order to pathologize indigenous religious statutes, but it shared the more general conviction circulating in the metropolitan press that "the colonized were to be regenerated in spite of themselves."[42] Another journal, the *Englishwoman's Review*, also recapped almost verbatim what had been written in the *Times* about the suit. Yet, the author of "Hindoo Marriage Law" for the *Englishwoman's Review* was virtually alone amongst the sources cited here in expressing concern about what would happen to Rukhmabai once the imprisonment order had been given. In this event, the author pointed out, "her troubles will not necessarily be at an end, for if her husband again requests her to live with him, and she again refuses, a fresh cause of action will arise, and the whole miserable business may be repeated over and over again after the expiration of each term of imprisonment."[43] If the *EWR* and the *Queen* were the only women's periodicals to follow the case, this was because they were among the few of their kind in this period. The *Women's Penny Paper* did not begin until the fall of 1888, and when it did, an advertisement of Rukhmabai's fund-raising efforts for her travel and medical education in Britain appeared in one of the first issues.[44]

Attention to the case was not, significantly, limited either to the London *Times* or to newspapers in the capital city of the empire. Papers as diverse as the *Daily Graphic*, the *Echo*, the *Aberdeen Observer*, the *Western Daily Press*, and the *Manchester Examiner* covered the story, and many of these were less restrained than the *Times* in the rhetoric they used to characterize Rukhmabai and Dadaji – who became tragic characters and figures of romance and melodrama in the provincial press. Although the *Bradford Observer* referred to Rukhmabai as "a Hindoo girl," most papers emphasized her lady-like status, her refinement and education. The *Bristol Evening News* called her "a damsel," and the *Scotsman*, "the heroine of a battle which is . . . fought not only for herself, but for her countrywomen."[45] Like the characterizations in the *Times*, the more cultivated Rukhmabai became, the further Dadaji sank into an irredeemably coolie-like status. A contributor to the *Western Daily Press* declared him an "ignorant and degraded peasant"; readers of the *Aberdeen Observer* were told that he was "an ignorant and idle boor"; and to the *Bradford Observer* he was "very vulgar indeed."[46] The language of class as marked by work (coolie labor), thus bears the burden of marking the masculine body as a carrier of disease and (sexual) violence – even as the pleasure to be derived from such a sexually charged spectacle was broadcast throughout metropolitan Britain.

Neither Rukhmabai nor Dadaji were unaware of these representations; and while the case was being turned into melodrama for British audiences at home, they were each publishing explanations of their conduct and defending their good names in newspapers in Bombay and all over India.[47] Some of the more unseemly details of the case – namely, that Dadaji lived with an uncle who had a mistress for fourteen years and that this was among the reasons that Rukhmabai judged him unsuitable – were kept from the British public, even though they were common knowledge to readers of the English-language press in India.[48] Indeed, in spite of the widespread coverage Rukhmabai's trial received in the British press, as much was suppressed about the context of the case as was broadcast.

Colonial knowledge, then, was not just circulated at the heart of the empire. In this instance its circulation was carefully managed, and in such a way as to suggest that Rukhmabai's case was the justification that Indian reformers needed to present a case against child-marriage to the Government of India – when in fact the mechanisms of its publicity and the disinterestedness of its publicizers were being interrogated throughout the subcontinent. Despite the control exercised in Britain over Rukhmabai's attempts to influence public opinion in Britain via her letters to the *Times of India*, Rukhmabai herself had made use of the public space afforded to her by metropolitan newspapers to articulate her own version of events and her own ideas about what kind of action was appropriate for ameliorating the condition of Indian women. The *Times*' Calcutta correspondent extracted only short selections from Rukhmabai's letters, which had been published in greater length in the *Times of India*.[49] Significantly, it was the National Indian Association which reprinted them in their totality in Britain. The first one appeared in the September 1885 issue of the NIA's journal, with the accompanying prefatory note:

> We mentioned in the last *Journal* a remarkable letter by a Hindu lady on Child Marriages which had appeared in the *Times of India*. We now give the [first] letter, as an important contribution to the discussion of the subject. A certain degree of exaggeration must, we are told, be allowed for in regard to the generalisations, which the writer makes from her own experience, and some of her suggestions might not be practical; but there must be much truth in the facts and arguments put forward, and we hope that this touching appeal will not be without effect in regard to customs which so greatly need reform.[50]

Thus was the "speaking voice" of "the Indian woman" stage-managed – that is, produced in specific institutional locations for specific colonialist purposes. In the body of her letter, Rukhmabai anticipated the possibility that her plea might be dismissed as hyperbole. "My English readers," she wrote, "can hardly conceive the hard lot entailed upon Hindu women by the custom of early marriage. They might think the picture a little too highly coloured, but I assure them that there is not, at least intentional, exaggeration."[51]

Rukhmabai's argument consisted of three interrelated parts: the differential effect on men and women of early marriage; the linkage between reform of the custom and female improvement through education; and finally, the need for government reform intervention. In her view, the disproportionately negative impact of child marriage on women was crucially linked to the question of female education. Early marriage rarely prevented boys from carrying on their studies, whereas girls who married at eight could continue their studies only until the age of ten (with the onset of puberty). If they wished to go on after that, they would need the permission of their husbands' families. "But even in these advanced times," she pointed out, "and even in Bombay – the chief centre of civilisation – how many mothers-in-law are there who would send their daughters to school after they are ten years old?" She chastised those indigenous elite reformers who championed women's education and yet resisted changes in marriage custom. "Unless this state of things is changed, all the efforts at higher female education seem like putting the cart before the horse."[52]

Rukhmabai returned several times to the idea that Hindu men failed to take debates about child-marriage seriously because they failed to understand its impact on women *as women*. Her claim that "as *men* among Hindus have much more freedom of action than *women*, they are indifferent to the social reforms which prejudicially affect the other sex," implied not just that male reformers did not see women as gendered beings who were discriminated against on the grounds of sexual difference, but that they did not see themselves as men with gender-specific privileges either – a rare enough kind of argument against patriarchy in the nineteenth century. Rukhmabai was persuaded that it was the duty of the British government in India to take action:

> If, Sir, Government shirks its responsibility and gives up this matter, it may be, in deference to the wishes of these gentlemen [male elites resistant to reform], there is not the smallest chance of our people taking it upon themselves for years to come, even if then; and in that case, though we are, by God's grace, living under the beneficent rule of her Most Gracious Majesty the Queen-Empress, there can be no one left to protect the women of India from the tyranny of these abominable customs.[53]

This was followed by a five-point outline of what such legislation might look like, including provisions to raise the age of marriage to 15 for girls and 20 for boys, and one to require young men who married below the stipulated age to give up their right to a university education. Although Rukhmabai's essay had begun as a letter to the editor (hence the "Sir" in the above citation) by the end she was addressing the leaders of the Hindu community who claimed to have the best interests of Indian women at heart:

> I entreat you, gentlemen ... to co-operate with Government in emancipating your sons and daughters from the social thraldom under which they groan. If you succeed in bringing about this salutary reform ... the mental and material prosperity of India, will follow as

> a matter of course, and India will revert to its once proud position in the scale of nations.[54]

In an era when speaking in public blurred the line between respectable and "public" women (prostitutes) in Britain – and when upper-caste Indian women's sexual respectability was contingent on seclusion – Rhukmabai's letters to newspapers must be viewed as both courageous and dangerous to her reputation as "a Hindu lady." Rukhmabai had another occasion during the height of attention to the court case to address the public in Britain. On April 9, 1887 a letter from Rukhmabai appeared in the London *Times*. It was printed with a cover letter by the Bishop of Carlisle, whose sister had been in correspondence with her. The Bishop prefaced the letter by indicating that Rukhmabai did not know that he was going to publish it. After giving a précis of the practice of child-marriage in India, Rukhmabai offered her own version of her life leading up to "my unfortunate trial." In her narrative, Dadaji is characterized not as a "coolie," but as a schoolboy who "fell into bad companies," "was attacked by consumption," and was so sickly that "he was confined to his bed for three continuous years, in such a state that he was not expected to live another season." She, meanwhile, left school at the age of eleven, but:

> began to learn English at home . . . day by day my love for education and social reform increased, and I continued to pursue my studies as much as I could . . . by aid of the little education which I had been able to gain, I began seriously to consider the former and present condition of our Hindoo women, and wished to do something, if in my power, to ameliorate our present sufferings. On the other hand . . . the habits of the man with whom I had been given in marriage added more to my natural distaste for married life.[55]

According to Rukhmabai, it was her stepfather who "resolved not to send me to his house to live as his wife." As for Dadaji, he "seemed indifferent to the matter . . . but by some former disputes between the leaders of our caste and the constant instigations of wicked people (very common in India), and in the hope of getting my little money, he was induced to file a suit asking me to go and live as his wife."

Where the *Times*' correspondent had cast her as simply a "refined" lady, Rukhmabai made it clear that she intended to be a reformer with the improvement of Indian women on her agenda. Rukhmabai suggested too that the trial itself was part of that work – an angle that had never been hinted at by the *Times*. Justice Pinhey's decision was "humane" and, in her view, "if it had been supported, would have altered the fate of millions of daughters of India, and the longed-for freedom would have been easily secured." In her concluding paragraphs, Rukhmabai appealed as she had in India to "our beloved Queen Victoria's Government, which has its world-wide fame for best administration." In a shrewd rhetorical maneuver, she reminded her correspondent that 1887 was the year of the Jubilee. "At such an unusual occasion," she wondered, "will the mother listen to an earnest appeal from her millions of Indian daughters and grant them a few simple words of change into the books on Hindoo law?"[56] The Bishop of Carlisle told the editor of the *Times* that "no words can plead [Rukhmabai's] case more eloquently than her own." But he was only partly right, because her speech was not purely her own. It had been both tampered with and re-presented before the public even read it. Carlisle's certainty "that I shall carry you, Sir, and all your readers with me, when I say that the appeal of the poor afflicted Hindoo woman to the Queen, with reference to the Jubilee, is infinitely pathetic" meant that Rukhmabai's own forceful words had to compete with his determination to recast her in the role of the pathetic and "defenseless" Indian woman.

Rukhmabai nonetheless demonstrated her determination to make her case in a metropolitan context where newspapers like the *Times* worked hard to control the kind of news about India which circulated via its columns throughout Britain. Most tellingly, the *Times* tried to use the outburst of opinion for and against Rukhmabai in India to discredit the claims for self-rule then being made on the British government by Indian nationalists. In the same columns where the *Times* gave updates on the trial between 1886 and 1888 it also reported a variety of "native" protests against the Government's legal interference with the custom of child-marriage throughout India. These were abbreviated stories which formed part of the longer daily report on events in India, but they consistently characterized the protests negatively as "agitations" and "outbursts of fanatical hostility" which were "boisterous" and "absolutely uproarious." Although the Indian National Congress, which had had its first meeting in 1886, was not mentioned by name, its meetings and activities were being covered elsewhere in the *Times* during the period of Rukhmabai's trial, and not in a very sympathetic manner. The Indian correspondent referred to it as "the so-called National Congress," and when Indian delegates visited Britain to enlist the support of sympathetic MPs, they were referred to as "ambitious agitators" who were unready for self-government. Most revealing perhaps is the editorial comment offered in March of 1886, in the wake of Dadaji's appeal, which advised that "native reformers... [should] direct their energies less to vague political aspirations and more to the pressing evils of their social system."[57]

For all that the *Times* tried to relegate debates about conjugality to the sphere of social relations and social reform, the publicity given to Rukhmabai's trial raised important questions about the rule of law in British India – questions that were *political* insofar as they threatened the tenuous balance of power the British had sought to maintain since 1857 by pledging (nominal) non-interference in religious customs like the age of marriage. Rudyard Kipling's poem, "In the Case of Rukhmibhaio," offered a view of the trial which was more satirical than that produced by the newspapers, but which made the connections between Indian nationalists' calls for self-rule and the debate about the trial in India unmistakably clear:

> Gentlemen reformers with an English Education –
> Lights of Aryavarta take our heartiest applause
> For the spectacle you offer of an 'educated' nation
> Working out its freedom under 'educated' laws....
>
> Gentlemen reformers, you have heard the story
> Weighed the woman's evidence – marked the
>   man's reply
> Here's a chance for honor, notoriety and glory!
> Graduates of culture will you let that chance go by?
>
> What? No word of protest? Not a sign of pity?
> Not a hand to help the girl, but, in black and white
> Writes the leading oracle of the leading city:
> 'We the Indian Nation, we hold it served her right....'
>
> It is then the brutal Briton feels an impulse, wild, unruly–
> That tingles in the toe nails of a non-official boot –
> Lumps in one mean heap of cruelty the graduate and coolie –
> And the old race-instinct answers to the clamour:
>   Hut you brute.[58]

Kipling's animosity toward the effeminate Bengali was, and is, well-known.[59] For him as no doubt for many metropolitan readers, the spectacle of Rukhmabai enabled the collapse of "the graduate" (Indian National Congressmen) into the coolie (Dadaji) and suggested that at stake in the display of the Hindu woman was the status and masculinity of Indian men – especially where masculinity was defined as a capacity to protect Hindu women.

Opinion in Britain during Rukhmabai's trial appeared to be both against legislation and "pro" Rukhmabai. This is at first glance a contradictory posture, since Rukhmabai herself called on the government repeatedly for legislative reform. But the disavowal of intervention produced, to borrow from Gyan Prakash, a kind of imperialist double-speak: those who sided with Rukhmabai did so to highlight the apparent barbarity of Indian male reformers who abandoned her to prison, not to criticize the imperial government for failing in its responsibilities.[60] Moreover, they dismissed legal intervention as only a temporary measure, pending the sufficient education of the indigenous population in the most civilized (read British) forms of conjugality. The coincidence of debates about Rukhmabai's trial with the tepid and at times outright hostile reception given to the activities of the Indian National Congress by the British press suggests that the case was being used to help solidify already implicit connections between the ability of Indian men to regulate female sexuality and their capacity for self-rule. Even, and especially, when they claimed to have the best interests of Rukhmabai at heart, her supporters in the metropole disparaged Hindu sexual mores by championing as a victim the woman whose very resistance made the court case itself an argument simultaneously against the violence of Hindu conjugality *and* colonial rule.

As in India, the debate on child-marriage in Britain was far from over when Dadaji and Rukhmabai reached their settlement in 1888. In 1890 a child named Phulmonee was "raped to death" by her husband, Hari Mati; she was a girl of 11, he a man of 35. According to Tanika Sarkar, "the event added enormous weight and urgency to Malabari's campaigns for raising the age of consent" in India. It did not go unnoticed in Britain either.[61] Encouraged by supporters of Rukhmabai in Britain, Malabari traveled to London in the spring of 1890, specifically to drum up support for consent legislation. This campaign revived the public debate in the *Times* and the *Englishwoman's Review* and carried it into new discursive spaces in a number of mainstream periodicals as well. Max Muller, Henry Cardinal Manning, and Millicent Garrett Fawcett all lent their support to his crusade. Fifty-five women doctors practicing in India petitioned the government, and Malabari flooded the British public with his treatise, *An Appeal on Behalf of the Daughters of India*.[62] He was hailed in Britain as the spokesman for the marriage reform movement and his book received favorable reviews in the press – while Tilak raised the cry of "Hinduism-in-danger" in Maharashtra and crowds were organized to protest the possibility of reform in the Indian Penal Code in several regions in India.[63] It was not Malabari's campaign in London alone but also the interest generated by the trial of Rukhmabai a few years earlier which helped to establish extra-parliamentary support for the reform of Indian law. And although Malabari dominated the debate in Britain in 1890, the impact of Rukhmabai's participation at this juncture must not be discounted. She was studying medicine at the time in London, where she published a lengthy piece in the *New Review* called "Indian Child Marriages: An Appeal to the Government." In it, she sounded her earlier themes – that child-marriage impeded women's educational progress, that women suffered as a result of it more than men, and that the only remedy could come from the British government. Those in Britain who had followed her trial no doubt recognized her ideological positions. They may also have sympathized with her lament: "Child marriage. Infant marriage. Cradle marriage . . . what a repetition of words, and how wearisome the sound of these words has become to some of us!"[64]

NOTES

1. Edward Said, *Culture and Imperialism* (New York: Vintage Books, 1993).
2. Anne McClintock, *Imperial Leather: Race, Gender and Sexuality in the Colonial Context* (New York: Routledge, 1995), 16.
3. This included the consummation of child-marriages when the bride was under the age of 12. According to Dagmar Engels, "such illegal sex was defined as rape and was punishable by a maximum of ten years imprisonment or transportation for life." See her "The Age of Consent Act of 1891: Colonial Ideology in Bengal," *South Asia Research* 3 (1983): 107.
4. See Behramji Malabari, *An Appeal from the Daughters of India* (London, 1890). His "Notes," together with a collection of his articles in the Bombay press on the problem of child marriage and the case of Rukhmabai, can be found in Dayaram Gidumal, *The Life and Life-Work of Behramji M. Malabari* (Bombay, 1888).
5. Padma Anagol-McGinn, "The Age of Consent Act (1891) Reconsidered: Women's Perspectives and Participation in the Child-Marriage Controversy in India," *South Asia Research* 12 (November 1992): 100–18; Charles Heimsath, "The Origin and Enactment of the Indian Age of Consent Bill, 1891," *Journal of Asian Studies* 21 (1962): 499–500; Radha Kumar, *The History of Doing: An Illustrated Account of the Movements for Women's Rights and Feminism in India, 1800–1990* (London: Verso, 1993), 27; Engels, "The Age of Consent Act," 107.

6. See Lata Mani, "Contentious Traditions: The Debate on Sati in Colonial India," in Kumkum Sangari and Sudesh Vaid, eds., *Recasting Women: Essays in Colonial History* (New Delhi: Kali for Women, 1989), 88–126; Lucy Carroll, "Law, Custom and Social Reform: The Hindu Widows' Remarriage Act of 1856," in J. Krishnamurty, ed. *Women in Colonial India: Essays on Survival, Work and the State* (Delhi: Oxford University Press, 1989), 1–26; Tanika Sarkar, "Rhetoric against Age of Consent: Resisting Colonial Reason and the Death of a Child-Wife," *Economic and Political Weekly* (24 Sept. 1993): 1869–78.
7. Sarkar, "Rhetoric," 1873.
8. See Vinay Lal, "The 'Rule of Law' and Modalities of Governance in Colonial India: The Trials of King Bahadur Shah (1858) and Mahatma Gandhi (1922)," paper presented at the Workshop on State Formation in Comparative Historical and Cultural Perspective (Oxford, 1997) and provided courtesy of the author. For another example of Lal's point, see Usha Thakkur, "Puppets on the Periphery: Women and Social Reform in 19th Century Gujarati Society," *Economic and Political Weekly* (4 Jan. 1997): 46–52. I am also indebted to John D. Kelly's study, *A Politics of Virtue: Hinduism, Sexuality and Countercolonial Discourse in Fiji* (Chicago: University of Chicago Press, 1991), p. x.
9. Meera Kosambi, "Anandibai Joshee: Retrieving a Fragmented Feminist Image," *Economic and Political Weekly* (7 Dec. 1996): 3193.
10. Anagol-McGinn, "The Age of Consent Act," esp. 103–5.
11. I draw here from Kali Israel's conclusion to "French Vices and British Liberties: Gender, Class and Narrative Competition in a Late Victorian Sex Scandal," *Social History* 22 (Jan. 1997).
12. See for example, Gyan Prakash, "Introduction: After Colonialism," in Prakask, ed., *After Colonialism: Imperial Histories and Post Colonial Displacements* (Princeton: Princeton University Press, 1994), 3–17; John Demos, *The Unredeemed Captive: A Family Story from Early America* (New York: Vintage Books, 1994); Dorothy Ross, "Grand Narrative in American Historical Writing: From Romance to Uncertainty," *American Historical Review* 100 (June 1995): 651–77.
13. See Mrinalini Sinha, *Colonial Masculinity: The 'Manly Englishman' and the 'Effeminate Bengali' in the Late Nineteenth Century* (Manchester: Manchester University Press, 1995), ch. 1.
14. Rukhmabai, letter to the *Times*, 9 April 1887. See also Sudhir Chandra, "Whose Laws? Notes on a Legitimising Myth of the Colonial Indian State," *Studies in History* 8 (1992): 187–211, and Anagol-McGinn, "The Age of Consent Act," 100–18.
15. A review of the (Anglo-Indian) *Bombay Gazette* law columns reveals that this was by no means the first such case. See for example, 6 Jan. 1884 and 3 Oct. 1884. In the latter case, *Jeewa Jussa* v. *Jalloo et al.*, Telang, who defended Rukhmabai, was also the defendant's counsel. Perhaps significantly, the *Bombay Gazette* began by headlining Rukhmabai's case as "A Novel Suit for the *In*stitution of Conjugal Rights," 4 March 1887; only after this was her case referred to as a *re*stitution of rights (emphasis mine). For a full discussion of Indian newspapers' responses to the trial, see Sudhir Chandra, "Rukhmabai: Debate Over Woman's Right to her

Person," *Economic and Political Weekly* (2 Nov. 1996): 2937–47. Thanks to Philippa Levine for this reference.
16. Chandra, "Whose Laws," 188.
17. See Chandra, "Rukhmabai," 2937.
18. Chandra, "Whose Laws," 189.
19. Edythe Lutzker, *Edith Pechey-Phipson, M.D.* (New York: Exposition Press, 1973), 207–9; "Dr. Rukhmabai," *World Medical Journal* (Jan. 1964): 35–6, and Meera Kosambi, "The Meeting of the Twain: The Cultural Confrontation of Three Women in Nineteenth Century Maharashtra," *Indian Journal of Gender Studies* 1 (1995): 1–22.
20. A. James Hammerton, *Cruelty and Companionship: Conflict in Nineteenth-Century Married Life* (London: Routledge, 1992), 1–2.
21. See Israel, "French Vices and British Liberties," and Judith Walkowitz, *City of Dreadful Delight: Narratives of Sexual Danger in Late-Victorian London* (Chicago: University of Chicago Press, 1992).
22. *Times*, 22 March and 12 April 1886.
23. Tanika Sarkar, "Bankimchandra and the Impossibility of a Political Agenda," *Oxford Literary Review* 16 (1994): 183.
24. See Geraldine Forbes, "Women and Modernity: The Issue of Child Marriage in India," *Women's Studies International Quarterly* 2 (1979): 408–9, and Barbara Ramusack, "Women's Organizations and Social Change: The Age-of-Marriage Issue in India," in Naomi Black and Ann Baker, eds., *Women and World Change: Equity Issues in Development* (Los Angeles: Sage Publishers, 1981): 198–219.
25. Rassundari Debi, *Amar Jiban* (*My Life*), excerpted in Susie Tharu and K. Lalita, eds., *Women Writing in India*, vol. 1 (New York: The Feminist Press, 1991), 193, and Tanika Sakar, "The Hindu Wife and the Hindu Nation: Domesticity and Nationalism in Nineteenth Century Bengal," *Studies in History* 8 (1992): 231.
26. Mani, "Contentious Traditions," 88–126, and Antoinette Burton, *Burdens of History: British Feminists, Indian Women and Imperial Culture, 1865–1915* (Chapel Hill: University of North Carolina Press, 1994).
27. Mary Carpenter, *Six Months in India*, vol. 1 (London: Longman's, Green and Company, 1868), 77–8.
28. For accounts of some of these Indian influences, see Meredith Borthwick, *Keshub Chunder Sen: A Search for Cultural Synthesis* (Calcutta: Minerva, 1977), and Antoinette Burton, "Fearful Bodies into Disciplined Subjects: Pleasure, Romance and the Family Drama of Colonial Reform in Mary Carpenter's *Six Months in India*," *Signs* 20 (1995): 545–74.
29. *Times*, 22 March 1886, and 14 March 1887.
30. "Judge," letter to the Editor, *Times*, 18 March 1887.
31. For an account of the relationship between English, Hindu and Muslim law in India, see Bernard S. Cohn, "Law and the Colonial State in India," in June F. Starr and Jane F. Collier, eds. *History and Power in the Study of Law: New Directions in Legal Anthropology* (Ithaca: Cornell University Press, 1989), 131–52.
32. Upendra Baxi, "'The State's Emissary': The Place of Law in Subaltern Studies," in Partha Chatterjee and Gyanendra Pandey, eds. *Subaltern*

Studies VII: Writings on South Asian History and Society (Delhi: Oxford University Press, 1993), 249–50.

33. F.L. Latham, letter to the Editor, *Times*, 18 March 1887.
34. Max Muller, letter to the Editor, *Times*, 21 April 1887. For a discussion of Muller's orientalism, especially with regard to Indian women, see Uma Chakravarti, "Whatever Happened to the Vedic *Dasi*? Orientalism, Nationalism and a Script for the Past," in Sangari and Vaid, *Recasting Women*, 27–87.
35. Max Muller, letter to the Editor, *Times*, 22 Aug. 1887.
36. Ibid.
37. J. Scott, letter to the Editor, *Times*, 24 Aug. 1887.
38. Max Muller, letter to the Editor, *Times*, 22 Aug. 1887.
39. Pandita Ramabai, letter to the Editor, *Times*, 27 Sept. 1887.
40. *Pall Mall Gazette*, 12 April 1886.
41. "A Disgusted Hindoo," letter to the Editor, *Pall Mall Gazette*, 27 May 1886.
42. Quoted in Chandra, "Whose Laws," 199–201.
43. "The Hindoo Marriage Law," *Englishwoman's Review*, 15 April 1887.
44. *Women's Penny Paper*, 10 Nov. 1888.
45. Quoted in Y.N. Ranade, *England in India: A Monthly Magazine Containing Extracts from English Newspapers on Indian Subjects* 1 (June 1887): 201, 205.
46. Ibid., 196, 203, 206.
47. Dadaji Bhikaji, *An Exposition of Some of the Facts of the Case of Dadaji vs. Rukhmabai* (Bombay: Advocate of India Steam Press, 1887), and Rukhmabai, *Rukhmabai's Reply to Dadaji's 'Exposition'* (Bombay: Bombay Gazette Steam Press, 1887).
48. See e.g. *The Mahratta* (English-language Hindu paper published weekly in Poona), 24 July 1887.
49. See the *Times*, 6 July and 28 Sept. 1885.
50. 'A Hindu Lady,' "Child Marriage in India," *Journal of the Indian National Association* (September 1885): 416.
51. Ibid., 416.
52. Ibid., 417.
53. Ibid., 420.
54. Ibid., 423.
55. Rukhmabai, letter in *Times*, 9 April 1887.
56. Ibid.
57. *Times*, 19 Aug. 1885; 22 March and 13 Sept. 1886; 22 Nov. 1887.
58. Rudyard Kipling, "In the Case of Rukhmibhaio," in Andrew Rutherford, ed., *Early Verse by Rudyard Kipling, 1879–1889* (Oxford: Clarendon Press, 1986), 374–5.
59. Thomas Metcalf, *Ideologies of the Raj* (Cambridge: Cambridge University Press, 1994), 166.
60. Gyan Prakash, *After Colonialism: Imperial Histories and Postcolonial Displacements* (Princeton: Princeton University Press, 1994), 7.
61. Tanika Sarkar, "Rhetoric Against Age of Consent: Resisting Colonial Reason and the Death of a Child-Wife," *Economic and Political Weekly* (24 Sept. 1993): 1873. See also the *Times*, 28 July 1890 and 29 Jan. 1891.

62. See Behramji Malabari's series in the *Times*: "Child Marriage and Enforced Widowhood in India," 13 Sept. 1890, 15 Sept. 1890, and 7 Oct. 1890. See also Henry Manning, "Indian Child Marriages: I," *The New Review* 3 (Sept. 1890): 447–9; Millicent Fawcett, "Indian Child Marriages: II," *The New Review* 3 (Sept. 1890): 450–4; and Max Muller, "The Story of an Indian Child Wife," *Contemporary Review* 60 (Aug. 1891).
63. See Meera Kosambi, *At the Intersection of Gender Reform and Religious Belief* (Bombay: Research Center for Women's Studies), 105–50.
64. Rukhmabai, "Indian Child Marriages: An Appeal to the Government," *The New Review* 3 (Sept. 1890): 263.

4 The English Dreyfus Case: Florence Maybrick and the Sexual Double-Standard

George Robb

"You may, if a person is addicted to the habit of reading novels, you can tell after reading only one or two pages not only who is going to marry who, but also who is going to poison who."

– Justice Stephen to the jury in the Maybrick trial (all *sic*)[1]

Florence Maybrick's 1889 trial and conviction for poisoning her husband was easily the most publicized and controversial murder case in Victorian England, dividing public opinion so violently that it came to be known as the "English Dreyfus Case." The case inspired a fifteen-year campaign to vindicate Maybrick spearheaded by English and American feminists. Those who championed Mrs. Maybrick believed that her conviction was unwarranted by any evidence in the case but was the result of Philistine prejudice against an adulterous woman. In resisting the sexual double-standard, which pilloried Florence Maybrick while turning a blind eye to her late husband's extra-marital affairs, Maybrick's supporters articulated a new, more outspoken feminist consciousness. Yet to more conservative elements in English society, Maybrick and her female supporters evoked deep-seated anxieties over women's changing roles. The anti-Maybrick forces feared the New Woman of the 1890s would stop at nothing to gain her ends, even murder.

The dramatic potential of the Maybrick case has inspired a number of fictional accounts, including Laura Dayton Fessender's *Bonnie Mackirby* (1898) and Dorothy Sayer's *Strong Poison* (1930). And yet the case itself seems a clear example of life imitating art, for Florence Maybrick's story reads like the plot of a Henry James or Edith Wharton novel: A vivacious American girl is married to a much older, wealthy Englishman. She later discovers her husband's business is on the brink of insolvency and that he has kept a mistress for years. In retaliation she begins a reckless affair with a young man and, when her husband suddenly dies, is accused of poisoning him.

The daughter of an American cotton merchant, Florence Chandler was born in Mobile, Alabama, during the Civil War. After the early death of her father, Florence's mother twice remarried – first to a Confederate officer, and following his death, to a Prussian aristocrat, the Baron von Roques. Florence now moved in fashionable, though not entirely respectable, circles. Most of her time, however, was spent at a series of boarding schools or being shunted from relative to relative. Her marriage in 1881 at the age of 19 to James Maybrick, a 42-year-old British cotton broker, probably represented a quest for stability and domesticity. The couple took up residence in a fashionable suburb of Liverpool in a large house with four servants. A son was born to them in 1882 and a daughter in 1886.[2]

In 1887 the bottom suddenly dropped out of Florence's world. She discovered that her husband's business was on the verge of bankruptcy and that he had been keeping a mistress for twenty years, by whom he had fathered five children. Possibly in retaliation for this betrayal, Florence began a dalliance with Alfred Brierley, a business associate of her husband. After months of flirtation, the affair became more serious. On 21 March 1889 Florence went to London, telling her husband that her aunt was having an operation. For two days she and Brierley lived in a hotel "as man and wife." Although he remained ignorant of his wife's adultery, James Maybrick had become suspicious of Brierley's attentions to Florence, and the Maybricks quarreled violently on March 29, after Florence had been seen walking alone with Brierley at the Grand National steeplechase. James gave Florence a black eye and she threatened to leave him, but their servants persuaded them to reconcile. A month later James Maybrick became profoundly ill with an intestinal complaint, taking to his bed on May 3 and dying on May 11.

During her husband's illness, Florence wrote a letter to Brierley which she asked her children's nurse, Alice Yapp, to post. Yapp opened the letter, and, alarmed by what she read, reported the matter to Mr. Maybrick's brothers, who immediately suspected foul play. The passage that struck them as most incriminating read:

> Since my return I have been nursing M. day and night. He is sick unto death. The doctors held a consultation yesterday, and now all depends on how long his strength will hold out. Both my brothers-in-law are here, and we are terribly anxious. I cannot answer your letter fully

today, my darling, but relieve your mind of all fear of discovery now and in the future.[3]

Did Florence know something the doctors didn't? At this point (May 8) no one considered death a possibility. Yapp then remembered that Florence had purchased arsenic-impregnated fly-papers in April, "when no flies were about." James's brothers banished Florence from the sickroom, not declaring their suspicions, but claiming that she had mismanaged her husband's household. The doctors were apprised of the situation and immediately tested James's urine for poison. None was found, but after his death an autopsy revealed traces of arsenic. A grand jury indicted Florence Maybrick for her husband's murder and she was brought to trial in late July, 1889.

The trial, which lasted from 31 July to 7 August, held the nation spellbound. Sir James Fitzjames Stephen was the presiding judge and Sir Charles Russell, one of the leading advocates of the day, defended Mrs. Maybrick. Ideally, to secure a conviction in a poisoning case, the prosecution had to prove 1) that poison was the cause of death, 2) that the suspect had acquired poison, and 3) that the suspect had administered the poison. In the Maybrick case, however, only the possession of poison was undoubted; the other points remained unclear and much of the trial was dominated by the conflicting medical testimony of several expert witnesses called by both the prosecution and defense.

There was considerable doubt whether or not Mr. Maybrick's death was occasioned by poison. Only one-tenth of a grain of arsenic was found in his body – far less than the 2–3 grains necessary to cause death. The defense marshalled an impressive array of medical witnesses, including Dr. Tidy, the official analyst for the Home Office, and Dr. McNamara, the chief physician of the Dublin Lock Hospital, both of whom declared their belief that James Maybrick had not died of arsenic poisoning. Dr. McNamara especially had had unique opportunities to observe the symptoms of arsenic poisoning since he had systematically poisoned his own patients (sometimes fatally) to test the effects of arsenic on venereal disease.[4]

Mr. Maybrick's own doctors testified that he was a notorious hypochondriac who habitually dosed himself with a wide array of drugs. A friend of the deceased reported that he had "a dozen drug stores in his stomach."[5] During his last days, Maybrick's doctors gave him, among other things, prussic acid, morphine, cocaine, strychnine, *and* arsenic. This was in addition to his "invalid's diet" of champagne, chicken broth, and brandy. Furthermore, the pans which prepared the sick man's food were found to have an arsenic glaze. As for the fly-papers, Mrs. Maybrick claimed that she had extracted arsenic from them for a cosmetic preparation, prescribed by an American doctor.[6]

As the Maybrick case made clear, Victorian society was awash in arsenic. The poison was easily obtainable and there were numerous legitimate reasons to acquire it. In addition to being an ingredient in many medicines, arsenic was found in common household articles. Wallpapers, curtains, upholstery, and carpets were saturated with arsenical dyes. Food and tobacco were often wrapped in arsenic-tinted papers. Most druggists and corner grocers sold arsenic over the counter as a poison for rats and mice or as an insecticide. Customers also requested arsenic as a cleaning agent and as a home remedy for toothache and "the itch."[7]

The most startling evidence presented by the defense was that James Maybrick was an "arsenic eater." Apparently he had taken daily doses of the poison for years as an aphrodisiac. A Liverpool pharmacist deposed to Maybrick frequently visiting his shop for arsenic "tonics," sometimes as often as three to five times a day. Such arsenic as was found in Maybrick's body had probably been put there by himself. Several pounds of arsenic were found in the Maybricks' house after James's death, which raised the question of why Florence would soak fly-papers for poison if so much were readily available? This arsenic was almost certainly her husband's, as it was found in boxes containing men's hats.[8]

As the Maybrick trial and other Victorian poisoning cases revealed, arsenic had numerous uses of an intimate, even sexual, nature. As a cosmetic preparation it was used to brighten the complexion, remove unwanted body hair, or, paradoxically, to promote a more luxuriant growth of hair. In addition to its supposed aphrodisiac qualities, arsenic was also used in the treatment of venereal disease and to induce abortions. It could also be employed, many feared, in eliminating unwanted husbands. Yet many of these uses were unknown to the general public, or at least its more respectable members. For instance, Dr. Thomas Stevenson, the medical expert for the prosecution, insisted that arsenic could not be used in cosmetics as it irritated the skin. The defense could only offer the testimony of an Italian hairdresser, James Bioletti, that arsenic was common in all sorts of beauty tonics and unguents.[9] If the Maybrick trial made anything clear, it was that medical and legal men knew next to nothing about the multifarious uses to which men and more especially women put arsenic.

By the end of the trial, the doubtful nature of the state's medical evidence and Sir Charles Russell's brilliant defense had turned the tide of public opinion in favor of Florence Maybrick, and there was a general expectation of acquittal, even on the part of the prosecuting lawyers. Indeed, acquittal was so firmly anticipated that on the last day of the trial some evening papers printed and sold a late edition announcing a verdict of "not guilty." They had reckoned without Sir Fitzjames Stephen, a dour moralist whose "constant preoccupation was with the vices that menaced society." His niece, Virginia Woolf, remembered him as "a living categorical imperative."[10] Justice Stephen's hostile summing-up to the jury dismissed the medical testimony and instead emphasized Mrs. Maybrick's adultery as a likely motive for murder.

In addressing the jury, Stephen declared "that he was very reluctant to deal with these scientific matters of which he knew nothing." In essence the prosecution and defense experts had cancelled each other out, he argued, and thus the case should be decided on other grounds. "You must decide it," Stephen urged, "as a great and highly important case, involving in itself not only medical and chemical questions, but involving in itself a most highly important moral question." "There is strong evidence," he suggested, "of the prisoner having been actuated by a motive at once strong and disgraceful." Stephen put great emphasis on Florence's letter to Alfred Brierley and the expression "sick unto death." "To put it bluntly," he asked the jury, "was not this letter a very strong and cogent reason to believe that she wished to be free and to be rid of her husband in order to live with the man for whom she had made the greatest sacrifice that a woman could make?"[11]

Adultery was not only a motive for murder in Stephen's view, it was evidence of a criminal nature. "There is no doubt," the judge maintained, "that the propensities which lead persons to vices of that kind do kill all the more tender, all the more manly, or all the more womanly feelings of the human mind." As upsetting to Stephen as Florence's adultery, was her aggressive role in the "Brierley episode," as the court and press euphemistically referred to her London tryst. In no way could she be constructed as the innocent victim of seduction, for not only had she made all the practical arrangements for the weekend in London, but, as Stephen took pains to point out, she had even paid the hotel bill herself. Alluding to another visitor Florence had received at her hotel, Stephen declared that Brierley was "not the first person who appeared at the hotel in London, or who appeared at the hotel in a very questionable position."[12] The gentleman in question was in fact an old family friend of the Maybricks and was simply making a social call, but Stephen further cast doubts on her moral character by implying that she was carrying on multiple affairs.

The fact that Florence hadn't burned Brierley's letters was to the judge yet another mark against her: "I confess that it is to me a most extraordinary thing that any woman having the least regard for her character and reputation should not have put the letters in the fire the moment she received them."[13] Such recklessness was only further confirmation of a desperate character. Continuing his hostile summation, Stephen dismissed many of Florence's statements in her defense. He was dubious of her claim that the fly-papers had been purchased for cosmetic purposes. If this were so, where was the alleged prescription for an arsenic-based face wash? And why hadn't Florence's mother testified to her daughter's cosmetic use of arsenic, supposedly so common in America? Unfortunately for Florence, the prescription was only found years later in a family Bible, and the Baroness had not been called as a defense witness because of wild rumors which had surfaced in Alabama around the time of the trial that she had poisoned her first two husbands.[14]

Stephen next dismissed Florence's statement that she and her husband had reconciled. "Can you think this reconciliation was true," he queried, "when on the 8th May she is writing to this man in terms of endearment and in the spirit of a lover?" Concluding his summation, he waxed indignant: " . . . it seems horrible to comparatively ordinary innocent people – a horrible and incredible thought that a woman should be plotting the death of her husband in order that she might be left at liberty to follow her own degrading vices…that was an awful thing to think of, and a thing you will have to consider in asking yourselves whether she is guilty or not guilty."[15] With Stephen's sermon ringing in their ears, it was little wonder that the jury returned a verdict of guilty after a mere 38-minute deliberation. The sentence of death was then pronounced.[16]

Florence Maybrick's conviction should not have come as a surprise. Throughout the nineteenth century, women had been convicted in poisoning cases on the flimsiest of circumstantial evidence. The very presence of poison in their husbands' bodies was often evidence enough. Women tried for poisoning their husbands in England between 1830 and 1900 were convicted 60 percent of the time – a much higher conviction rate than Victorian murder trials in general, where only 40 percent of the accused were found guilty.[17]

Whether or not the judge and jury gave a suspected husband murderer the benefit of the doubt often depended less on the facts of the case than on the woman's previous character and marital history. Several women were convicted of poisoning their husbands less on the basis of sound evidence than because of their "improper intimacies" with other men. For example, at the trial of Sarah Barber in 1851, more witnesses were called to detail the accused's adultery than to connect her to her husband's poisoning.[18] In 1869 Fanny Oliver was convicted in spite of the fact that only one-fourth of a grain of arsenic was found in her husband's body. Although the medical evidence was doubtful, her fate was sealed when the prosecution read in court a series of love letters she had written to another man.[19] As the *Times* summarized the Oliver case, "a married woman who dictates love letters to a former lover ...cannot be surprised if society considers her a dangerous person and disposes of her accordingly."[20] Florence Maybrick's conviction was far from anomalous, but the public outcry against it was something altogether new.

After pronouncing sentence on Mrs. Maybrick, Justice Stephen was hooted and jeered by crowds outside the court and had to be escorted by the police to his lodgings. Public meetings were held across the country to agitate for a reprieve and petition drives netted tens of thousands of signatures, principally from the middle classes. On 10 August a mass meeting was held at the Great Eastern Hotel in London, organized by Alexander McDougal, a Scottish lawyer who had become obsessed with Mrs. Maybrick's plight.[21] Among the many professional groups who drew up petitions were the physicians of Liverpool, who no doubt felt that their collective expertise had been impugned by the judge and jury's casual dismissal of so much medical testimony.[22]

In Liverpool, the Maybrick controversy took on an unexpected political flavor – with Unionists favoring execution and Liberals and Irish Nationalists against it. In a city with a large Irish population, the case became intertwined with the contemporary issue of Home Rule, for Maybrick's counsel, Charles Russell, was a leading advocate of Irish autonomy while Justice Stephen was a staunch Tory opponent.[23] Florence Maybrick's body had become another battleground in British imperial politics.

Newspapers were flooded with letters concerning the case; the *Times* reported that two-thirds of its correspondents opposed the verdict. Numbers of armchair detectives rushed forth with their support. Women wrote in to affirm that fly-papers were commonly used cosmetically while other letters maintained that "sick unto death" was merely an American figure of speech. The *British Medical Journal* also criticized the verdict and published the opinions of seven professors of medical jurisprudence, five of whom questioned the verdict on medical grounds.[24]

The bulk of Maybrick's supporters were probably motivated by genuine doubts about the case, but her youth and beauty also inspired a chivalrous, masculine desire to protect a friendless woman. In the words of one chronicler of the case, Florence was offered aid "by every type from crusty old noblemen to pimply office boys." As a testament to her romanticized stature, she actually received several proposals of marriage following her conviction.[25]

Middle-class prejudice made it difficult for many to believe that a lady could be guilty of so heinous a crime. Witnesses had testified to Florence's attentiveness to her husband during his illness and her evident distress at his death. Was this merely the act of a calculating woman? Few thought it possible. Commenting on this class bias, one contemporary observed, "one thing is certain, had Mrs. Maybrick been a poor, illiterate woman, instead of an educated 'well-placed' one, she would have been dust years ago."[26] Indeed, there had been a sensational case in Liverpool only five years earlier, in which Margaret Higgins was convicted of poisoning her husband with arsenic extracted from fly-papers. Higgins, however, was working-class and middle-aged, and she was duly hanged.[27] There was no national outpouring of support to save her from the gallows.

No doubt in response to the many appeals in favor of Mrs. Maybrick, the Home Secretary, Henry Mathews, commuted her death sentence to life imprisonment. However, he foolishly justified his decision by arguing that, although the evidence pointed to Florence poisoning her husband, there was considerable doubt whether his death was actually caused by arsenic. In essence she was given a sentence of life imprisonment for attempted murder – a crime for which she was not tried and which never carried such a heavy sentence regardless. Mathew's decision was far from a happy compromise, and was to haunt the government for years.[28]

During the two-week interval between her sentence of death and reprieve, the nation seemed crazed with Maybrick mania. In addition to the meetings and petition drives, a hastily produced melodrama based on the case played in the West End and a hastily produced wax figure of Florence went on display at Madame Tussauds, where it was viewed by thousands. Street ballads relived the various incidents of the case, including one that celebrated Mrs. Maybrick's reprieve: "She will not have to climb golden stairs."[29] Of course this level of interest could not long be sustained, and support for Maybrick dropped off precipitously after the commutation of her death sentence. In an act emblematic of public disinterest, Madame Tussauds melted down Maybrick's effigy.

Fortunately for her, Florence Maybrick's family, like the Dreyfuses, was well-connected and kept her case alive for years. The Chandlers were related to two United States Supreme Court justices, and the American government made repeated interventions to secure her release. In 1891, Robert Lincoln, the American ambassador to Great Britain and son of the late president, appealed to the prime minister on Maybrick's behalf. In 1897, President McKinley sent a request to the Home Office through Ambassador Hay, asking that she be released as a matter of international courtesy. This appeal was made on the occasion of Victoria's diamond jubilee and, like earlier efforts, was curtly rebuffed by Her Majesty's government.[30] Official American appeals were resented by the British, who characterized them as attempts by "jingoes" to "supervise the administration of the criminal law in England."[31]

The American public also rallied behind its countrywoman languishing in a British prison. During the 1890s there were petition drives and benefit concerts across the United States in support of Maybrick. Patriotic resentment against her treatment at the hands of the British found expression in American papers. The *New York Tribune* maintained that "no American judge would have ventured to sum-up the Maybrick case with such boldness and license," while the *New York Herald* insisted that "no American jury would condemn a woman to the gallows on the evidence produced in this case." The presumed superiority of American justice was also invoked by Florence's mother, who, in writing to a supporter, exclaimed: "Your American blood would boil at the injustice, the cruelty which has been done to this delicate, innocent girl."[32]

At a time when the United States was struggling for a sense of its own national identity and for a place of prestige in international affairs, Florence Maybrick became emblematic of many national concerns. To the Secretary of State, James G. Blaine, she was a tragic symbol of America's subservience to degenerate European culture. She "may have been influenced," Blaine suggested, "by the foolish ambition of too many American girls for a foreign marriage and have descended from her own rank to that of her husband's family, which seems to have been somewhat vulgar..."[33] To a journalist writing in the *North American Review*, she was a symbol of a new America:

> Mrs. Maybrick, in her sufferings, as in her blood, unites the North and the South, the Democrat and the Republican, the old slave-holder, the old abolitionist, and the new nation which embraces both; the old Confederate, the Old Unionist, and the new American, who knows but one flag.[34]

In a nation still scarred by the Civil War, Florence Maybrick offered a cause around which the whole country could rally.

Unquestionably the most enthusiastic and sustained opposition to Maybrick's imprisonment came from a group of English and American feminists who kept her cause before the public until 1904, when the Home Office finally released her from prison. The Women's International Maybrick Society was founded in 1891 at the urging of Mary Dodge, a well-known American journalist. The Society's president was Helen Densmore, an American physician living in London, and its executive committee included Elizabeth Cady Stanton, Julia Ward Howe, and Ida Trafford Bell. The organization raised enough money to mount its own legal enquiry led by the eminent lawyer Harry Bodkin Poland. In addition to its efforts to petition the government and work through official channels, the Maybrick Society also made use of the extensive networks of women's clubs that existed in Britain and America. For instance, the poet Ophelia Laurence Blair wrote an ode, "God's Justice Will Be Done," in support of Maybrick, which was recited at a number of women's clubs to publicize her plight.[35]

Mary Dodge and Helen Densmore were especially active in pleading Maybrick's case. Dodge, who wrote under the name Gail Hamilton, already had a distinguished career as a journalist and philanthropist extending back to the 1850s. A regular contributor to the *National Era*, she had been a leading anti-slavery activist and an advocate of women's rights, having published a feminist tract, *Woman's Wrongs: A Counter Irritant* in 1868. She was also a cousin of James G. Blaine, Secretary of State in the Harrison administration and erstwhile presidential candidate, and therefore well connected to the Washington political scene. Dodge brought to the Maybrick cause "the tremendous vitality and activity" which were her "recognized qualities."[36] Densmore was a pioneering woman doctor who had been active in diet reform. Along with her husband, Emmet, she had founded the Natural Food Society in England, which advocated a diet of fruits and nuts. The Densmores were also enthusiastic supporters of women's rights, Emmet later penning the feminist tract *Sex Equality*.[37]

The careers of Helen Densmore and Mary Dodge were indicative of the more active role middle-class women were playing in public life in the latter half of the nineteenth century, a phenomenon that was also reflected in the large numbers of women who attended public meetings and rallies in support of Maybrick. In its coverage of one such meeting in August 1889, the *Times* remarked, somewhat in surprise, that "a large number of ladies were also present." Indeed, the chair of the meeting, Alexander McDougal, called attention to the female presence, commending the women who had come "and were not afraid to act the part of a Samaritan to a fallen sister," at which point the crowd cheered the women in the audience.[38]

Much of the women's campaign focused on the issue of the sexual double-standard which, in the eyes of many, was what really convicted Florence Maybrick. This had been alluded to by Charles Russell when he addressed the jury in his closing remarks:

> Ah, gentlemen, for faults of this nature, the judgments of the world are indeed unequal. In a man such faults are too often regarded with toleration, and they bring him often but few penal consequences. But in the case of a woman, it is with her sex the unforgivable sin.[39]

Press commentary on the trial also called attention to this issue. The *Saturday Review*, while generally hostile to Maybrick, argued that too much had been made of her adultery. "No one who is not a happy compound of Pharisee and fool would say that a man or woman who, in the French phrase, 'puts a knife into the contract,' [commits adultery] is therefore necessarily or even probably minded to put a knife into his or her partner." The *Pall Mall Gazette* asked whether Maybrick would have been convicted had her position and that of her husband been reversed and had the judge and jury been all women.[40]

Letters to newspapers from women decried the double-standard. One woman wrote: "I feel certain that no jury would on such evidence have convicted a man for the murder of his wife and I venture to doubt whether a jury of six men and six women would have agreed in this case." Another woman lamented: "Of course the jurors decided for their sex. Doubtless each was a husband and became bitter on the dishonouring wife."[41]

The last two decades of the nineteenth century witnessed a growing challenge to a Victorian sexual code that had demanded a higher standard of behavior from women than from men. Most notable was the repeal of the Contagious Diseases Acts in 1886 after a protracted feminist campaign against them led by Josephine Butler. The Acts, which had been passed during the 1860s, enshrined the sexual double-standard by subjecting prostitutes to forced medical inspections for venereal disease while leaving their male clients unmolested.[42] Fresh from her victory in the repeal campaign, Josephine Butler commented on the Maybrick case, declaring her disgust "that such strong expressions should be reiterated *ad nauseam* when dealing with a woman, while they are not made use of at all in the case of men...."[43] Florence herself expressed her frustration with this situation when she wrote to a friend: "Because I have sinned once, must I be misjudged always?"[44]

Literary attacks on the double-standard were also raised by a number of *fin-de-siècle* writers, such as Thomas Hardy in *Tess of the D'Urbervilles* (1891) and Oscar Wilde in *A Woman of No Importance*, first performed in 1893. In Wilde's play, the title character, Mrs. Arbuthnot, has led a blighted and guilt-ridden life since having a child out of wedlock, while her seducer went on to a brilliant political career. Commenting on this hypocrisy, Mrs. Arbuthnot declares: "I am disgraced: He is not. That is all. It is the usual history of a man and a woman as it usually happens, as it always happens. And the ending is the ordinary ending. The woman suffers. The man goes free." Although she accepted this situation with fatalistic resignation, the play's young American heroine, Hester, does not. "You are unjust to women in England," she charges a group of cynical aristocrats, "and until you count what is a shame in a woman to be an infamy in a man, you will always be unjust."[45]

Some commenters on the Maybrick case were angry that James Maybrick's adultery was barely mentioned in the trial or by the press, as if it were irrelevant. W.T. Stead focused on this hypocrisy in an 1892 article for the *Review of Reviews*, "Ought Mrs. Maybrick to be Tortured to Death?" Stead, who had achieved considerable notoriety during the 1880s for his journalistic crusade against child prostitution, argued that Florence Maybrick's single weekend in London with Brierley was "a trifle light as air compared to the debauchery in which her husband lived and moved and had his being." According to Stead, James Maybrick was "habitually and notoriously immoral...a roué who used arsenic as part of his daily diet."[46] Stead even implied that Mr. Maybrick's arsenic habit began as a means to counteract venereal disease. James Maybrick's adultery was central to the case in Stead's view since it gave Florence grounds for divorce, thus eliminating her supposed need to murder him.

In presenting Florence Maybrick as more sinned against than sinning, Stead was of course drawing on a view of women as victims of male viciousness who were in need of pity and protection, a view Stead himself had done much to promote over the years. As Kali Israel has argued, "sweeping attacks by feminists and others on the sexual double-standard had created new narrative possibilities for 'fallen women,' not only as reformed sinners but as victims of male lust."[47] Thus Florence Maybrick was constructed by her supporters (and herself) as an innocent abroad who was caught-up in a world of masculine viciousness: first deceived by a profligate husband and later trifled with and abandoned by Brierley, who becomes yet another villain in the case when he flees the country at the first sign of trouble. In contrast to the "debauched" James Maybrick, Florence was depicted as a trusting wife who sacrificed her life to uphold her late husband's honor. W.T. Stead maintained that evidence of James's infidelity was omitted from the trial due to "the chivalrous anxiety of Mrs. Maybrick to shield the reputation of her dead husband." Supposedly she had instructed her solicitors "to spare Jim as much as possible. I know he has done many wrong things, but he is dead now, and I would be distressed if his life were to be made public." Thus was a "deeply injured woman" destroyed by her own "loving heart."[48]

Although Maybrick's supporters frequently employed the language of melodrama in her defense, they also remained deeply rooted in the prosaic world of politics. In 1892 there was a change of government in England, with H.H. Asquith succeeding Mathews as Home Secretary, and a determined attempt was made to procure the release of Maybrick. Helen Densmore published a book-length appeal, *The Maybrick Case; English Criminal Law*, and Dodge used her Washington connections to request another reprieve through Ambassador Lincoln.[49] Asquith proved no more amenable than Mathews, and Dodge complained to Lincoln that he was not being zealous enough on Maybrick's behalf. His task, she somewhat hyperbolically instructed him, was "greater in your way than was that of your father in setting free 3,000,000 slaves."[50]

The State Department was hampered by the fact that Florence had lost her American citizenship upon marriage, a fact that Maybrick's women supporters saw as symbolic of how married women's identities were effaced by the law. Somewhat frustrated by official channels, Dodge took the Maybrick Society's case to Caroline Harrison, the first lady, who petitioned Queen Victoria directly for Maybrick's release. The petition, which was actually written by Dodge, was later published in the *North American Review* along with "An Open Letter to the Queen," also by Dodge. The petitioners declared their love and respect for Victoria: "Confiding in the power of your Majesty and in the power of your goodness, we pray your grace in behalf of our young countrywoman, Florence Maybrick, a widow, a mother, fatherless, brotherless, wearing out in prison a life sentence of penal servitude." Lacking male protectors, Maybrick was being championed by her American sisters. Besides the first lady, the petition was signed by the "ladies of the cabinet," that is the wives of the Secretaries of State, the Treasury, and Agriculture.[51]

In another petition to the queen by American women, Victoria was informed that "there is one woman in England who has the power and the right to interfere and do justice in this case. We remember her long and splendid reign, unsullied by one unwomanly act...and we appeal to her to end this unfortunate controversy by granting a full pardon to this unfortunate woman."[52] Again, the mothers of America were appealing to the Mother of the Empire.

In 1896 the continuing pressure of public opinion and the repeated petitions of Charles Russell, who had become Lord Chief Justice in 1895, caused the new Home Secretary, Sir Mathew White Ridley, to promise a further review of the case. Despite serious doubts raised by senior officials in the Home Office, Ridley resisted further commutation of Maybrick's sentence. Instead he referred the case to the Lord Chancellor, Lord Halsbury, for "unofficial review." Halsbury responded with a "lengthy justification of the original verdict" and of Stephen's conduct of the trial. In 1900, the year of his death, Charles Russell visited Maybrick in prison and again petitioned yet another Home Secretary, Charles Thompson Ritchie, for her release. This latest petition was no more successful than its numerous predecessors.[53]

The decade long tug-of-war over Florence Maybrick reminded many of the contemporary Dreyfus Affair. Helen Densmore spun out this analogy at length in an 1899 article in *Arena*, "The English Dreyfus Case":

> In the French Dreyfus case we have a conspiracy and an innocent person accused, tried, and condemned by a prejudiced tribunal. When the friends of Dreyfus attempted to get a new trial for him, they were confronted by a secret dossier, and by the "honor of the army," which was felt to be at stake. In the English Dreyfus case we have likewise a conspiracy and an innocent person accused, tried and condemned by a prejudiced tribunal...In France they have the army staff; in England they have the permanent officials of the Home Office.[54]

The similarities did not end there, for like the Dreyfus case, the Maybrick controversy revealed more about the values and anxieties of the pro- and anti-Maybrick factions than it did about the woman herself and her alleged crime. If anti-Semitism was at the heart of the Dreyfus Affair, the Maybrick case centered on controversies surrounding the New Woman of the 1890s and changing gender roles. The determined efforts of the Women's International Maybrick Society and their challenge to the sexual double-standard were indicative of a growing militancy among middle-class women on both sides of the Atlantic. And yet, paradoxically, Florence's women supporters, even as they lashed out at a patriarchal legal system, frequently invoked the most traditional images of female passivity and martyrdom in her defense. Mary Dodge characterized Maybrick as "a woman, frightened, shrinking, fainting." While in this case it was rather problematic to play on Maybrick's widowhood for sympathy, her motherhood was beyond reproach. She was often referred to as the *mater dolorosa*, the sorrowful mother weeping for her lost children. In a letter to Queen Victoria from the Maybrick Society, "the great Queen and tender mother" was implored "to rise up and give back this hapless and innocent young mother to the light of day and the sunshine of her children's faces!"[55] Such language was in part a rhetorical strategy for appealing to the widest possible audience, but it was also characteristic of Victorian feminism's emphasis on motherhood and women's innate nurturing qualities. The supposed moral superiority of women thus required them to take a more active role in social reform and social justice.

As a mirror image to the "mother of sorrows" created by her supporters, Maybrick's detractors spun out incredible fantasies of female depravity and linked them to her. The rumor was started that she had given birth in prison to a child fathered by a high official. Others whispered that the Home Office had a "secret dossier" on Maybrick brimming with immorality.[56] Indeed, the Home Secretary had tried to silence Mary Dodge by showing her a secret report that Florence had wounded herself in prison by inserting a knife into her vagina.[57] Whether or not the story was true, it was taken by the government as proof of her perversity.

The wrath of the anti-Maybrick forces was directed as much at Florence's partisans as at the condemned woman herself. Even many who questioned the verdict were appalled by the outspokenness of Maybrick's female supporters, whom they frequently designated "ladies." That women could be so sympathetic to an admitted adulteress and suspected husband poisoner was nothing short of alarming. As one correspondent to the *Times* declared, "I object, as a man, to the sickening sentimentality evoked in favour of an abandoned woman."[58] The *Saturday Review* sarcastically noted that adultery "would appear in the eyes of some Liverpool 'ladies' and others to be a virtue entitling the person committing it to a reprieve for possible murder." The journal further condemned "the intolerable and, in some cases, positively loathsome folly of her partisans…no depth of folly or height of extravagance or excess of indecency has been left unexplored by the unlucky woman's defenders."[59] This seems rather strong language to describe public meetings and petition drives. Clearly much of this disapproval was really directed against the more active, public roles British women had assumed during the 1880s.

The decade which saw the passage of the Married Women's Property Act and the repeal of the Contagious Diseases Acts was an important one for British feminists.[60] A backlash was inevitable, and the Maybrick trial presented an opportunity to condemn the New Woman by associating her with sexual impropriety. The *Spectator* argued that "in the Maybrick case there has been an element of partisanship which we can hardly be mistaken in referring to something like a claim for women of the right to observe or disregard the obligations of marriage at their own pleasure." Another journal mocked the "ladies" who "may not have expressed indifference to the Sixth Commandment [which forbade murder], but certainly took scant notice of the Seventh [which forbade adultery]."[61] Ironically, and unbeknownst to the public, one of Maybrick's greatest detractors was Queen Victoria, the very person to whom so many women had addressed their petitions on Florence's behalf. Convinced of the guilt of "so wicked a woman," Victoria had regretted the stay of execution and insisted that "her sentence must never be further commuted."[62] It was only after the queen's death in 1901 that the government dared reverse itself.

Maybrick's foes were motivated not only by contempt for her adultery, but also by the deeply irrational fears that domestic poisonings evoked. Florence Maybrick was but the latest in a long line of suspected Victorian poisoners that included Madeleine Smith, Fanny Oliver, Florence Bravo, and Adelaide Bartlett. In total numbers, cases of husband poisonings were small, amounting to less than fifty for the century, but in the minds of many they loomed large. Public hysteria found expression in headlines like "More Poisonings by Arsenic" or "Another Husband Poisoned in Norfolk."[63] The female poisoner especially created anxiety since she symbolized a perversion of woman's caregiving role as the nurturer, the provider of food and medicine. The belief in confederacies of women sharing poison recipes with one another had remarkable staying power in the popular imagination. Not only did rumor have it that Florence's mother had poisoned two of her own husbands, but a story was circulated that a novel about the celebrated French poisoner Marie LaFarge had been found in Maybrick's bedroom and that it was full of underlinings and marginal notes.[64]

Florence Maybrick's trial opened in the summer of 1889, in the wake of another Ripper murder, and trial reports from Liverpool appeared in newspapers next to coverage of the Whitechapel slayings. If Jack the Ripper came to represent some monstrous example of male violence against women, Florence Maybrick's alleged poisoning of her sick husband seemed to embody the dark possibilities of female rage against men. If the Ripper was some demon of the night, then Maybrick and her sister poisoners were witches, practicing their arcana on guileless men. While the Ripper asserted control over what was traditionally male space, butchering women in the streets, poisoners committed their crimes in the feminized space of the Victorian home.[65]

Although poisoners were demonized in court and by the press, some women may have found the image empowering, allowing them to manipulate male fears to their own advantage. In evidence given at poison trials, witnesses repeatedly testified to threats made by wives to "white powder" their husbands, to "give him a pill," "give him a dose," or "season a pie" for him.[66] It seems unlikely that women actually planning a murder would have incriminated themselves so overtly and carelessly. Rather, the threat to poison was probably a common form of intimidation – the wifely equivalent of the husband's threat of physical abuse. As Judith Walkowitz has shown, husbands in the 1890s frequently threatened to "Whitechapel" their wives, invoking the mythic terror of the Ripper murders.[67] Women's threats to "white powder" their husbands could likewise draw upon the fear of poisoning that was so apparent in the reception of poison cases, like that of Florence Maybrick.

Maybrick herself never fully escaped the stigma of poisoner. Although released from prison in 1904, her name was not officially cleared and her life remained blighted. She never again saw her children, who had been brought-up by her husband's family in belief of her guilt. She toured England briefly, lecturing on her prison experiences which were also the subject of a memoir, *Mrs. Maybrick's Own Story: My Fifteen Lost Years* (1905). The book offered little new about the case, and was significantly silent about her liaison with Brierley. Thereafter Florence Maybrick vanished from the public gaze until news of her death in 1941. She had been living for years in South Kent, Connecticut in obscurity and poverty. Known to her neighbors as Mrs. Chandler, they found next to her dead body "a scrapbook, thick with saffron clippings, telling who the recluse really was."[68]

The Maybrick case clearly resonated far beyond the Liverpool courtroom where it was tried, highlighting anxiety over the viability of marriage and changing gender roles at the end of the nineteenth century. The Maybrick trial and its aftermath also exemplified the growing contestation of women's subordination within the patriarchal family structure.

The harsh judgment meted out to Florence Maybrick by the presiding judge and the jury who convicted her follows patterns of similar cases during the century. However, the outcry on Maybrick's behalf points us in new directions. This agitation was in part an attack on the double-standard and in part a characterization of Florence Maybrick by her defenders that drew upon the special claims of women to the status of victim.

Attempting to reconfigure Victorian gender roles was certainly no easy matter, as Florence Maybrick's partisans learned. By attacking the double-standard, were they claiming for women the same sexual license enjoyed by men? This certainly was the fear of conservatives who equated support for Maybrick with an attack on hearth and home. To imagine Maybrick as an active woman, one who could give as good as she got, was to imagine an entity to be feared – the New Woman as virago. Ironically, it was only by redrawing her portrait in a posture of submission that Maybrick could be differentiated from other criminal women sufficiently to merit sympathy and protection. By styling her "the modern Iphigenia," after the legendary Greek maiden sacrificed by her father Agamemnon, Maybrick's supporters probably hoped to evoke an archetypal, mythic image of fragile womanhood and martyrdom.[69] Unfortunately *that* myth doubtless caused others to remember Iphigenia's mother, Clytemnestra, an adulteress and husband murderer.

NOTES

The writing of this article was supported by a grant from the Huntington Library.

1. H.B. Irving, ed. *Trial of Mrs. Maybrick* (London: William Hodge, 1927), 320.
2. Materials for this narrative are drawn primarily from Irving's *Trial of Mrs. Maybrick*, part of the Notable British Trial Series and the most extensive transcript of the case. The Maybrick Case has been explored in a number of popular books, most notably in Trevor Christie's *Etched in Arsenic* (Philadelphia: Lippincott, 1968). The only scholarly treatment is Mary Hartman, *Victorian Murderesses* (New York: Schocken, 1977), ch. 6.
3. *Trial*, 45–6.
4. *Trial*, 203–20.
5. Hartman, *Victorian Murderesses*, 303.
6. *Times*, 2 Aug. and 6 Aug. 1889.
7. For discussion of the Victorians and arsenic, see Peter Bartrip, "A 'Pennurth of Arsenic for Rat Poison': The Arsenic Act, 1851 and the Prevention

of Secret Poisoning," *Medical History* 36 (1992): 53–69, and idem, "How Green Was My Vallance?: Environmental Arsenic Poisoning and the Victorian Domestic Ideal," *English Historical Review* 109 (1994): 891–913.

8. *Trial*, 196–203.
9. *Trial*, 180, 228.
10. Quentin Bell, *Virginia Woolf: A Biography* (New York: Harcourt Brace Jovanovich, 1972), 8.
11. *Trial*, 321 and 343; *Times*, 8 Aug. 1889.
12. *Trial*, 172, 322, and 344.
13. *Trial*, 322.
14. *Trial*, 323–5; Hartman, *Victorian Murderesses*, 250.
15. *Trial*, 327, 344–5.
16. Stephen's hostile intervention in the Maybrick trial bears many striking similarities to a case he had tried in London only two years earlier. In 1887, Israel Lipski, a Jewish emigrant from eastern Europe, was tried and convicted of murdering a neighbor woman, Miriam Angel, by poisoning her with nitric acid. Although the evidence in the case was circumstantial and confusing, Stephen became preoccupied with the idea that Lipski had raped Angel and his hostile summing-up of that case sealed Lipski's fate. See Martin L. Friedland, *The Trials of Israel Lipski* (London: Macmillan, 1984).
17. Poison cases were compiled by the author from Victorian Criminal Registers and Calendars of Prisoners, Home Office Papers, Public Record Office, and from newspaper accounts of poison cases. See also, George Robb, "Circe in Crinoline: Domestic Poisonings in Victorian England," *Journal of Family History* 22 (April 1997): 176–90.
18. Trial of Sarah Barber, 25 July 1851. Summer Assizes. Minutes of Midland Circuit. Public Record Office. Assi 11.
19. Trial of Frances Oliver, 20–1 July 1869. Summer Assizes. Minutes of Oxford Circuit. PRO. Assi 1.
20. *Times*, 6 Aug. 1869.
21. See the *Times*, 11 Aug. 1889. Alexander McDougal later wrote a book in favor of Maybrick in which he painstakingly rehashed every detail of the case over 600 pages: *The Maybrick Case* (London, 1891).
22. *Times*, 12 Aug. 1889.
23. Christie, *Etched in Arsenic*, 155–6.
24. See the *Times*, 9 Aug.–5 Sept. 1889, and *British Medical Journal*, 17 Aug. 1889.
25. Christie, *Etched in Arsenic*, 154.
26. Hargrave Adam, *Woman and Crime* (London: T.W. Laurie, 1912), 87.
27. Roger Chadwick, *Bureaucratic Mercy: The Home Office and the Treatment of Capital Cases in Victorian Britain* (New York: Garland, 1992), 305.
28. Ibid., 190–1.
29. W. Henderson, ed., *Victorian Street Ballads* (London: Country Life, 1937), 48–9.
30. Christie, *Etched in Arsenic*, 308.
31. *Times*, 13 April 1896.
32. Christie, *Etched in Arsenic*, 158, 205.

5 Did "My Lord Gomorrah" Smile?: Homosexuality, Class, and Prostitution in the Cleveland Street Affair

Morris B. Kaplan

My Lord Gomorrah sat in his chair
Sipping his costly wine;
He was safe in France, that's called the fair;
In a city some call 'Boo-line'
He poked the blaze and he warmed his toes,
And, as the sparks from the logs arose,
He laid one finger beside his nose –
And my Lord Gomorrah smiled.

He thought of the editor clapped in a cell,
And the Bow Street Bail refused,
While he and his "chappies" got off quite well,
Though a "leg-bail" was all that they used.
And my Lord Gomorrah has cause to thank
His stars for the privilege of rank;
His luxorious couch he preferred to a plank –
So my Lord Gomorrah smiled.

Englishmen, men of cash, class, and clan,
Who can say of yourselves, at least,
Your vices bear the stamp of the man,
And not the mark of the beast,
Will you suffer that justice stint its stroke,
Or speak out strong as you oft have spoke?
Or do you, *mes amis*, relish the joke?
My Lord Gomorrah smiles.[1]

The Cleveland Street affair of 1889–90 in London provides a rich site for historicizing sexuality by focusing on Victorian figures of male homoeroticism.[2] Much of the recent literature in lesbian and gay studies has paid increasing attention to historical issues around the "social construction" of sexuality. This work helps to situate norms of freedom and equality, such as those defended by John Stuart Mill, within a complex cultural context. Historians have debated when modern homosexual "identities" and subcultures in Western Europe may be said to have appeared. Many follow Foucault in locating the point of origin in the discourses of nineteenth-century science and medicine, especially in the shift from sodomy as a category of prohibited *behavior* to the construction of the homosexual as a distinctive kind of *person*.[3] Social historians underline the increased mobility and urbanization of capitalist industrial societies in Western Europe and North America as a crucial factor in the development of distinct homosexual communities.[4] Either way, London in the nineteenth century was a crucial site for the emergence of a modern homosexual identity and of a generalized ethos of individuality. Public trials and political campaigns for law reform provide especially rich texts for reading the historical interaction of law, culture, and society. When they are concerned with sex, they sharply focus general theoretical issues about the boundaries between private and public, the intersections of sexuality with gender and social class, and the strange combination of indeterminacy and overdetermination that attends the use of law to control personal lives.

The Cleveland Street Affair, or the "West End scandals," as the episode came to be known, was the first public scandal to involve the application of section 11 of the Criminal Law Amendment Act of 1885 banning "gross indecency between men." This provision, known as Labouchere's Amendment, transformed the legal treatment of same-sex conduct by men. The Act resulted from campaigns for moral purity directed at the condition of poor women and their exploitation through prostitution, in part as response to W.T. Stead's series on "The Maiden Tribute of Modern Babylon."[5] Its implementation intensified police control over both prostitutes and men who had sex with other men; both groups were seen as threats to moral order and normal family life.

The West End scandals provide a rich focus for inquiring into the social expressions of male homoeroticism and the politics surrounding the legal enforcement of sexual morality. The status of homosexuality as an attributed social identity and as an available self-definition appears somewhat problematic for this period. Foucault's insistence on the emergence of the homosexual as a "new species" in the late nineteenth century depends on discursive developments in medicine and the sciences that seem rather distant from the social realities on display at Cleveland Street. Public discussion constructed the participants primarily in terms of their age, social status, and economic condition; their sexual desires and activities were interpreted and judged in relation to more complex identities and ways of life. The "sodomite" was embodied quite differently in the representation – and experience – of Lord Euston and Lord Arthur Somerset, the "Lord Gomorrah" of my title, and of John Saul, a male prostitute who testified in the affair, describing himself as a "professional sodomite."

Although the West End scandals filled the papers from the fall of 1889 through the winter of 1890, they began quietly enough on 4 July 1889 during the investigation of some petty thefts in the Central Post Office. In the course of interrogating a telegraph messenger boy named Charles Swinscow about his access to more cash than his salary at the Post Office could account for, Police Constable Luke Hanks learned that several young men in the employ of the Post Office picked up extra money by moonlighting at 19 Cleveland Street, where they were paid 4 shillings a session for engaging in "indecent acts" with adult males from the middle and upper classes. Swinscow revealed that he and some of the others were recruited for this activity by Harry Newlove, once a messenger boy, now employed as a clerk elsewhere in the Postal Office. Swinscow admitted that prior to his employment at 19 Cleveland Street, he had engaged in sexual acts with Newlove and others in the lavatory at the Central Post Office. Hanks' investigation led him to two other messengers, George Alma Wright and Ernest Thickbroom, who had similar stories in which sexual play with other youths led to proposals that they earn extra income by making themselves available for similar activities with the customers at Cleveland Street. Statements by the telegraph boys are quite matter of fact about their activities and their willingness to have sex with older men in exchange for ready cash. Newlove admitted his own activities with clients at Cleveland Street and to recruiting colleagues from the Postal Service for the same. Finally, only Newlove and an associate named G.D. Veck were arrested and charged in the affair. They both pled guilty in Magistrates' Court: the older Veck got nine months at hard labor; the 19-year-old Newlove, four months.[6]

Hardly the stuff of major scandal, but rather more was going on than met the public view. As W.T. Stead commented in *The Pall Mall Gazette* on the Director of Public Prosecution's presence in court at the arraignment of Veck and Newlove:

> The question ... Stephenson will have to answer is whether two noble Lords and other notable persons in society who were accused by witnesses of having been principals in the crime for which the man Veck was committed to trial are to be allowed to escape scot free. There has been too much of this kind of thing in the past. The wretched agents are run in and sent to penal servitude: the lords and gentlemen who employ them swagger at large and are even welcomed as valuable allies of the administration of the day.[7]

The crusading reformer here echoes the attitude of Newlove himself: "I think it very hard that I should get into trouble while men in high position are allowed to walk about free," he said to the police just before naming Lord Arthur Somerset, younger son of the Duke of Beaufort and an equerry to the Prince of Wales; the Earl of Euston, heir to the Duke of Grafton; and other less well-known figures from the nobility, military, and middle classes. After arresting Newlove, Chief Inspector Frederick Abberline, already a public figure as a result of his efforts to track down Jack the Ripper, followed the leads to Cleveland Street only to find that the proprietor Charles Hammond had got away. He sent two of the telegraph boys with a police constable to identify Somerset at his club in Piccadilly. The arrest of Veck resulted in the discovery of letters from a youth named Algernon Allies referring to a "Mr. Brown," who had provided ongoing financial assistance. Allies admitted that his benefactor was Lord Arthur Somerset, who had paid him in exchange for ongoing sexual favors. Proof that Somerset had been a frequent visitor to Cleveland Street brought the West End scandals perilously close to the royal family. Stead's editorial publicized speculation that had been circulating in London circles for some weeks. Concern about who might be touched by a public trial informed discussions among the highest legal officials in the land. Hamilton Cuffe, assistant to the Director of Public Prosecutions, wrote to his chief: "I am told ... that Newton [attorney for Somerset] has boasted that if we go on a very distinguished person will be involved (P.A.V.). I don't mean to say that for one instant I credit it – but in such a case as this one never knows what may be said, be concocted, or be true."[8] "P.A.V." refers to Prince Albert Victor, older son of the Prince of Wales, and as "heir presumptive," second in line to Queen Victoria's throne.

Speculation about sexual goings-on in high places has always been grist for the rumor mills – the higher the place, the more unorthodox the doings, the more productive the mills. When files on the Cleveland Street affair became available to scholars in 1976, two books on the subject appeared: H. Montgomery Hyde's *The Cleveland Street Scandal* and *The Cleveland Street Affair* by Colin Simpson, Lewis Chester, and David Leitch. Although they disagree on crediting allegations of a full-scale cover-up, both works present elaborate documentation of an extraordinarily complex round of policy discussions in which the Home Secretary, Chief of Police, Attorney-General, Director of Public Prosecutions, Lord Chancellor, and even the Prime Minister played a role. The Prince of Wales himself intervened through two courtiers. By the time Lord Arthur Somerset was indicted in November, he had left his position in the Prince of Wales' household and absconded to France. Simpson, Chester, and Leitch argue that the documents support the conclusion that there was an enormously successful cover-up, directed by the Prince of Wales with the complicity of the Prime Minister, Lord Salisbury. On the other hand, Hyde, himself an attorney and Member of Parliament who assembled *The Trials of Oscar Wilde*, is willing to see legal and bureaucratic complexities where Simpson and his colleagues find conspiracy.

Throughout the fall of 1889, the radical press especially harped on allegations of unequal justice and implied the existence of a far-reaching cover-up in the case. When the affair was no longer in the courts, Henry Labouchere presented a full case against the administration in the House of Commons, and he was suspended from Parliament for a week for publicly declaring that he did not believe the Prime Minister Lord Salisbury's explanations. Some rumors die hard: in 1994, Theo Aronson published *Prince Eddy and the Homosexual Underworld* in which the allegations as to Prince Albert Victor, known to his family as Eddy, are once again rehearsed. Aronson's case is weakened somewhat by his equal sympathy for theories that Prince Eddy may have committed the crimes attributed to Jack the Ripper, or protected the one who did.

The legal effects of the Cleveland Street scandal are rather surprising. It resulted in three separate criminal proceedings. Veck and Newlove pled guilty to "gross indecency" and received relatively light sentences. The other trials were not prosecutions for sexual wrongdoing. The attorney Arthur Newton and his associates, who acted for the absent Somerset, were tried for obstructing justice by offering to finance the emigration and resettlement of the telegraph boys before they could testify further in court. Newton pled guilty, while the charges against his subordinates were dismissed. To the surprise of all the attorneys involved, an angry judge sentenced Newton to six weeks in jail and refused to recommend lenient treatment. The only proceeding to go to trial was the libel case brought by Lord Euston against Ernest Parke, editor of the *North London Press*. The radical newspaperman had published an editorial deploring the special treatment of prominent persons and claiming that the administration had enabled Somerset to flee to France and Euston to Peru. Although he had been named to the police, Lord Euston had not left the country and came forward to vindicate his name. At Parke's trial John Saul, identifying himself as a "professional sodomite" or "Mary-ann," testified to the truth of the allegations about Euston's visits to Cleveland Street. Nevertheless, the jury convicted the editor, and Judge Henry Hawkins sentenced him to one year in prison. The most severe penalty in the affair was suffered by a journalist who sought to publicize the events rather than anyone directly involved. This outcome reflects widespread social attitudes such that even the highest legal officials deliberated whether it might not be better to allow the guilty to go uncharged rather than publicize the commission of such acts.[9]

The "new misdemeanor" of "gross indecency between men" was defined as a crime by Labouchere's amendment, clause 11 of the Criminal Law Reform Act of 1885, which reads:

> Any male person who, in public or private, commits, or is party to the commission by any male person of, any act of gross indecency with another male person, shall be guilty of a misdemeanor and being convicted thereof shall be liable at the discretion of the court to be imprisoned for any term not exceeding two years, with or without hard labour.

This provision was added late to extensive legislation designed to raise the age of consent for young women from 13 to 16 and to increase penalties for brothel keepers and those who otherwise profited from prostitution. Labouchere claimed that his only interest was in protecting young men from sexual exploitation to the same extent that the act protected young women, but Clause 11 appears to prohibit all sexual activities between men of whatever age, whether in private or public.[10]

The crime of "gross indecency" perpetuates the legacy of "the sin not fit to be named among Christians" in its indeterminacy and inclusiveness. The laws against sodomy, prohibited since 1533, applied to behavior between men and women and men and animals as well as against male same-sex behavior.[11] Sodomy was a capital offense in the "Buggery Act" of Henry VIII and remained so until 1861. This fact partially explains the tendency of judicial construction to require elaborate proof that was difficult to come by. As a result, convictions for sodomy were rare. More frequently persons were prosecuted for "attempted sodomy," which was easier to prove and carried a punishment of up to ten years' imprisonment. When Parliament repealed the death sentence, the penalty became imprisonment from a minimum of ten years up to life, at the discretion of the court. During this time, some sexual offenses between men were prosecuted as "sexual assaults" which carried lesser penalties and lower burdens of proof. In order to accurately assess the impact of the Labouchere Amendment, it is important to learn more about the routine enforcement of laws against same-sex behavior between men before and after its passage to determine whether they reached activities that could not have been charged as attempts at sodomy or sexual assaults under the prior law. Evidence is also lacking as to the percentage of convictions and the severity of the sentences meted out under the different regimes (pre- and post-Labouchere).[12]

* * *

The concept of the homosexual as a specific kind of person does not appear to figure in the press accounts or in the court proceedings; neither mentions medical or psychiatric perspectives of any sort.[13] Of course, the only actual trial in the Cleveland Street affair was Lord Euston's prosecution of Ernest Parke for libel. However, no contemporary efforts elucidated the affair in terms of pathology.[14] Rather, the traditional moral condemnation of sodomy was asserted with considerable vigor, often conjoined with a powerful civic republican discourse that figured aristocratic license as moral corruption and challenged governmental complicity with social privilege. The image of aristocratic clients ready to pay for sexual favors was juxtaposed in the popular press with the contrasting image of the sons of working-class families eager to improve their lot. Much was made of the youths' employment in the Postal Service, adding a suggestion that their corrupters posed a threat to the nation itself. In police reports, each of the telegraph boys was asked whether or not he wore his uniform when performing indecent acts for pay.

The public controversy distinguished the situations and character of the male prostitutes and their clients. The telegraph boys already had full-time jobs and social roles, which marked their sexual activities as mercenary and their prostitution as temporary. Saul identified himself as a "professional" walking the streets in search of sex for pay with other men; he appeared to fully occupy a stigmatized social role and sexualized personal identity. In less obvious ways, the two noble lords named in the press complicated the image of the sodomite as upper-class sexual predator. Whereas the absent Somerset was matched with the telegragh boys and systematically represented as their corrupter, Lord Euston came forward publicly to vindicate himself and was dramatically confronted by an unrepentant but marginalized Saul. Not surprisingly, Euston emerged the victor in the legal proceedings and court of public opinion, while Somerset lived out his life in exile and died in disgrace. Although *The North London Press* explicitly targeted Somerset's escape to France, it was Lord Euston who "got over" while "my Lord Gomorrah" had little cause to smile.

As the West End scandals developed, the telegraph boys were quickly cast in the role of victims, capitalizing on the fervor to combat the sexual exploitation of children that animated the social purity movement and led to the passage of the Criminal Law Amendment Act of 1885 in the first place, despite the fact that, with one exception, they were all in their late teens. The illustrated London papers featured drawings on their front pages, showing the lads as handsome, clean-cut, and respectable.[15] The conjunction of moral and political discourses relieved the younger men from any imputation of irregular sexuality. The Director of Public Prosecutions summed up his reasons for proceeding with the Cleveland Street Affair in these terms:

> Whatever may be said, and much may be said – as to the public policy of allowing *private* persons – being full-grown men – to indulge their unnatural tastes – in private – or in such a way as not to come to public knowledge – in my judgement, the circumstances of this case demand the intervention of those whose *duty* it is to enforce the law and protect the children of respectable parents taken into service of the public as these unfortunate boys have been, from being made the victims of the unnatural lusts of full-grown men – and no consideration of public scandal – owing to the position in society or sympathy with the family of the offender should militate against this *paramount duty*.[16]

The only thing that distinguished this argument from that of the editorials in the radical press was the latter's emphasis on the social class of the corrupting adult males. Labouchere, editorializing in his paper *Truth*, provided the missing note: "very possibly our Government of the classes is of the opinion that the revelations which would ensue, were the criminals put on trial, would deal a blow to the reign of the classes, and to the social influence of the aristocracy." He concluded: "It would be really too monstrous if crimes which, when committed by poor ignorant men, lead to sentences of penal servitude were to be done with impunity by those whom the Tory government delights to honour."[17]

Despite the repeated emphasis on their youth and respectability, the evidence in the police files shows the telegraph boys to be something other than sexual innocents. Two of the three who made statements to the police admitted that they had "behaved indecently" with Newlove (himself nineteen) in the lavatory at the Post Office *before* he recruited them for Cleveland Street. In fact, George Wright described acts that amounted to "attempted sodomy" under the law.[18] None of the publicity suggested that these boys should have been prosecuted for gross indecency, much less attempted sodomy. Both their acts and their identities were insulated against condemnation by their construction as diligent sons of the working class eager for a leg up in the economic struggle and vulnerable to corruption as randy young males. The fact that *both* participants in the earlier acts were relatively young is taken as a defense against legal and moral culpability.[19] To mark such practices *between* young men as seriously deviant would be a risky undertaking in a society where young men were quite often segregated in such intense same-sex settings as boarding schools, army barracks, navy ships, and universities.

John Saul represented a social status and personal identity quite different from that of the telegraph boys. He was the only witness in the affair at Cleveland Street actually to present himself in court, testify against a nobleman, and be subject to judgment by jury, court, press, and public. Saul, the "professional sodomite" or "Mary-anne," worked as a male prostitute like the delivery boys, but his activity was not a temporary measure.[20] His sexual contacts with clients amounted to more than an opportunistic aberration from a life otherwise characterized by working-class normalcy. Indeed, Saul seems to have fallen outside the dominant structure of class relations in Victorian England. Perhaps more accurately, he represents the emergence of a new urban underclass marked by its connections with crime, vice, and especially sex. In response to police questions, he recited a proliferation of addresses between Soho and Leicester Squares which he had occupied together with a variety of others similarly situated – female prostitutes, men with women's names, theater people, muggers and blackmailers. Saul's "professional" status does not simply qualify the traditional conception of the sodomite with the addition that he performed forbidden acts for money. Rather, the "Mary-anne" was a new figure; he was a "professional of desire" whose sexual contacts define a distinctive social status and perhaps even a personal identity. Although his self-description linked him to female prostitutes with whom he shared a demi-monde, Saul also adumbrates more recent conceptions of sexual identity.[21] When he said that he has worked hard cleaning the houses of "gay people," "gay" referred to female prostitutes among whom he lived, not men marked by their same-sex desires and activities. Labouchere's Amendment defined all sexual interaction among men, in private or public, regardless of age, and whether cash was exchanged or not, as outside the law and equivalent to prostitution. Note also that the Criminal Law Amendment Act did not outlaw same-sex activities between women; rather it targeted "gay women" – prostitutes – and "gross indecency between men" – the defining activities of those who were to become "gay men."[22] John Saul's life was a site at which prostitution and same-sex activities converged.

How are we to understand the role of same-sex desire in contributing to the social and personal identities of the upper-class clients at 19 Cleveland Street? Given the opprobrium visited upon them by press and society, and despite their escape from legal punishment, these men were indeed stigmatized by their sexual desires and activities. However, the stigma was crucially inflected by their class and the fact that their partners in sex were poor and young. The precise character of their vicious propensities was never defined in the press attacks. Indeed, their offenses were compounded by the fact that they directed public attention to such things in the first place. To provide a bill of particulars would only add to the damage. In his statements to the police, Saul described the clients at Cleveland Street as "sodomites." In Foucault's terms, he used the older discourse of sinful or criminal acts, for which sexual practices rather than identities were at issue. However, the discourse of sodomy was traditionally linked to a conception of *character*, if not of identity. The "sodomite" was a figure of *excess*. He posed a danger of corruption to all with whom he came into contact because he was driven by his desires to disregard all social and moral restraints.[23] One of the most notorious sodomy trials in the early modern period, that of Lord Castlehaven, accused the nobleman of acts of buggery against both his wife and his pages. Castlehaven exemplified the sodomite in his excessive and uncontrolled desires and in his willingness to use anyone in his power to satisfy himself.[24]

In this context it is important to remember that the Labouchere Amendment was passed in a climate of widespread outrage at tales of the sexual abuse of children. Although Stead's vivid exposures detailed the mistreatment of girls and young women, a pervasive theme – for journalists and for feminists and other campaigners for moral purity – was unbridled male lust, especially that of those in position to use money or power to exploit the vulnerable children of the lower classes.[25] Recognizing the sodomite as a figure of unrestrained male desire and of upper-class corruption rather than of same-sex desire as such, the animus against him cannot simply be identified with contemporary "homophobia." The clients at Cleveland Street cannot yet be regarded as examples of modern homosexuality – with its confused, and perhaps incoherent, joining of same-sex object choice and inversion of sex/gender identity. Hostility towards them is fraught with the politics of social inequality and the morality of sexual purity.

The sexual issues raised by Cleveland Street are deeply implicated with the politics of party and social class. It is hard not to sympathize with the radical press's demand for equality before the law. At the same time, the editorials repeatedly emphasized the heinous character of the unspecified underlying sexual offenses: egalitarian hostility towards the aristocracy was linked with a pervasive suspicion of deviant desires and practices. In the *North London Press*, Parke sounded the alarm about inequality and corruption with a national and imperial inflection:

> a minister at Hackney had been condemned to penal servitude for life; with the special warning from the judge that he could have no hope of a mitigation of his dreadful doom. Yet there was no trace in his case, as there is in this, of a foul and widespread plot to poison the morals of the community, and make the name of England a hissing and reproach in Christian Europe.[26]

The editorial concluded on an almost apocalyptic note: "If half of what we know, and are learning from day to day, comes out in a court of law, there has been accumulating under our feet a store of moral dynamite sufficient to wreck the good name of the nation."[27] The sexual peccadilloes of the clients at Cleveland Street were blown up into the moral equivalent of the Gunpowder Plot. In a lower key, one working-class spokesman addressing a mass meeting of Radical Clubs at the Shoreditch Club in North London suggested that gross indecency was congenital in the upper classes but could only be acquired by the sons of the working class through the temptation of rational economic interest: "Bringing up our boys as we have to do, we should not submit to a state of things which might end in their temptation, for their tempters are men of position and wealth. Working men are free from the taint, and for gold laid down our boys might be tempted to this fall."[28]

Very little effort was made in the public debate occasioned by the "West End scandals" to separate distinct issues that appear conflated from a contemporary point of view. John Stuart Mill's influential essay *On Liberty* had been published in 1859 and clearly influenced the Public Prosecutor's distinction between what adult men might do together in private and the sexual exploitation of the young and underprivileged. However, no voice was raised in public to defend the liberty or privacy of the clients at Cleveland Street. The necessary distinctions were certainly available in 1890, but there was no political interest in articulating them. George Bernard Shaw saw some of this very clearly. Early in the emerging scandal, on 26 November 1889, he wrote a letter to Labouchere's journal *Truth* insisting on the difference between the abuse of minors and the consensual activities of adults:

> we may presently be saddled with the moral responsibility for monstrously severe punishments inflicted not only on persons who have corrupted children, but on others whose conduct, however nasty and ridiculous, has been perfectly within their admitted rights as individuals.[29]

Shaw insistently defended a "liberal" perspective that was eclipsed by the intersection of class, party, moral, and sexual issues in the controversy. His argument was not free of the conventional prejudices of his time, but he insisted on distinguishing these social attitudes from their enforcement by the criminal law. Alone among the voices raised in response to the Cleveland Street affair, Shaw recognized an issue of human rights:

> I appeal now to the champions of individual rights . . . to join me in a protest against a law by which two adult men can be sentenced to twenty years penal servitude for a private act, freely consented to and desired by both which concerns themselves alone. There is absolutely no justification for the law except the old theological one of making the secular arm the instrument of God's vengeance.[30]

Shaw underestimated the power of the forces of moral purity and the hypocrisy of a society that tolerated deviance only so long as it remained secret. Sexual activities between men remained crimes in Great Britain until 1967. Millean arguments finally carried the day with the Wolfenden Committee of 1957 that recommended decriminalizing private consensual acts between adult men, but they were not even heard in 1889. Shaw's letter to *Truth* was not published.

* * *

The most dramatic court proceeding in the Cleveland Street affair was the trial of *Euston* v. *Parke*, the libel action initiated by the noble lord against the editor of the *North London Press*. On 18 November 1889, that paper declared that the Earl of Euston had fled to Peru to avoid arrest. Unfortunately for editor Ernest Parke, Lord Euston was very far from Peru, at home in London. While Lord Arthur Somerset followed the case from France, safe from prosecution, Euston confronted his accuser in court. Ironically, the paper's portrayal of a smiling "Lord Gomorrah" applied more convincingly to Euston, whose victory at the libel trial left him free to continue his life, rather than to Somerset who ended his days under a cloud and never returned from exile. Lord Euston was the oldest son and heir of the Duke of Grafton. He was first mentioned by Newlove after his arrest, along with Somerset and others, as a patron of the house at 19 Cleveland Street.[31] In his memoirs, Frank Harris described Euston as "decidedly manly looking, the last person in the world to be suspected of any abnormal propensities."[32] Euston, however, was not a model of rectitude and respectability. His marriage to chorus girl Kate Cook had ended after seven years. During the divorce proceedings in 1884, it emerged that Kate had been married to someone else when she wed Euston. The noble lord only escaped prosecution for bigamy because Kate's first husband had himself been married to another when he married Kate. Clearly Euston moved in fast company. In court he denied the allegations against him although he admitted that he once visited 19 Cleveland Street. Certainly part of the attraction of this case for the press and public was the highly-charged courtroom encounter between Lord Euston and the man who appeared to accuse him of indecent acts.

John Saul's statement to the police spelled out particulars of his contact with Euston: "He is not an actual sodomite. He likes to play with you and then 'spend' on your belly."[33] The newspapers did not print anything so explicit as this. Despite their uniform reticence in reporting the details Saul offered ("After saying what we cannot report"), the press played up the drama of the confessed "professional sodomite" accusing Lord Euston to his face. We get a vivid sense of Saul's personality from the newspaper reports. Although doubly contained – by the formal constraints of acting as a witness in a criminal trial and by the press narration of the scene – something irrepressible about Saul emerges: a high theatricality, making the most of his day in court, a gentle and generous responsiveness to the police and the defendant, a touch of irony, an occasional flare of anger and self-pity, and sometimes, a sad note. The reporter for *The Star* was struck by these effects: "Dramatic indeed was the situation when this young man, asked whether he recognized anyone in court as having been to Hammond's house, pointed to Lord Euston, and in his effeminate voice, said distinctly 'Yes, that one. I took him there myself.' It seemed minutes before another question was asked. So intense was the thrill which this declaration caused."[34] And that was certainly no accident. The description of Saul's *coup de théâtre* betrays the ambivalence of the observer; not even "his effeminate voice" undermines the powerful effect when conjoined with the pointing and distinct articulation. Saul goes on to relate his initial encounter with Euston: "I picked him up, just as I might have picked any other gentleman up." Having met on the street in Piccadilly, "he laughed at me, and I winked at him." According to Saul, the two men then took a hansom cab to Cleveland Street. Saul's genteel descriptions of the house provoked laughter in the courtroom that must be chastened by the judge:

> ... Mr. Lockwood addressing his lordship expressed the hope that his task would not be made more difficult by such expressions of feeling. The whole thing was too horrible.
>
> The Judge said such levity was brutal and disgusting, and he trusted it would not occur again.[35]

Lockwood was Parke's attorney; Saul was his witness. Clearly, he felt that laughter in the courtroom could only work to undermine Saul's credibility. But there are multiple displacements at work here. The expressions are overdetermined: "The whole thing was only too horrible." Was the laughter "brutal and disgusting?" Or were the acts between Saul and Lord Euston? Or was it Saul's effrontery in coming forward to testify about them?[36]

Of course Lord Euston had a different tale to tell. Taking the stand after the defense had presented its case, he denied that he had ever seen Saul or heard of other witnesses against him. Euston claimed that he had once visited 19 Cleveland Street by accident. He went in the mistaken belief that a staged display of nude women (*poses plastiques*) would take place there, but upon learning "the real character of the house," he stormed out in a rage.[37]

While the press were somewhat skeptical of Lord Euston's account, the radical *Reynold's Newspaper* even calling it a "cock-and-bull story," Mr. Justice Hawkins had no doubts at all.[38] Nor did he disguise his hostility to John Saul. *The Standard* reported the following from the judge's summary of the evidence for the jury:

> As to the witness Saul, a more melancholy spectacle he could not imagine. Was Saul's story true? Lord Euston said it was as foul a perjury as a man could commit. Of course directly they could only have the

> oath of Lord Euston against the oath of that man. It was necessary to speak out, and they would have to ask themselves which oath they preferred – the oath of the man who, according to his own account, if he spoke the truth, was liable to be prosecuted, or the oath of the Prosecutor [Lord Euston]. So far he marveled that no one suggested that the man should be prosecuted.[39]

One is not surprised that the judge in these circumstances should side with the heir to a dukedom rather than with a self-described "professional Mary-anne." But his vehemence in dealing with Saul expressed unusual hostility and contempt: he referred to Saul repeatedly as "that creature." He argued that Saul should not be believed because, if he were telling the truth, he would be subject to severe penalties; whereas Lord Euston should be believed because his denials established his innocence. The law usually regards this as a powerful motive to lie. But of course, Euston was a gentleman and a noble lord ...

The jury believed him. They found Ernest Parke "guilty of libel without justification." Hawkins sentenced the journalist to a year's imprisonment claiming that "a more atrocious libel than that of which you have been found guilty has never been published by any man."[40] It is not surprising that conservative papers should welcome the verdict and sentence as a vindication of a sound social order more threatened by muckraking journalists than by highly placed malefactors, but they were not alone. The populist *Daily Telegraph* declared: "The condemnation of Parke to imprisonment for twelve calendar months prevents for that time, and perhaps for all future time, a foul-mouthed slanderer from inflicting any further injury on society and poisoning the very air we breath."[41] The outrage generated by the activities at the male brothel was now directed against those who accused pillars of the Victorian social order of patronizing such an institution. Had popular hatred of sexual deviance so colored class indignation that it contributed to a whitewash of the powerful and privileged? Many in all walks of life preferred to believe that radical journalists fabricated the charges to sell papers than that the sons of Dukes paid for sex with young men. One interested party, Lady Blanche Waterford, sister to Lord Arthur Somerset, wrote privately: "So *thankful* poor Lord Euston has won his trial, and only *wish* it were poor Arthur. However, it is a mercy that somebody is made happy."[42]

Somerset had been paired with Lord Euston by the *North London Press* and in the gossip generated by the West End scandals. Evidently he suffered rather more as a result of the Cleveland Street affair than

Euston, whose vindication at the libel trial permitted him to get on with the business of his life, whatever that may have been. Euston remains an opaque figure. We may speculate about the actual extent of his involvement with activities at Cleveland Street, but we cannot settle questions about his behavior, much less more complex issues about his desires and self-conception. Lord Arthur, driven into exile to avoid prosecution, left rather more in the way of personal correspondence with friends and family which, although governed by concerns of prudence and propriety, provides a glimpse of his own experience and response to the affair.

The evidence against Lord Arthur Somerset paints a different character, altogether more complex in his desires and sense of self. Not only was it strong enough to lead to his indictment, but it led Somerset to conclude that he could not face down the charges and to flee to France. The plain fact is that Somerset faced overwhelming evidence that he had committed acts of "gross indecency" with a number of young men whom the police had interviewed and who were available to testify against him. The stories they told are richer and more interesting than the case against Euston. Somerset had been named by Newlove immediately after his arrest and was consequently identified by two of the telegraph delivery boys as a frequent client at 19 Cleveland Street. The case against him was solidified by the discovery of Algernon Edward Allies, whose letters had been found on Veck upon his arrest. Allies was the son of a coachman in service in Suffolk. He had been employed as a houseboy at the exclusive Marlborough Club, founded by the Prince of Wales, of which Somerset had been a member. When Allies was convicted of stealing at the club, Lord Arthur appeared on his behalf and secured his release on "good behavior." He promised the boy he would help him find work and arranged with Hammond for Allies to live at 19 Cleveland Street. Allies had already returned to his parents' home when Newlove was arrested. However, he remained in touch with both Veck and Somerset. He admitted to the police that the "Mr. Brown" with whom he had a long-term association and who provided him with money was actually Lord Arthur. Tipped off about the police interest, Allies had destroyed his letters the day before Police Constable Hanks arrived. As the Cleveland Street affair developed in the following months, after Somerset fled the country, Allies went to live in London under the auspices of the police. However complex the questions about Allies' conduct and motivation during the investigation, there can be no doubt that he had been involved with Somerset in an ongoing connection that went beyond the casual encounters reported by the telegraph boys.

In his correspondence with his friend Reginald Brett, Lord Arthur allowed himself some irony regarding these developments, at one point writing about Allies: " ... I trust [Inspector] Abberline is seeing that A. is comfortable for the rest of his life, and the other youths. I am quite surprised that they have not applied to me for pensions."[43] As indeed, Allies eventually tried to do. In a letter to the Duke of Beaufort written 6 July 1890, Allies asked for Somerset's address and for help from the Duke himself: "I am Destitute. I ask you kindly to do something for me. And if this does not meet with your approval, I shall not ask anything more because I shall think you blame me for what has been done. But am sure his Lordship would help me a little."[44] Allies may have been right about Lord Arthur. His letters to Brett reveal him to have maintained sentimental attachments to many of the men in his life. Even in his most self-pitying moments, he continued to express concern for the manservant who accompanied him into exile: "I cannot bear to think of parting with him, but he would be miserable living abroad with one always without a soul to speak to." The most gentle and disinterested manifestation of his emotional connection and practical concern with younger men from the working class appears in regard to one working in the regimental stables. On 21 October 1889, Somerset wrote to a friend: "there is a boy in my stable in Barracks named Barrett. He comes from Little Bad Minton and his parents are wretchedly poor and I took him because he was so starved. I wish you ... would take him and keep him as a helper or get him a place."[45]

Somerset's letters from exile provide a chronicle of considerable suffering. Although coming from a family of wealth and status, he had only limited means as a younger son. Work was an issue from the beginning; his difficulties resulted from social ostracism: "I have wandered about all day for two days trying to think what employment I am fit for and am still undecided. You see, if I got a promise of employment, I should require a reference. To whom am I to refer?"[46] Somerset traveled to Constantinople in the hopes of being hired to help the Sultan with his horses. Failing in that, he went on to Budapest, Vienna, and eventually back to France. It became clear that no one associated with his old regiment or with the household of the Prince of Wales would intervene on his behalf. As one whose life had been shaped by the institutions and associations of aristocratic birth, Lord Arthur Somerset was now a man without a place.

Publicity about the scandal followed him to Europe, where he adopted pseudonyms and avoided others from home in fear of being shunned, or worse. He wrote of his efforts to hide the day's *Le Figaro* from an

American guest at a hotel where he stayed because it contained "miles of Labouchere, Euston, and Somerset – all about a '*tendresse étrange pour les jeunes telegraphistes*' which I was supposed to have." In Vienna he felt harassed by the police and believed they were having him followed by street boys to provoke an incident. The recurrent theme in his letters is an abiding loneliness with little prospect of relief: "Constantinople was very interesting, but I rather wanted a friend to go with me to see all the things. Can not I find any luckless devil like myself who wanted a friend to talk to?" Although his brother Henry was in Monaco, and Lady Blanche traveled to visit him, he felt cut off from his family: "My poor father and mother, it is too awful for them and I suppose I shall never see them again nor shall I see any of my many friends . . ."[47] Lord Arthur Somerset remained in exile until his death in 1926 at Hyeres on the French Riviera, where he was buried.

In the West End scandals, the treatment of Somerset by officials in the highest reaches of government became the primary evidence of official complicity in protecting highly placed sexual offenders from the full measure of legal punishment. In hindsight it is hard to see that Somerset got away with anything. His life was ruined as a result of his desires to have sex and establish friendships with young men from the working classes. No doubt it could have been even worse if imprisonment had been added to his disgrace. The fate of Lord Arthur should caution us against measuring the social impact of laws simply in terms of the frequency of prosecution, chance of conviction, and severity of sentence. Laws against same-sex behavior clearly exercised a chilling effect out of all proportion to their actual enforcement and worked to reinforce and legitimate informal social sanctions against men known to prefer unorthodox sexual activities.[48] Did "my Lord Gomorrah" smile? As Shaw's Eliza Doolittle might have said, "Not bloody likely!"

NOTES

1. First, third, and fifth stanzas of a five stanza poem, published in *The North London Press*, 11 Jan. 1890.
2. This essay is based on archival research conducted during the summer of 1995 under the auspices of the NEH seminar on "The Culture of London, 1850–1920" directed by Michael Levenson. I am grateful for their assistance to the staffs at the Public Record Office, Chancery Lane; the British Library, including the newspaper collection at Collindale; and the

archives at Churchill College, Cambridge University. Michael Levenson and the members of the seminar provided a supportive and challenging setting in which to pursue and reflect on this work. Special thanks to William Cohen, Geoffrey Field, and Michael O'Loughlin for helping me to get this project off the ground.

3. See for example, Michel Foucault, *The History of Sexuality: An Introduction* (New York: Random House, 1978), and David F. Greenberg, *The Construction of Homosexuality* (Chicago: University of Chicago Press, 1988).
4. See especially Jeffery Weeks, *Coming Out: Homosexual Politics in Britain from the Nineteenth Century to the Present* (London: Quartet Books, 1977), and George Chauncey, *Gay New York: Gender, Urban Culture and the Making of the Gay Male World, 1890–1940* (New York: Basic Books, 1994).
5. For an illuminating and provocative discussion of that episode, see Judith Walkowitz, *City of Dreadful Delight: Narratives of Sexual Danger in Late-Victorian London* (Chicago: University of Chicago Press, 1992), ch. 3.
6. For good general narratives of the Affair, see H. Montgomery Hyde, *The Cleveland Street Scandal* (New York: Coward, McCann and Geoghegan, 1976), and Colin Simpson, Lewis Chester, and David Leitch, *The Cleveland Street Affair* (Boston: Little, Brown, and Co., 1976).
7. Simpson, *The Cleveland Street Affair*, 68.
8. Ibid., 74.
9. The Lord Chancellor Lord Halsbury himself wrote in his official capacity to the Assistant Director of Public Prosecutions in charge of the case, Mr. Cuffe: "The offense alleged to have been committed is an offense created by the recent statute and only a misdemeanour. The punishments already inflicted seem to me very inadequate and are likely to do more harm than good. If as is alleged in the papers, the social position of some of the parties will make a great sensation, this will give very wide publicity and consequently will spread very extensively written matter of the most revolting and mischievous kind, the spread of which I am satisfied will produce enormous evil." Simpson, *Cleveland Street Affair*, 105.
10. Labouchere had showed little enthusiasm for moral purity campaigns, and Frank Harris believed that the proposal was designed to undermine support for the bill as a whole. Labouchere later claimed that he was persuaded by officials in the administration to reduce his original seven years to the two authorized. However, the parliamentary record reveals that there was no debate on the subject, and that Labouchere proposed a sentence of one year that was raised to two as a result of amendment from the floor.
11. Although the crime was not spelled out in the statute, authoritative court interpretation restricted the crime of sodomy to anal intercourse and required proof of penetration. In 1781 the courts began to demand proof of "emission of seed" as well as of penetration. Carrying forward prohibitions of the canon law, the crime of sodomy was defined in terms of sexual intercourse that defeated the procreative possibilities of the act. In principle, any person could commit the crime or sin of sodomy with any other; those who preferred sex with others of their own gender were not singled out as the target of these laws.

12. There are no systematic surveys of prosecution for homosexual offenses during the earlier or the later period. It is hard to get data on offenses based on the crime charged except anecdotally, as in the scandalous trials of Boulton and Park in 1871, Cleveland Street, and Oscar Wilde.
13. This fact is in marked contrast to the 1871 trial of Boulton and Park in which medical evidence of a very specific and highly controversial sort figured centrally.
14. There is one exception to this generalization. In private correspondence now available in the archives at Churchill College, Cambridge, the sister of Lord Arthur Somerset writes to a friend that if there is any truth to the allegations, her brother must be mad. However, this judgment is not very specific and makes no reference to medical opinion.
15. See e.g. *The Illustrated Police News*, 18 Jan. 1890.
16. Simpson, *Cleveland Street Affair*, 73.
17. Ibid., 123.
18. Although at first he admits only that Newlove attempted to sodomize him, towards the end of his statement, in response to an assertion by Newlove, he admits that he did the same in return.
19. The following exchange between Newlove's attorney and the prosecutor when Newlove pled guilty reveals something about the legalistic and moralizing scrutiny of what we might call adolescent sexual experimentation or play:

    "... he does admit that he did take them to this house, knowing what might happen to them. On the other hand, the three boys had admitted that they had all indulged in indecent practices before Newlove approached them ..."

    "In justice to the boys," Poland broke in here, "I wish to say that they had played with other boys but had not committed these acts."

    "They said they had done such acts with boys before but not with men," Matthews retorted. "That goes to the degree." Quoted in Hyde, *Cleveland Street Scandal*, 53.
20. John Saul's testimony from his two statements to the London Police on 10 and 12 Aug. 1889, Public Record Office, DPP 1/95/4.
21. Jeffrey Weeks has argued for the importance of the links between male homosexuality and male and female prostitution in the development of modern gay subcultures and identities. See Weeks' essay, "Inverts, Perverts, and Mary-Annes: Male Prostitution and the Regulation of Homosexuality in England in the Nineteenth and Early Twentieth Centuries," *Journal of Homosexuality* 6 (1980–1): 113–24.
22. Note also that clause 11 applies only to conduct between men. The available legal history of Labouchere's amendment forces one to conclude that a much-repeated episode must be apocryphal: i.e., that the law originally defined a crime of gross indecency between women as well, but that this provision was withdrawn when Queen Victoria herself insisted that such a thing was impossible.
23. In work on the treatment of sodomy in the early modern period, historians like Alan Bray, Jeffrey Weeks, and Randolph Trumbach have shown that sodomy itself was defined in a fuller social context than that of theological proscriptions on non-procreative sex. Indeed, Foucault himself, in

his later work explicating the specific sexual ethos of ancient Greece and Rome, portrays a conceptual framework quite similar to that at work in the Renaissance. See e.g. Alan Bray, *Homosexuality in Renaissance England* (New York: Columbia University Press, 1982); Jeffrey Weeks, *Sex, Politics and Society: the Regulation of Sexuality Since 1800* (New York: Longman, 1981), and Randolph Trumbach, "London's Sodomites: Homosexual Behavior and Western Culture in the 18th Century," *Journal of Social History* 11 (Fall 1977–8).

24. The sodomite is a close relative of the rake, and virtually indistinguishable from him. And the rake is godfather at least to the nineteenth-century dandy. See Randolph Trumbach, "The Birth of the Queen: Sodomy and the Emergence of Gender Equality in Modern Culture, 1660–1750," *Hidden From History: Reclaiming the Gay and Lesbian Past*, eds. Martin Duberman, Martha Vicinus, and George Chauncey (New York: New American Library, 1989).
25. It is sometimes alleged that Stead provided Labouchere in 1885 with a dossier on boy prostitution that he had withheld from publication. I can find no authoritative evidence for this, although it is often repeated in the secondary literature. No one claims to have seen it.
26. Hyde, *Cleveland Street Scandal*, 111.
27. Ibid., 112.
28. Simpson, *Cleveland Street Affair*, 131.
29. George Bernard Shaw, *Bernard Shaw: Collected Letters*, ed. Dan Laurence (New York: Dodd, Mead and Co., 1965), 230.
30. Ibid., 231.
31. A difficult question about the conduct of Parke's defense is why they failed to call Newlove, who had named Euston and should have been available since he was in jail as a result of his guilty plea. Euston was also named by Frank Hewitt, another telegraph delivery boy working at Cleveland Street. Hewitt was named in Parke's plea of justification, which suggests that his attorneys had spoken with him. Saul testified that Hewitt had "been sent" abroad.
32. Frank Harris, *My Life and Loves* (1925) reprint (New York: Grove Weidenfeld, 1992), 336.
33. Saul's police statement, PRO, DPP 1/95/4.
34. *The Star*, 16 Jan. 1890.
35. Ibid.
36. Oddly enough, we have more evidence about John Saul than that discussed so far. He must be one of the very few figures in social history who has been immortalized in a work of pornography. *Sins of the Cities of the Plain; or, Confessions of a Mary-anne* was privately printed in London in 1881. It opens with the narrator's account of his encounter with John Saul of Lisle Street, a "professional Mary-Anne" whom he meets in Leicester Square. The succeeding chapters purport to be based on information that Saul provided about his life.
37. Simpson, *Cleveland Street Affair*, 144.
38. *Reynold's Newspaper*, 24 Jan. 1890.
39. *The Standard*, 17 Jan. 1890.
40. Hyde, *Cleveland Street Scandal*, 156.

41. *Daily Telegraph*, 17 Jan. 1890.
42. Hyde, *Cleveland Street Scandal*, 157.
43. Ibid., 126.
44. Ibid., 214.
45. Somerset, letters. The Lord Esher Papers, Archives, Churchill College, Cambridge.
46. Hyde, *Cleveland Street Scandal*, 99.
47. Somerset, letters. The Lord Esher Papers.
48. See data collected in the early chapters of Louis Crompton, *Byron and Greek Love: Homophobia in 19th-Century England* (Berkeley: University of California Press, 1985).

6 A Shock to Marriage?: the Clitheroe Case and the Victorians

Ginger Frost

Emily Hall married Edmund Haughton Jackson in 1887 in the town of Clitheroe, Lancashire, but the couple never cohabited. In fact, except for a few days immediately after the ceremony, Emily refused to live with her husband for four years, ignoring his many requests to do so and defying a court's judgment in his successful suit for restitution of conjugal rights in 1889. According to English law, her flouting of the order for restitution could have landed her in prison. However, Parliament abolished the penalty of imprisonment in the Matrimonial Causes Act of 1884, so by the time Emily and Edmund Jackson became embroiled in their battle of wills, there was little Jackson could do. Thoroughly frustrated, and convinced that her family was influencing her against him, Edmund kidnapped Emily in public on March 10, 1891. Her sisters immediately sued for a writ of *habeas corpus* to gain her release. A court case ensued, and in the original judgment, justices Cave and Jeune found against Mrs. Jackson, but the Appeals Court reversed that decision. Emily returned to her family amid public outcry.[1]

Many Victorian feminists, as well as some historians of women's history in recent years, have viewed this case as a benchmark in the evolution of British married women's legal rights.[2] After all, the Appeals Court decision in favor of Emily Hall and her family seemed to say that husbands no longer controlled their wives' bodies. In order to assess the significance of this case, an exploration of its background and context is necessary. First, I would like to examine the relationship between the couple before the case ever came to court to uncover the lesser known complications of it. Second, I want to analyze the many-sided public debate sparked by the Appeals Court decision, which was carried out in the popular press, legal reviews, and suffragist journals of the period. Both parts of my investigation will reveal that the Clitheroe case was symptomatic of an array of contemporary social problems and cannot be reduced to a simple conflict between proponents of institutional male dominance and advocates of women's independence.

* * *

Emily Maud Hall was the youngest of three sisters, the children of Henry Hall, a fairly prosperous solicitor in Clitheroe. In 1860, when Emily was fifteen, her oldest sister married Hartley Baldwin, her father's law partner. Her other sister did not marry. Emily, too, seemed well on the way to permanent spinsterhood, as she was still unmarried in 1881, at the age of 36. When their father died in 1875, the Hall sisters had each inherited an equal portion of his estate; Emily's share was enough to give her an annual income of £600. Despite this potential for independence, the three sisters remained close. Emily and her older sister lived together in their parents' house after the death of their mother in 1878, and the Baldwins lived nearby.[3]

Emily met Edmund Haughton Jackson (whom she always called Haughton in her letters) at a picnic in 1881. Haughton was the youngest son of a navy officer; his brother was a colonel. He appeared to be an entirely suitable partner for the daughter of a solicitor. Emily concluded "that he was living upon his means," since he did not appear to have a business or to need to work.[4] She continued to meet him at social events for the next few years. Emily insisted in the account of her life published after the 1891 trial that she saw Haughton merely as a friend and social acquaintance during this time, but that he acted like a suitor and repeatedly asked her to marry him. Because she did not share his feelings, she always refused. Haughton himself admitted that he had proposed several times but attributed her reluctance to the disapproval of her sisters and brother-in-law rather than any lack of reciprocity.

In October 1887, Emily discovered that Haughton and his best friend, Dixon Robinson, intended to go to New Zealand to take up farming. Rather than see him go without her, she at last consented to marry him. But she was still hesitant and within two days she had broken the engagement off, afraid to marry a man who was not going to stay in England. Indignant, Jackson and his friend both berated her for her weakness, and Emily and Haughton argued. After another two days, however, Jackson wrote to her in a conciliatory tone, begging her to reconsider. As a result, the two made up their quarrel. More importantly, Haughton again persuaded her to marry him, largely by painting a bright picture of his future in New Zealand. With Emily at last agreeable, the two were married on November 5, 1887 in London, witnessed by

Haughton's friend and business partner, Robinson, but not by any members of Emily's family.[5]

Immediately after the ceremony, Emily returned to Clitheroe and her family. Robinson had telegraphed a friend about the marriage, who then informed Emily's married sister. Both Mr. and Mrs. Baldwin were distressed at the news. Her brother-in-law, Hartley, in fact, told Emily that he hoped she would not regret her hasty actions. According to Emily, this gloomy remark led to an exchange with the groom: "Mr. Jackson said, 'What is your objection to me?' and Mr. Baldwin answered, 'You have no business or occupation; what have you got to keep a wife on?' He replied, 'I have got enough to keep myself always in bread and butter.'"[6] Emily then asked her brother-in-law, who was an attorney, to prepare a separate settlement for her property, to which her new husband made no objection. By the time Haughton left for New Zealand on November 8, her family had agreed to make the best of the situation and Mrs. Baldwin wrote a conciliatory letter to Jackson before he left, receiving a friendly note in return.[7]

Almost as soon as her husband and Dick Robinson left, Emily was assailed by renewed doubts. She became ill, and her friends pointed out to her that her health had not been good for some time. As she put it, "I realized that it would be impossible for me to hope to endure the rough life of a colonial settler, and this necessitated a complete change of plans." Emily then wrote to Haughton in January 1888 asking him to return. She then busied herself finding a place for the two of them to live, deciding to rent a "nice detached house" in Southport.[8] She received Haughton's reply in March. He agreed to return, since he did not want to live without her. This promise reassured his anxious wife but the rest of the letter's contents, however, became a serious bone of contention between them. He wrote:

> So darling, we give up N.Z., but cannot go home without means, and that is a hundred pounds and a little more ... Darling, I could not leave Dick behind; it would kill him. You know, dear, it is through him that we are together, and that I am so happy. When we get home, we can settle what is to be done. What Dick and I should like would be a nice little farm, near a town, anywhere you like; and, if it can be managed, a little place for Isabel [Haughton's unmarried sister] near, and Dick would stay with her. We should all be then so happy ...[9]

Emily was horrified by the letter. She interpreted his request for funds as a confirmation that he had married her for money and not for love. Possibly, her sisters and brother-in-law encouraged her in this interpretation. She was also unenthusiastic about sharing a home with Dixon Robinson, which was how she read Haughton's discussion of finding a farm in England. Although his words were ambiguous, Emily saw them as a suggestion that she support not only Haughton, but his sister Isabel and his best friend as well. Isabel Jackson's behavior did not contradict this view, since she constantly urged Emily to send money to Haughton and was quite content to have her brother and sister-in-law provide her with a home.[10] Isabel also gave her the impression that she thought her new sister-in-law had definitely come up in the world with her marriage, an attitude unlikely to endear her to the Halls and Baldwins. In the end, Emily came to see the entire Jackson brood as money-hungry upstarts.[11]

In April, she replied to Jackson's letter in terms that were certain to cause conflict: "Now, about your coming home, of course I shall be glad to see you, but as to Dixon, I think it a most absurd idea following you back when he went away for a purpose, and has never yet given it a trial. But I have nothing whatever to do with him, therefore he must do as he likes and as he thinks best." In other words, Emily made it clear that she did not intend to support his family or friends. Then she went even further. She reminded him that farming in England cost money and snapped, "If you go in for it you must be sure and make yourself responsible for it, for I shall advance you no money whatever." She also flatly refused to live with Dixon or anyone else. As she wrote, Emily seemed to become more and more indignant with the "slights" she had suffered, and her tone became increasingly cold. She accused Haughton of marrying her for her money, and added that she was "very sorry I was Blind enough before not to find it out. If you think you have any prospect of making money if you remain where you are for a time you had better do so... I must tell you I don't think I have raised myself in the eyes of the world by marrying you."[12]

Not surprisingly, Haughton replied to this letter in an equally hostile manner, beginning his answer with the bold statement that "Your letter is an insult to me and mine." He denied strenuously marrying her for her money or suggesting that Dixon live with them. All the same, he defended Dixon, claiming that his friend had saved his life when he became ill on the voyage to New Zealand. He tried to regain his authority by appealing to his rights as her husband:

> Do not make any mistake; there shall be a perfect understanding between us, but I will make it, not you. It is most ridiculous for you to say you will have this or that; it depends upon whether I approve or no... And how dare you say I married you for your trash, when you

> know it is a lie? As for not raising yourself by marrying me, that is quite a matter of opinion ... You say you do not wish to quarrel, yet you insult me in every way you can.[13]

One can understand Jackson's frustration with his new wife. However, his peremptory letter, full of husbandly commands and authority, served to confirm Emily's suspicion that marrying him had been a terrible mistake. She replied huffily, "I received your very insulting and unmanly (I won't say ungentlemanly, but unmanly) letter yesterday ... it is very evident to me that we shall never get on together ... If you are capable of addressing such a letter to me before we have lived together a single day, it plainly shows me what you will say or do afterwards." From that point on, she refused to see Haughton or speak to him. He returned to England on July 17, but was at first unable to see her. She refused to meet him, and her sister and brother-in-law physically restrained him from rushing into their house to get her alone.[14]

Haughton Jackson was indeed in an impossible situation. He had gone to New Zealand, apparently with his wife's approval and had agreed to return to England as soon as she urged him to do so. Having spent a great deal of money traveling, however, he needed help returning. Nor was his defense of his friend unreasonable. Robinson had helped him to marry Emily and had stood by him during the difficult sea voyage. Probably Robinson would not have tried to go to New Zealand alone, but only in partnership with his friend, so how could Jackson leave him? But Emily insisted on seeing his loyalty to his male friend as disloyalty to her. And she refused to have anything to do with him or to let him speak to her and explain. He could not repair his marriage, nor could he dissolve it. To add insult to injury, his appeal to the law court in 1889, through the writ for restitution of conjugal rights, proved to be a pointless expense, since the state no longer enforced it.

When Haughton finally did persuade Emily to meet with him for a discussion, his attempts to win her back were futile. She insisted that she could never live with him, for she had no respect or love for him. As she recalled: "... I was not going to run the risk of a cat-and-dog life with him, and that, after what had happened, I should be afraid to live with him. I said we were unsuited for each other and must live apart."[15] She also resented his legal proceedings, which she called "unpardonable." Any coercive action to get her back was in her eyes more evidence of his unsuitability as a husband. Yet if he did nothing, she was equally lost to him. He could not win.

Although these circumstances do not excuse his response, they do at least explain why he resorted to violence. Though Emily deeply resented the kidnapping, she did admit later that he did not try to force himself on her or seriously injure her in their scuffle. For his part, Jackson always insisted that he just wanted to be alone with her to try to effect a reconciliation without her family's interference. But, in the end, his rash action made reconciliation impossible. Emily characterized it as the act of a "coward," adding that "she loathed him for what he had done, and told him so." Rather touchingly, Haughton remained convinced of his powers of persuasion. He insisted that had he just been able to spend some time alone with her, he could have repaired their relationship. "I fully believe," he wrote after her release, "if her friends had not always been about the house and signalled to her continually she would have come round and I should have gained my point."[16] Jackson was either still thoroughly deluded, or perhaps was hoping to make a further appeal to the House of Lords and considered this statement useful to any future legal actions.[17] Either way, the outcome of the case left him with severely limited options.

While their correspondence is very revealing, none of their letters played a part in the court case, and thus some of the complexities of their relationship and estrangement have not been taken into account by analysts of the trial. Their differences over money, for instance, were generally ignored by contemporary commentators and later historians. I believe that Emily Jackson's income was clearly of ultimate importance in the breach between the couple. There are several concrete social factors that contributed to their estrangement. First of all, although Haughton and Emily socialized together and had similar backgrounds, her family did not see him as acceptable marriage material, probably because he had such a small income. He had enough money to live by himself (enough to "keep himself in bread and butter"), but not to support a wife. He had to find a way to work with his hands (farming), while Emily lived in leisure. Besides a gap in income, he was culturally different from the Halls and Baldwins. His love of his male companions is reminiscent of the hard-riding aristocratic culture of earlier times or the pub culture of working-class men.[18] He wanted his best friend as a neighbor, either in New Zealand or England, and would not dream of leaving him when he returned to England. Dixon was also one of the men who helped him kidnap Emily; their relationship was far stronger and longer-lived than his marital tie to Emily. His attempt at kidnapping also indicates his assumption that coercion of one spouse by another was acceptable, as a last resort. And life on a small farm near his friend and sister was enough for him, while Emily was busy finding a "nice detached house" in Southport for the two, clearly envisioning a different social life than her new husband.

Though his age is never mentioned, one could speculate that Haughton was also younger than his wife. This might explain why he was planning to go to New Zealand to make his way in the world and why Emily feared that he had married her for her money. Whatever his age, her family certainly saw him as a fortune hunter and his sister Isabel as little better. That Emily came to share their view was his downfall. Isabel apparently believed that Emily was fortunate to marry into and thus share the prestige of a naval family, even if Haughton was a younger son. But Emily used income and stability to determine social prominence, thus her remark about not raising herself by marrying Haughton. Further, Emily appeared to have little compassion for her sister-in-law, an unmarried woman who had not inherited a family home and an income and so was dependent on her brother. Although Emily appeared psychologically dependent on the Baldwins, she apparently did not consider her tie to them on the same level as Isabel's tie to Haughton. Despite her disdain for the alleged mercenary motives of the Jacksons, Emily seems equally concerned with financial matters, at least in her interest in status.

Of course, gender considerations were hardly absent from the couple's conflict. Emily's use of the word "unmanly" in one of her letters showed her contempt for a husband who would not or could not provide for his wife. Haughton, despite his lack of funds, tried to use his socially and culturally sanctioned authority as Emily's husband to regain the initiative in the relationship. James Hammerton has argued that two models of marriage existed side by side during the late nineteenth century – companionate marriage, championed by middle-class women, and the old patriarchal model, supported by many men.[19] The Jacksons clearly showed a gender divide on their opinions about the way marriage should be. However, the class difference between them intruded in their most stereotypically gendered exchanges. For example, when Emily called her husband "unmanly" but also added the jibe that she would not use the word "ungentlemanly," she implied broadly that gentility was not something he possessed. For his part, Haughton was unable to translate his claims of authority into reality as long as Emily could afford to live apart from him. The story of their torturous relationship shows that even the smallest degrees of status distinctions could affect middle-class individuals' ability to negotiate marital unions. Edmund Jackson was not significantly poorer than Emily Hall and the couple certainly had little difference in background. But his ties to his male friends, his violence, and his lack of a steady income were enough to make him unacceptable to Emily's family and, ultimately, Emily herself.[20]

An equally divergent picture emerges from the public reaction to the decision of the Appeals Court. In many ways the arguments, although ostensibly about different issues, reflected the same complicated allegiances to class and gender. Most of the law journals as well as many of the era's popular writers were appalled at the judgment, since they were convinced that it would destroy the institution of marriage. In the most famous phrasing, Eliza Lynn Linton announced, "Marriage, as hitherto understood in England, was suddenly abolished one fine morning last month!"[21] Although most commentators avoided such hyperbole, they certainly agreed with the sentiment. Several assumptions underlie this attitude. First, these writers saw marriage more as an institution than a relationship. Couples got along if they had to, but separated if circumstances permitted it. As Lord Penzance, a Divorce Court judge, put it, "It is the knowledge that man and wife must live together that induces both to make that life as tolerable as mutual concession can make it." A second assumption of such writers was that individual happiness was less important than the health of one of the pillars of society. The editors of the *Saturday Review* lamented, for example, that the sacredness of marriage was gone and nothing comparable had been put in its place. The result, they concluded, was an inevitable decline and the "ruin of domestic happiness."[22] Such writers agreed more with Edmund Jackson's understanding of the marriage bond than with Emily's.[23]

Those who condemned the decision also protested that it gave far too much power to women. Many foresaw scores of women leaving their husbands on the slightest of whims. "Now, if she is offended – if she is crossed in her desires or thwarted in her actions – she may carry her 'huff' into a wider region and graver issues than mere peevish discontent. She may take herself away if she have a mind, and no law exists that can bring her back," Linton complained. Though an overstatement, Linton's point was more relevant to the Jackson case than it might be to many others, since Emily's reasons for refusing to cohabit with Haughton could be interpreted as trivial. In addition, some questioned the role of Emily's two sisters in contributing to the couple's estrangement and thus focused attention on the role of assertive women. Interestingly, the complaints about outsiders' interference in the courtship were strongly split along gender lines. Not one of the commentators mentioned the role of Hartley Baldwin, although he too was a strong influence on Emily. Justice Cave, in fact, singled out the Hall sisters and scolded them in his original opinion, saying they had behaved very foolishly.[24]

Articles printed in the legal journals and newspapers centered on the potential difficulties the decision posed for deserted husbands, who were by law still responsible for their wives' maintenance but had no grounds for divorce. G.H. Wrey wrote to the *Law Times* that "it would seem clear the Legislature must interfere either in the direction of giving a husband *some* right and remedies as such, or of providing him with the means of revoking the onesided bargain." In short, this writer saw women as the aggressors and men as the victims in this scenario. In addition, many expounded a traditional view of the status of married women. The editors of *Law Notes* bluntly insisted that "by the marriage contract, the wife voluntarily parts with her full liberty."[25] A married woman was not in the same position as a single woman and should not be. Such opinions were not only unusually frank, but also ignored the considerable progress in married women's legal rights by 1891.[26]

Finally, critics of the decision were distressed by the "chaos" they saw in the marriage laws. In other words, they showed tremendous concern over the *laws* governing marriage as well as the institution of marriage itself. In their view, numerous inconsistencies and "unfair" practices abounded. For example, many otherwise conservative writers proposed adding desertion (of two to four years) to the grounds for divorce, so that a deserted man did not have to live the rest of his life celibate.[27] Other suggested reforms included exonerating husbands of their wives' debts and abolishing suits of breach of promise to discourage unhappy unions.[28] There was a split within the critics' camp, however. Though some insisted on further changes within marriage laws, others were against any more tampering. Lord Penzance, for instance, disapproved of the movement to allow divorce for desertion, saying "To enact that a husband whose wife has left him may claim a divorce will only increase the present evil." He particularly feared that couples would use the law to get collusive divorces, a problem with which he was familiar as a Divorce Court judge.[29]

Although outnumbered, other writers, even those who were not involved in the feminist movement, voiced their approval of the decision. In contrast with those who disliked it, these commentators felt that the decision could only strengthen marriage. They argued that marriage was a relationship between two individuals. If one partner did not wish to cohabit, then the marriage was already dead, since it could not survive by force. In other words, these commentators sided with Emily's view of marriage. Edward Manson, for instance, argued that "It is because it is so sacred and intimate a relation that people begin to see the folly, not to say the cruelty of compelling cohabitation against the will of either of the parties. What husband indeed, of any delicacy or decency of feeling, would wish to compel a reluctant wife to live with him, or wife a husband, except out of vindictiveness or mercenariness or some other discreditable motive?"[30] These writers also viewed marriage as sacred, but they saw equality within marriage as the only way to achieve it. As the *Spectator* insisted, "marriage, to be sacred, must be voluntary."[31] They supported the new vision of companionate marriage.

Those who applauded the decision had a less exteme view of the potential outcome, especially regarding married women. They pointed out that men deserted their wives far more often than the other way around so they did not foresee a rash of abandoned husbands. Furthermore, they noted that a wife seldom had an income or occupation that would enable her to leave an unhappy marriage without maintenance payments. She also usually had children she was reluctant to lose. The editors of the *Spectator*, in particular, ridiculed the overreactions of Linton and others: "To hear them talk ... half the wives in England would in a few weeks be taking themselves away from their husbands' sides, – whither, no one was at any serious pains to explain." They concluded that the vast majority of women would stay with their husbands, particularly in the lower classes, so that the consequences of *R.* v. *Jackson* would be limited indeed.[32]

Naturally, feminist periodicals centered on the case's liberating aspects, seeing it as, in the words of the *Englishwoman's Review*, "the charter of the personal liberty of married women." The *Personal Rights Journal* called it "a humane, broad verdict, whereby the wife is no more to be considered by law ... the slave of the husband."[33] Almost all these writers, in agreement with some of their conservative opponents, urged Parliament to use the decision as a springboard for more legal reforms. For instance, they, too, argued for divorce reform, but they also demanded women's suffrage, an end to the remaining bits of "coverture" in the law, and equality in custody of children.[34] In fact, Elizabeth Wolstenholme Elmy assumed that these changes were inevitable after the Clitheroe verdict. She wrote to a friend, "Let us rejoice together ... coverture is dead and buried."[35] Even some working-class women seized upon the case as a new way to demand help from the magistrates. One woman in London, who wanted protection when she tried to leave her abusive spouse, received little encouragement from Mr. Denham until she complained, "The law is all for the men, and none for the women. I wish I was Mrs. Jackson." Her knowledge of the action intrigued the magistrate, who eventually did order a constable to help her.[36] Although this reaction was seldom repeated, and thus Elmy's optimism proved to be misplaced, most feminists saw the case as an advance, a decision which made any kind of "slavery" unacceptable in English law.

Many of those who supported the decision, even if they did not support the goals of the feminist movement, agreed that the marriage law was in a bad state, but they tended to see this as an opportunity rather than a lamentable problem. Still, just as in the more conservative ranks, some of those who applauded the decision did not believe that further change was necessary or valuable. The editors of the *Spectator*, for example, firmly opposed any changes in the grounds for divorce, insisting that "The real and only great inducement [to try to make a marriage work] must be the firm conviction, that if they desert each other, they cannot at least contract any other marriage during the lifetime of the deserted partner."[37] Others felt that women now had everything that they could possibly want, so that further reform was unnecessary – this at a time in which women could not divorce on equal terms with men, could not vote in national elections, and had far fewer economic opportunities. For instance, Edward Manson insisted that "The advocates of women's rights have really hardly a grievance left."[38] They saw Emily's victory as an example of the viability of the current system.

In fact, the divided loyalties of both sides revealed many shared preoccupations. First, proponents and opponents of the decision expressed tremendous concern about marriage. Both groups, but particularly the opponents, saw marriage as terribly fragile, likely to be destroyed by the slightest breath of wind. Almost all had suggestions on how to "fix" marriage, but, as stated above, their visions of reform were not univocal by any means. For instance, even the most trenchantly conservative spokesperson, Eliza Linton, argued for numerous additions to the grounds for divorce, including drunkenness, madness, felony convictions, and desertion, thus distinguishing herself from many conservative allies. In fact, many of her suggestions were similar to those advanced by the much more liberal writer Elmy.[39] On the other hand, even some feminists who applauded the decision were leery about further change in the marriage law, putting them in agreement with many staunch conservatives.

The argument for easier divorce, in particular, provoked an ambivalent reaction. Most feminists wanted equal grounds for men and women and some general liberalization. Yet male desertion was far more common than female, and men had a much greater possibility of earning a living wage and supporting themselves than women, should a divorce occur. The editors of the *Saturday Review* put it bluntly: "Few rational beings can deny that, if marriage fell into general disfavour ... it would be, all things considered, decidedly easier and pleasanter for men to provide themselves with substitutes for a wife than for women to provide themselves with substitutes for a husband. From no point of view whatever have men so much to lose as women by the disuse of marriage."[40] Several magistrates began refusing to grant separation orders to women, arguing that the Jackson case made them unnecessary. Perhaps technically this was true, but without such an order, the woman could not receive maintenance.[41] Emily, of course, did not need maintenance; most other women did, though, and they probably felt little gratitude for the "freedom" her victory brought about. Legal equality without economic and social equality caused more harm than good, which made decisions like *Jackson* problematic.

The effect on marriage law was also a cause for concern. The *Times*, though generally in favor of the action, was dismayed at its effect on marital law; cases like *Jackson* made "the English law of marriage a medley like nothing ever before heard of. What a mass of confusion and contradictions it contains!" J. Edmondson Joel characterized the law as "one of growing perplexity and confusion," and the *Saturday Review* called it "hopelessly irrational and muddled."[42] Most were unhappy that the common law allowed suits for restitution of conjugal rights but no enforcement of them. They pointed out that Jackson's rash actions were partly a result of his having no other way to enforce his writ. Others centered on the fact that husbands had to maintain wives who fled. The *Law Times* even complained about widows inheriting from husbands with whom they had refused to cohabit.[43] In addition to these problems, some writers pointed out that the English and Scottish marriage and divorce laws were not the same. Some of the English commentators on the case began to wonder publicly, perhaps for the first time, if the Scottish or American laws were superior their own, an idea distressing to English pride and insularity. Indeed, the reaction of Canadian, American, and Scottish law journals at the time was one of amusement that the English even had a court case on this issue.[44] All of this caused considerable chagrin.

As in the relationship between Haughton and Emily, anxiety over gender roles was paramount in the decision, though it was complicated by several other factors. Naturally, those who opposed the decision were most concerned with its effect on married women. The prediction that hordes of "wild women" would rush out the door and leave an unhappy marriage for the merest caprice showed fear and resentment of possibly unfettered women. Several opinions also expressed a sense of longing for the "good old days" of complete husbandly authority. The editors of *Law Notes*, for example, huffed that "In olden times, the law was much more masculine in this respect." They went on to reminisce longingly about husbands' powers of "correcting" women, as well as praising the practice of imprisoning recalcitrant wives.[45]

Yet, despite these expressions of misogyny, both sides showed far more concern with men than women in their analysis of the case. Unsurprisingly, those who supported Emily Jackson highlighted men's tendency to desertion and violence which had to be restrained by law. Even the conservatives distrusted men's "nature." One sees this most clearly in their assumption that marriage was doomed unless men had complete control. That is, they argued that men would not marry if they could not enjoy patriarchal privileges. The *Illustrated London News* airily charged that "if the marriage market is a little 'flat' for some time to come, women will have to trace this depression to the story of Mrs. Jackson."[46] Blended with this was the assumption of the naturalness of male sexual aggression. Men would not be celibate; instead, they would pursue sexual partners outside of matrimony. In other words, the male sex drive was unstoppable, but monogamy was purely a result of social and legal incentives. Without them, women faced two options: concubinage or spinsterhood. These arguments highlight again the concern with masculinity that was a constant in late Victorian family law. Was a "manly" man authoritarian, sexually adventurous, even violent? Or was he domesticated, paternal, and loving? Or could he be both? These competing definitions of masculinity brought confusions about gender roles to the forefront in discussions about marriage and the family.[47]

Though these gender concerns were pervasive, they were complicated by class issues, just as the Jacksons' marriage was. As a man, Haughton Jackson should have been able to make his way without his wife's help, but as a younger son in a naval family, he was unable to do so. In contrast, Emily's assured income allowed her to chose to live apart from him. Thus, Jackson could not exercise his husbandly prerogatives in part because of his lesser financial resources, in other words his weakness. Another way that class concerns interacted with gender issues was in the decision itself. The Appeals Court referred to Emily constantly as a "lady," obviously distressed that someone of her station had been kidnapped in public. Although the violence was minimal, the judges expressed outrage all the same.[48] One doubts they would have expressed as much concern about the ill treatment of a poor woman, since Victorian judges were notoriously unsympathetic to brutalized working-class wives.[49]

In the contemporary press, both sides showed considerable class bias, too, although the arguments of opponents of the decision were more overt. In general, they assumed that because Emily Jackson was well off, all married women had settlements like hers that would enable them to live on their own, or that all widows had estates to inherit. There were some exceptions, however. As the *Spectator* pointed out, the lower classes found extra-legal ways to work out marital difficulties and these options were unlikely to change because of the *Jackson* decision. The *Law Journal*, too, admitted that "the classes in whom the reluctance [to use force] is not so strong ... not infrequently exercise the marital right of custody; but their disputes are mostly settled in the police courts."[50] Indeed, some lower class people in Clithoroe, as many historians have noted, publicly sided with Mr. Jackson, mobbing Emily's carriage and rioting outside her home when she returned to town. Perhaps they recognized that Jackson's behavior fit more with their rowdy culture than with that of his in-laws. In this sense, reaction to the ill-fated marriage was an example of a union between the upper and lower classes against the middle.[51]

This mixture of class and gender concerns made for curious legal muddles, bringing into question the stability of the common law in general. The Appeals Court's opinion had insisted that husbands had never been given the right to imprison their wives under the English common law. The justices dismissed most of the precedents cited by Mr. Jackson's barristers, including the most relevant one, *Cochrane's Case* (1840). The reaction of legal experts was swift and unambiguous. The *Law Journal* stated flatly, "Perhaps never in the history of judicial decisions has authority been so boldly overruled and disregarded as in *Jackson's Case*." The *Solicitor's Journal and Reporter* complained, "The manner in which the common law has been dealt with by the Court of Appeal ... gives a rude shock to the current ... theory as to its nature."[52] Law journal editors professed to be horrified that judges used their personal preferences in deciding a case, rather than precedent and statutes. They declaimed against "judge-made law," ignoring the obvious point that following precedent itself was a socially determined action. The *Law Journal* complained, "Reluctance on the part of a judge to accept conclusions which may be out of harmony with the sentiment of the day is a frame of mind likely to produce bad law," and the *Solicitor's Journal* agreed, calling the Court of Appeal "careless of maintaining the consistency of the common law."[53]

With such arguments, the critics of the decision showed remarkable (and probably deliberate) naiveté about the workings of the common law courts, one that had been made many times before, whenever judicial activism flourished. Judges throughout the nineteenth century (and before) made decisions that conformed to current social conventions, though masked with the language of legal formalism.[54] Writers on both sides found legal justifications for their prejudices as well.[55] However, the original court also knew of the 1884 Matrimonial Causes Act, yet its decision was the exact opposite. Obviously, both groups of judges used legal language to justify decisions based at least in part on their own social views. This was yet another unpalatable fact for conservatives. Though it had always been true, the glaring inconsistencies in the Jackson case forced them to acknowledge it. Common opinion had turned against the conservatives by the late Victorian period, and the law had followed suit.

Finally, all of the commentators showed a distaste for the publicity surrounding the suit. The *Spectator*, in particular, complained about people going to newspapers and open court to find vindication. Mrs. Jackson had the approbation of the Appeals Court judges; Mr. Jackson was supported by the "mob," as well as many of the elite. Both found a sort of validation from these sources, which was why they were both willing to publish vindications and their letters in the local newspaper, which were then reprinted in the *Times*. The editors of the *Spectator* disapproved of such exhibitionism: "Representative institutions have resulted in making a sort of god of even the coarsest and least intelligent expressions of public opinion ... There seems to us something very pitiful in this ... public sophistry."[56] As more and more people used the court system, this public "confessional" became commonplace, a process accelerated by the creation of the Divorce Court in 1857. Most observers saw nothing but evil in these appeals to the public, while at the same time they themselves capitalized on the reading public's interest by printing stories and opinions about the case.

All the publicity gave the public a pleasurable sensation of participating in controversies, or, perhaps, even contributing to them. This frisson was not limited to the "great unwashed," but extended to newspaper and journal editors, divorce court judges, and law journal writers. The main problem with this publicity was that it meant that neither Emily nor Haughton could completely control or eradicate the perceptions of their viewers; they became in a sense what the public made them. Thus, for many Victorian feminists, Haughton Jackson was a wife-beater and for many conservatives, Emily Jackson was a "wild woman," when both were considerably more and less than these sweeping characterizations.

The reactions to the Clitheroe decision demonstrate a complex mixture of anxieties in late Victorian culture. Even those who saw the action as a victory were not satisfied with the state of the law or with marriage. Marriage, indeed, was a primary concern, an institution that seemed doomed to decline. Yet the elite could not agree on how to save it – further surgery or complete cessation of treatment? Both the fascination of the public with matrimonial cases and the great influence of Emily's family on the course of her courtship and marriage call into question family historians' assumption that community controlled marriage was out of date by the Victorian period. Emily was 36 and financially independent when she met Haughton, yet she remained under the influence of her sisters and brother-in-law, even after her (possibly rebellious) marriage. The community at large, through letters-to-the-editor, attendance at court, or even public riots, made their opinions known as well. These controls may not have been all-pervasive, but they were certainly still in force. This case suggests that the waning of the era of communal courtship and family control was much more gradual, and extended even into the twentieth century.

Beliefs about gender roles undoubtedly were a major factor in marital disputes in the *fin-de-siècle* and Emily and Haughton clearly had different opinions about their marital obligations and the proper behavior of husbands and wives. Similarly, commentators on their case held divergent views. Reformers argued for a more domesticated man and more egalitarian marriage, while conservatives insisted that such outcomes were impossible. In many ways, class distinctions heightened these gender role disparities. For instance, Edmund Jackson was poorer than his wife and could be seen as a fortune hunter. He may have had the right as a man to control her, but his wife's higher status prevented him from succeeding, since she was "a lady." Emily Jackson was able to exploit gendered expectations and class divisions to evade one of the remaining rules of coverture, but precisely because of her class affiliation, the decision in her case was less ground-breaking for English women *per se*.

Nevertheless, because of cases like *R.* v. *Jackson*, the English began to express doubts publicly about the validity of their marriage laws by the 1890s. Judges became more open about ignoring precedents, while Americans, Canadians, and Scots derided "outmoded" English practices. It was no wonder that many of the commentators predicted further breakdowns in the legal system. On the eve of the twentieth century, the *Jackson* case could be seen in two radically different ways: as a harbinger of decline or as an opportunity for endless improvement. And however the public reacted, Haughton Jackson was still without recourse in the courts for his permanent quasi-married status. Nothing shows the difficulties of a would-be patriarch more than Jackson's inability even to speak to the woman he had married with such optimism in 1887. For those who cherished the old domestic order, the Jacksons represented the dark side of the evolution of social mores at the end of the century.

NOTES

1. For the decision, see *Law Times* 64 (25 July 1891), 679–85; 1 *Law Reports, Queen's Bench Decisions* (1891), 671–86.
2. Mary Lyndon Shanley, *Feminism, Marriage, and the Law in Victorian England, 1850–1895* (Princeton: Princeton University Press, 1989), 177–83; David Rubenstein, *Before the Suffragettes: Women's Emancipation in the 1890s* (Brighton: Harvester Press, 1986), 55–7; and Maeve Doggett, *Marriage, Wife-Beating and the Law in Victorian England* (Columbia, SC: University of South Carolina Press, 1993), 1–15; 134–41. Doggett has insisted that the decision was much less liberating than previously argued, but still centers on the same feminist issues.
3. *Times*, 18 April 1891.
4. *Times*, 10 March and 18 April 1891.
5. *Times*, 20 April 1891.
6. *Times*, 20 April 1891.
7. The texts of the letters are reprinted in the *Times*, 20 April 1891.
8. *Times*, 20 April 1891.
9. Ibid.
10. This was not an unusual request of an unmarried sister upon her brother, although tensions were inevitable when the brother married. See Leonore Davidoff and Catherine Hall, *Family Fortunes: Men and Women of the English Middle Class, 1780–1850* (Chicago: University of Chicago Press, 1987), 348–53.
11. *Times*, 21 April 1891.
12. Ibid.
13. Ibid.
14. *Times*, 22 April 1891.
15. *Times*, 2 May 1891.
16. *Times*, 28 April and 2 May 1891.
17. For the posibility of an appeal, see *Law Journal* 26 (25 April 1891), 284.
18. Ellen Ross, *Love and Toil: Motherhood in Outcast London, 1870–1918* (Oxford: Oxford University Press, 1993), 848–86; Keith McClelland, "Masculinity and the 'Representative Artisan' in Britain: 1850–80," and Pamela Walker, "'I Live But Not Yet I For Christ Liveth in Me': Men and Masculinity in the Salvation Army, 1865–90," in John Tosh and

Michael Roper, eds., *Manful Assertions: Masculinities in Britain Since 1800* (New York: Routledge, 1991), 74–112; David Roberts, "The Paterfamilias of the Victorian Governing Classes," in Anthony Wohl, ed., *The Victorian Family: Structure and Stresses* (London: Croom Helm, 1978), 59–81.

19. A. James Hammerton, *Cruelty and Companionship: Conflict in Nineteenth-Century Married Life* (London: Routledge, 1992), 82–101.
20. For more on how small distinctions could derail relationships, see Ginger Frost, *Promises Broken: Courtship, Class and Gender in Victorian England* (Charlottesville, Va.: University Press of Virginia, 1995), 80–4; and F.M.L. Thompson, *The Rise of Respectable Society: A Social History of Victorian England, 1830–1900* (Cambridge, Mass.: Harvard University Press, 1988), 103–6.
21. Eliza Lynn Linton, "The Judicial Shock to Marriage," *Nineteenth Century* 29 (May 1891), 691.
22. Lord Penzance, "The Law of Husband and Wife," *Times*, 30 April 1891; "The Future of Marriage," *Saturday Review* (28 March 1891), 370–1.
23. For a similar argument about the nature of marriage, see Frost, *Promises Broken*, 141–55.
24. Linton, "Judicial Shock to Marriage," 697; *Law Times*, 64 (25 July 1891), 679–80.
25. Linton, "Judicial Shock to Marriage," 697; *Law Times* 90 (11 April 1891), 433; *Law Notes* 10 (1891), 113.
26. Shanley, *Feminism, Marriage and the Law*, 103–55.
27. See e.g. Linton, "Judicial Shock to Marriage," 698–700; Alexander Robertson, "The Reform of the Marriage Laws of Great Britain and Ireland," *Law Magazine and Review* 4th series, 17 (1891–2), 12–13; *Law Journal* 26 (1891), 249, 343–4.
28. *Law Journal* 26 (1891), 249.
29. Ibid.
30. Edward Manson, "Marital Authority," *Law Quarterly Review* 7 (July 1891), 251.
31. *Spectator* 66 (21 March 1891), 397. See also "The Law of Husband and Wife," *Law Journal* 26 (23 May 1891), 354. For the companionate ideal, see Joan Perkin, *Women and Marriage in Nineteenth-Century England* (London: Routledge, 1988), 233–56; Davidoff and Hall, *Family Fortunes*, 321–56; and Judith Rowbotham, *Good Girls Make Good Wives: Guidance for Girls in Victorian Fiction* (Oxford: Blackwell, 1989), 50.
32. "Husband and Wife," *Spectator* 66 (March 28, 1891), 439; 66 (March 21, 1891), 397.
33. "The Clitheroe Abduction Case," *Englishwoman's Review* (15 April 1891), 107; M. Sevasly, "Marriage and Divorce," *Personal Rights Journal* 110 (April 1891), 37.
34. See especially Elizabeth Wolstenholme Elmy, *The Decision in the Clitheroe Case and Its Consequences: A Series of Five Letters* (Manchester: Guardian Printing Works, 1891), 10–17.
35. Elmy, *The Decision in the Clitheroe Case*, 10–17. Her letter to Harriet McIlquaham quoted in Lucy Bland, *Banishing the Beast: Sexuality and the Early Feminists* (New York: The New Press, 1995), 136.

36. Quoted in George Behlmer, "Summary Justice and Working-Class Marriage in England, 1870–1940," *Law and History Review* 12 (Fall 1994), 250.
37. "Lord Penzance on Husband and Wife," *Spectator* 66 (2 May 1891), 615.
38. Manson, "Marital Authority," 255.
39. Linton, "Judicial Shock to Marriage," 698–700; Elmy, *The Decision in the Clitheroe Case*, 10. For similar arguments about divorce reform, see Gail Savage, "'Equality from the Masculine Point of View . . .': The 2nd Earl Russell and Divorce Law Reform in England," *russell: the Journal of the Bertrand Russell Archives* 16 (Summer 1996): 67–84.
40. *Saturday Review* (28 March 1891), 371.
41. See "The Clitheroe Case," *Englishwoman's Review* (15 July 1891), 186–7; and *The Spectator* 66 (April 1891), 530.
42. *Times*, 23 April 1891; Joel, "On the Present State of the Law Relating to the Married," *National Review* 17 (May 1891), 310; *Saturday Review* (28 March 1891), 371.
43. *Law Times* 90 (25 April 1891), 473.
44. See *American Law Review* 25 (1891), 454–5; *Juridicial Review* 13 (1891), 157; and *Canada Law Journal* 27 (1891), 356.
45. "The Last of the Marital Rights," *Law Notes* 10 (1891), 112.
46. "The Rights of Husbands," *Illustrated London News*, 28 March 1891.
47. For debates about masculinity, see Hammerton, "Manliness and Marriage: Resisting the 'Flight from Domesticity' in Late Nineteenth-Century England and Australia," Unpublished Paper, 1994; Frost, *Promises Broken*, 40–57.
48. See *Times Law Reports* 7 (1890–1), 386–8, for examples.
49. See Hammerton, *Cruelty and Companionship*, 34–67; Ellen Ross, "'Fierce Questions and Taunts': Married Life in Working-Class London," *Feminist Studies* 8 (1982): 575–602; and idem, *Love and Toil*, 84–6.
50. *Spectator* 66 (28 March 1891), 439–40; *Law Journal* 26 (27 June 1891), 433.
51. See Hammerton, *Cruelty and Companionship*, 38–9; and Doggett, *Marriage, Wife-Beating and the Law*, 136.
52. *Times Law Reports* 7 (1890–1), 386–7; *Law Journal* 26 (26 March 1891), 207; *Solicitor's Journal and Reporter* 35 (28 March 1891), 357.
53. *Law Journal* 26 (20 June 1891), 416; *Solicitor's Journal* 35 (28 March 1891), 359.
54. For more on the arguments about judicial activism, see Stephen Hedley, "Keeping Contract in Its Place – *Balfour* v. *Balfour* and the Enforceability of Informal Agreements," *Oxford Journal of Legal Studies* 5 (1985): 391–415; and Frost, *Promises Broken*, ch. 9.
55. Historians have, on occasion, repeated this disingenuous argument. Maeve Dogget insists that the decision was not a significant change in the law, since the Appeals Court justified its actions by claiming that the Matrimonial Causes Act of 1884 was the main reason they decided against Mr. Jackson. Doggett, *Marriage, Wife-Beating and the Law*, 134–41.
56. "The Public as Confidant," *Spectator* 66 (2 May 1891), 620–1; for the newspaper exchange, see *Times*, 18 April 1891; 20 April 1891; 21 April 1891; 22 April 1891; 23 April 1891; 28 April 1891; 2 May 1891.

7 Books on Trial: Prosecutions for Representing Sapphism in *fin-de-siècle* France

Nicole Albert

"Do you honestly believe that everything can be said, can be described, can be revealed as long as afterwards the feelings of disgust that result from debauchery and the illnesses that are its just reward are described too?"[1]

SAPPHISM ON TRIAL

At the turn of the century Paris was the capital of sapphism.[2] It attracted expatriate women seeking greater sexual freedom, including Renée Vivien and Natalie Barney, who lived openly as lesbians but were never harassed or penalized by the French authorities because of it.[3] Yet even though women like these pursued their pleasures and lived out their lives without real constraints, the French criminal justice system made lesbianism itself invisible and surrounded the topic with a thick veil of secrecy. In particular, the prosecutions of authors and attempted censorship of texts which depicted lesbianism became a principal strategy of the judicial authorities by the late nineteenth century. In fact, the targeting of books with homosexual themes and the subsequent trials of their authors was more frequent than actual prosecutions for sexual misconduct. This essay will focus on two such censorship trials – the attempts to ban the novels *Deux Amies* by René Maizeroy in 1885 and *Jouir... Mourir* by Victorien du Saussay in 1894 and to prosecute the authors on the grounds of obscenity. In both cases the novel's central figure was a lesbian. At the very time the law ignored lesbianism as a reality, it felt compelled to sue writers for giving sapphism a name and for granting it visibility.

There was no law at this time that explicitly forbade sexual relations between women. The French legal code was silent and thus powerless against what some observers called a scourge of society; it was so helpless that as a contemporary fictional character declared, every "mentally disturbed woman who was no less than the incarnation of Vice itself was innocent of any crime" and absolutely immune from prosecution.[4] Nevertheless, despite the law's silence about it, many contemporary observers – sociologists, authors of literary and medical texts – did protest against what they perceived as an astonishing increase in sapphism and the equally disturbing inaction of the imperial authorities, who constructed no legal barriers against it.

In fact, French law was somewhat unique in Western Europe. The Napoleonic Code adopted in 1804 tacitly approved any and all homosexual acts committed in private between adults, recognizing as criminal only acts committed in public or relations with a minor partner.[5] Thus, in France, adultery, for example, although categorized as an offense in the code, was not considered to be such if an unfaithful wife were found in bed with another woman.[6] France's legal code was not the only one to ignore acts between women; lesbian sexual relations were not mentioned and thus not classified as a criminal act, in several European countries. In 1931 the writer Marise Querlin noted that since the adoption of the Napoleonic Code:

> French laws have made a distinction between crime and vice. Homosexuality is thus free of criminal penalties in cases where there's no violence, no offense to public decency, no lack of mutual consent or no minor partner. In those instances it would be subject to the penalties specified in article 334 of the Penal Code. The possible penalties ranged from a prison term of up to five years and a fine of a maximum of five hundred francs. The laws were the same in Belgium, Holland, Spain and Portugal. In Switzerland the laws varied from canton to canton, but in Germany, as in Austria and England, homosexuality was severely punished. One could say that these laws were intended for male homosexuals... except in Austria, where they applied to women and men.[7]

It should also be noted that in England Queen Victoria purportedly refused to sign Section 11 of the Criminal Law Amendment Act of 1885 penalizing homosexual acts unless all references to women were removed, since she claimed that women didn't do such things.[8]

Moreover, the ground for the invisibility of sapphism, ratified by the Napoleonic code, had been prepared by the emperor-to-be as early as

1800 in an official proclamation that stipulated that women could not wear men's clothing. This prohibition would be revived at the turn of the century when emancipated women and female cycling enthusiasts decided to adopt male attire.[9] Thus, lesbians would be as invisible as lesbianism itself. Or, outward signs of gender transgression were thereby erased from official view, as the lesbian act itself had been, from the legal code.

Around 1898 Charles Virmaître published a book about lesbians in which he decried the laws that protected them from prosecution. He believed that this had created a hospitable environment for the growth and increase of sapphism:

> Dr. Martineau ... has observed that from one year to the next there has been a violent upsurge in the sapphic passion. Isn't this proclivity an offense to decency as it's commonly understood? Our legislators didn't think so, since our legal code is silent in this area, if the acts aren't committed *in public* ... For this reason, sapphists don't come under the purview of articles 330 and 334 of the Penal Code ... But if an attempt were made to extirpate this evil invading us, spreading its rot and putrefaction throughout society, people would protest against such a blow to personal freedom, since we all have the right to pursue our pleasures wherever we wish, and in fact women who do this sort of thing are committing no offense.[10]

It is true that according to journalists and proto-sociologists of the 1880s, lesbians could gather in "specialized cafés" like *Le Rat Mort* or *La Souris* near the Place Pigalle.[11] And they could even go to brothels, an act the law apparently prohibited but the authorities in fact tolerated, as Jules Davray, a commentator on contemporary morals, lamented in 1890. "When scandals come to light ... they reveal – to the outrage of our virtuous public – that titled ladies, noblewomen, have not hesitated to partake in lesbian dalliances in brothels, where women's presence is strictly forbidden by the laws governing such establishments."[12]

Clearly, lesbians were not totally ignored since their social customs and mores were repeatedly mocked and criticized in contemporary articles and novels. But it seemed that their existence would be tolerated as long as they kept out of sight of the public. At least, that's what numerous turn-of-the-century commentators oberved with a trace of rancor. For instance, in 1908 Doctor Gallus published a work about male and female homosexuals and in the section on sapphists, he noted a particular police action. He observed that the police would sometimes visit brothels to make sure prostitutes didn't sleep in the same bed, as it was often the case that these women, disgusted by men and heterosexual love because of the work they engaged in, would turn to their own sex for solace.[13] The author added that this was the only official act of repression against sapphism that he could identify. "Women may openly express their affection for each other in any byway of the city without fear of reprisals. No one sees any problem with that."[14] This sort of tolerance can no doubt be attributed to the fact that the behavior he discusses is a private matter between individuals, even if it occurred on the street, and does not have overt sexual overtones. In contrast, the same conduct occurring on stage would have provoked negative reactions and repressive measures. In any event, if actions that appeared to be sapphic were not castigated because they were not overtly sexual, they could be condemned because they represented a taboo sexuality. This was the case with two contemporary music hall performances.

The turn-of-the-century French music hall was famous for frivolous and "naughty" entertainment such as the cancan, suggestive song lyrics (like those in Polaire's repertoire), and outrageous depictions of women. Even though its shows were meant for a popular crowd that was not easily offended, two scandals involving music hall performances illustrate the aforementioned distinction between private practices and public representation. One scandal occurred in 1907 and the other the following year; the second resulted in a trial and penalties. One involved an actual lesbian couple, the other, two actresses performing a scene of lesbian sex. Both raised anew questions about how the authorities determined when sapphism was scandalous *per se* as well as the issue of limits on representation in general.

The Moulin Rouge scandal (1907) is remembered mainly because of its protagonists, or at least one of them – the writer Colette. At the time, the press gave the performance a great deal of attention. It was preceded and followed by numerous caricatures and insulting articles targeting the scandalous and supposedly ludicrous couple Colette and her lover, the Marquise de Morny, made. The Marquise, who preferred using her family name "de Belbeuf," was notorious as a lesbian who dressed mannishly and lived a bachelor's life, even though she was a married woman separated from her husband. Colette too was married to a well-known popular journalist and music critic who went by the pen name Willy.[15] At the end of 1906 the Marquise wrote a pantomine called *Rêve d'Egypte* (Egyptian Dream) that she wanted to perform with Colette. In it, the Marquise would play a male archeologist who discovered a female mummy who sinuously undid her wrappings in order to seduce him. After that, the two would exchange a kiss. The performance took place on January 3, 1907 at the Moulin Rouge. Attended by the Mornys, the Marquise's family, and Willy, Colette's estranged husband, the pantomime provoked a scandal. The incident was front-page news the following day; and Lépine, the police prefect of Paris, under pressure from the Morny family, threatened to close the music hall if the two performed again.[16] As a result, the Marquise withdrew from the performance and on the second night Colette's mime teacher Georges Wague took on her role in the pantomime, which itself was renamed *Songe d'Orient* (Oriental Reverie.) This did little to calm the public furor and the performance was definitively banned in Paris by the prefect after the second night.[17]

A year later, in May 1908, another scandal originated in a music hall called the Little Palace. It resulted in fines and a prison term. The show called *Rêverie d'Ether* (Ether Intoxication) consisted of a scene of "ether inebriation and lesbian passion" played with an unusual dedication to verisimilitude and very skimpy costumes by two protagonists. Monsieur Chatillon, the manager of the Little Palace, was judged the chief instigator of this shocking performance and condemned to three months' imprisonment and a 200 franc fine. The two performers, Mademoiselles Bouzon and Lepelley, were given suspended one-month sentences and fined 50 francs each. The court explained its ruling in strong language: "Such exposure of bare flesh and such embraces, such kisses or feigned ones intended to excite nervous passions cannot be considered as anything less than an appeal to the grossest, most excessive and dangerous lubricity."[18]

In general, however, lesbian couples or lesbianism were tolerated as long as they remained invisible and secret, an attitude consistent with the time-honored distinction between public and private matters in France. Yet, at the turn of the century the boundary between the two became blurred – as far as sapphism was concerned – when many novelists started to write more openly about it and disclose sapphic mores. Their rationale was basically that to be fought against and possibly eradicated, sapphism had to be discussed. Others, in contrast, held to the principle that "the best way to eliminate it would be to ignore it."[19] These were empty words indeed in an era when the writers of sensational literature saw enormous profits to be made from certain titillating subjects. And sapphism was unquestionably one of them, if one judges from the titles of books listed in publishers' catalogs. Homosexuality was there alongside fetishism, bestiality, and necrophilia; "the lesbian thrill" was associated with "the most extreme sadistic practices" in the extensive "Satanic Bible" produced by fiction writers and scientific experts at the turn of the century.[20] The time was well past for the type of discretion exercised by a medical expert like Ambroise Tardieu, for instance. The 1862 edition of his *Etude médico-légale sur les attentats aux moeurs* (1857) included a section on "Assaults by Women on Women" for the first time. It covered the few new cases observed by the author, but, wary of the attention given to such "moral depravity and physical monstrousness" Tardieu recommended legal and medical intervention only in cases of violence. In all others, he advised, it was better not to "probe too deeply into these shameful matters."[21]

While medical studies of the time were turning their attention more and more to sexual perversion and especially to sapphism, a flood of fictional works on the same topic were published also.[22] They were of uneven literary quality and destined for a popular readership. This literary phenomenon reinforced a certain image of lesbians which drew on a variety of stereotypes and was informed in part by the descriptive categories developed by sexologists.[23]

Then again, as the number of contemporary figures who were lesbians (including members of Paris society such as the Marquise de Morny, Colette, and Natalie Barney) seemed to increase and sapphism became an important social and sexual phenomenon, it became more popular as a theme of male fantasy and as a symbol of *fin-de-siècle* decadence and sexual depravity. As a result, lesbians and lesbianism became the focus of studies such as Charles Virmaître's reportage, *Mlles Saturne* (1898), or of novels like Catulle Mendès' masterpiece *Méphistophéla* (1890), the story of a lesbian who was the spawn of Satan himself. The topic also appeared in many short stories, columns, and illustrations in periodicals in the 1890s and after.

Sexual topics once considered taboo seemed to be so ever-present in contemporary writing that in 1911, Curnonsky observed in a tone of feigned shock and disdain that "nowadays there is no vice that hasn't already been the subject of a monograph. Bookshops' shelves are filled with novels with suggestive covers, novels on sadism, masochism, fetishism, uranism, and other varieties of human behavior."[24] Nevertheless, it should not be assumed that the significant role sapphism played in popular literature escaped the attention of the authorities who assessed the moral content of works sold in humble bookstalls as well as those arrayed in the bookshops. In fact, the legal void that enclosed sapphism was accompanied by a legal arsenal that made it easy to impose a code of silence on the topic. By using the penalties intended for "offenses to decency" the authorities were able to single out and punish offending texts.

TRIALS AND TRANSGRESSIVE WRITING

The legal complaints at the heart of literary trials at the end of the nineteenth century were based on new laws which punished "offenses to decency" more severely than in the past. For instance, the authors Gustave Flaubert and Charles Baudelaire were both summoned into court in 1857 to answer charges of offenses against Christian morality under the law of May 17, 1819. But then that law was superseded by the law of July 29, 1881, known as the "law of press freedom"; its article 28 enabled the state to prosecute "offenses to decency" and punish the guilty with penalties that could go as high as two years in prison and a 2,000 franc fine, compared to the former penalty of one year in prison and a 500 franc fine.[25] The Third Republic's lawmakers thus established a distinction between "offenses to decency" made in the iconographic mode (sketches, engravings, paintings, etc.) which were in the purview of the Correctional Court and those in other modes of reproduction. The latter was addressed by the Assizes Court, which took longer to decide cases because of its more complicated procedures. In addition, an 1882 law specified that "offenses to decency" committed by periodical publications, whether illustrated or not, were to be judged by the Correctional Court while obscene books remained in the purview of the Assizes. As a result, the Correctional Court prosecuted certain publications and meted out its punishment more swiftly – by banning them – even to the extent of demanding that printing be suspended or distribution be stopped if the offending material were in a serial novel or serial publication. This potential threat of legal action undoubtedly resulted in self-censorship by the least courageous contributors to journals, who adapted to the current climate rather than risk tangling with the criminal justice system. Some writers even incorporated disclaimers into their work, as in an article published about the well-known *demi-mondaine* Liane de Pougy in the journal *Le Fin de Siècle* in 1892. The writer, who used the pen name "Bonne Amie," pointed a finger of blame at the authorities who prevented a frank discussion of Pougy's sapphic liaisons. (Pougy would later be known as the lover of Natalie Barney, whom she met in 1899.[26]) The journalist explained that this repression was exercised by "Dame Blanche" (meaning the Correctional Court's ninth chamber). "The white lady . . . claims to be rooting out Vice by mercilessly condemning indiscreet journals that have parted the bed curtains which conceal feminine love nests, love affairs that exclude men. It's ostrich-like behavior, putting your head in the sand so as not to see the danger rather than confronting it head-on in order to ward it off or fight it."[27]

Literary trials did not deal with transgressive sexual behavior, as was the case with Fersen's "Satanic masses" for instance, but with transgressive representation.[28] In fact, writers and publishers were brought to trial for having represented, written about, or printed works in which a certain kind of sexuality and/or sexual practices, such as sapphism, were shown and described in an overly detailed manner. Therefore, the offense was to have violated the moral strictures more or less implicitly set down in the law, and especially to have spoken overtly about something that legally did not exist.

It is difficult to analyze particular trials in detail for several reasons. In general, trials were conducted quickly, especially in the Correctional Court to which infractions like vagabondage, fraud, thievery, insults to police, etc., were assigned. In addition, the judges' language was always somewhat formulaic and vague since they were guided by the principle that the proper way to dispose of an offense against decency and morals in the law courts was to avoid the same wordy style as the literary disquisitions that were on trial. Besides, transcripts of these trials have not generally been kept. What remains is a statement of the charges and the details of the fines the authors and/or publishers paid.[29] Moreover, these trials usually did not make headlines or create extensive publicity, except that generated by the authors and publishers themselves. Therefore, what is in fact interesting in these cases is the problematic relationship between law and literature, between social reality and the representation of sapphism as well as the dead-end situation of the law confronted with something it is supposed to condemn when represented but to ignore as a reality. Both served the same purpose: to keep sapphism silent and unnamed. Also, with the exception of a few notable works published between 1833 and 1835, such as the ones by Alfred de Musset (*Gamiani*, 1833),[30] Honoré de Balzac (*La Fille aux Yeux d'Or*, 1835), and Théophile Gautier (*Mademoiselle de Maupin*, 1835–6), sapphism was absent from literature until the publication of Charles Baudelaire's *Les Fleurs du Mal* in 1857, a collection that was originally and provocatively titled "Les Lesbiennes."

In his review of the play *Sapho* by Philoxène Boyer in 1850, Théodore de Banville rightly observed that sapphism was "an awful and awe-inspiring subject that even the bravest among us hardly dares to broach."[31] A few years later, precisely because they did confront it, some famous writers were prosecuted and publicly condemned. Indeed, the literary trials launched against Charles Baudelaire and his Belgian publisher Poulet-Malassis in 1857 for six selections in *Les Fleurs du Mal*, among them "Lesbos" and "Femmes Damnées," made France notorious.[32] In England, Algernon Charles Swinburne would face the same kind of threat after he published his *Poems and Ballads* (1st series, 1866), which included "Anactoria" and "Sapphics," two poems dealing openly with Sappho and lesbianism. After the collection was published, Swinburne was attacked by moralistic critics who asked him to explain this "deification of incontinence," "unclean for the mere sake of uncleanness".[33] Swinburne replied directly to these accusations of blasphemy and obscenity in *Notes on Poems and Reviews* in words reminiscent of Baudelaire's lawyer at his trial: "What is there now of horrible in this? The expression of fierce fondness, the ardours of passionate despair? Are these so unnatural as to affright or disgust? Where is there an unclean detail? Where an obscene allusion? A writer as impure as my critics might of course have written, on this or on any subject, an impure poem; I have not."[34] For his part, Baudelaire was accused of having written poems which "necessarily lead to the excitement of the senses through a gross realism which offends decency."[35] The poet Paul Verlaine was next, charged in 1868 for having published the six erotic sapphic poems "Les Amies," which would later be included in *Parallèlement* (1889).[36]

Similar pursuits on moral grounds would begin again at the end of the century. Although involving lesser known authors, the charges and trials were no less virulent. There is a specificity in French literature and juridical attitudes as opposed to England, for example, where no explicit depiction of sapphism, except in some medical treatises, is to be found before the publication of Radclyffe Hall's *The Well of Loneliness*, a novel that would be charged under the "Obscene Publications Act" in 1928.[37] Thus, if sapphism is not mentioned in the British penal code, it was hardly ever mentioned in literature either. There was then a more homogenous attitude toward its supposed invisibility, or non-existence, as opposed to France, where *fin-de-siècle* literature and iconography turned it into one of the most widespread topics of the time. There were many literary trials in France at the turn of the century and there were also many sapphic novels. Victorien du Saussay, a popular writer now completely forgotten, and Baron René Jean Toussaint, a prolific novelist who published titillating novels under the pseudonym René Maizeroy, faced charges for writing about lesbianism and vividly depicting lesbian sex and what could be termed sapphic debauchery. Their trials implicitly raised the issue of invisibility versus representation, since to grant sapphism visibility, even by depicting it negatively, was considered dangerous by the legal authorities. It was as if sapphism, being "hors nature" or "unnatural," had to be excluded from representation as well.[38]

The first trial took place in 1885 after the publication of René Maizeroy's *Deux Amies* (Two Girl Friends), a decadent best-seller about sapphic love, and the second in 1894 when Victorien du Saussay's novel *Jouir... Mourir* was published in installments in *Le Fin de Siècle*. The book's title, "To Climax... To Die", was scandalous in itself because of its sexually explicit meaning; however, du Saussay was cited for the seventeenth chapter only, which dealt with sapphism and was called "In Excelsis." It was obviously the climax of the narrative. One might wonder why these two specific works were targeted when so many other novels of the period dealt as explicitly with sapphism. Were these two meant to be examples not to be followed? Did they have more subversive aspects? Or were they simply poorly written? Indeed, the aesthetic qualities of a literary work were always important in France, where style could be a rationale that could help an accused author be acquitted.[39]

The reasons why some novels caught the eye of the authorities and others did not are problematic and probably due to unlucky accidents in some instances and to the wrong kind of publicity in others. Otherwise, how can one explain the widely divergent treatment of two other contemporary novels: *Méphistophéla* and *Zé'Boïm*? Catulle Mendès' *Méphistophéla* (1890) failed to provoke the wrath of the authorities while the prosecutor was alerted to the reprehensible content of another novel whose very title, *Zé'Boïm*, would be incomprehensible to anyone not schooled in Semitic languages. *Zé'Boïm* is a slightly erotic novel with a sapphic theme; signed by "Maurice de Souillac," apparently the pen name of a woman, Madame Lefèbvre, its title means "Gomorrah" in Hebrew. It was first published by Piaget in 1877 with a rather unobstrusive cover which didn't attract the attention of the authorities charged with upholding the moral order. However, when Félix Brossier took over Piaget's stock the following year, he decided to try to sell the book off quickly and changed its cover. The task of designing a new illustration went to Jules Roy, who "had made a name for himself in outrageous cover design," most notably with his work for *Gomorrhe* (1888) by Henri d'Argis.[40] *Zé'Boïm*'s new cover featured a semi-nude woman dressed only in black stockings. She was lying down, her legs parted, a finger of her left hand airily pointing upwards. Her right hand seemed to be aimed at her pubic area, but it was partially obscured by an explosive flash of light emanating from her crotch. When the book with its new cover was displayed in bookshop windows in 1889, the suggestive artwork caught the eyes of passers-by and did not go unnoticed by the authorities, who considered it an affront to public decency. In an 1890 article devoted to the prejudice that licentious dust jackets, added by editors with few scruples, could bring to novels like *Zé'Boïm*, Camille de Sainte-Croix attacked the remarks of a prosecutor from the ninth chamber who had declared that "a book, however immoral, was not a public offense against decency if it was published discreetly and sold to connoisseurs."[41] In the spring the entire stock of the book was seized and the Assizes Court held a closed door trial. The author of *Zé'Boïm* received a one-month prison term and a 100 franc fine and the publisher was sentenced to two weeks in prison and a 1,000 franc fine.[42] But this would not be the last time the book ran foul of the authorities. Léon Genonceaux acquired Boissier's publishing firm and once again *Zé'Boïm* appeared in the bookshops. It went on sale in November 1891 with yet another cover that hardly differed from the previous one, except that the pubic light-burst had been replaced with the image of a cat's head.[43] This time the Correctional Court charged the publisher with offenses under the August 2, 1882 law, that is, an offense to public decency because of the book's cover. Genonceaux fled but was nonetheless condemned in absentia to thirteen months in prison and a 3,000 franc fine.[44] Still, if the authorities found that *Zé'Boïm*'s contents were less offensive than its cover, this was not the case for other novels published in the era, such as those by René Maizeroy and Victorien du Saussay.

MAIZEROY'S *DEUX AMIES* (1885)

In his book about literary trials, Alexandre Zévaès reminds us that Maizeroy's novels "always have a perceptible flavor of sensual languor and lasciviousness. The author's craft is particularly evident in his descriptions of love scenes and luxurious sensuous settings."[45] Zévaès adds that most of Maizeroy's heroines are young and pretty, which is partly true for some of the lesbian characters in *Deux Amies*. What was the subject of this scandalous novel whose author was condemned to a fine of 1,000 francs, while his editor Victor Havard was acquitted? It is the story of two young girls meeting in a convent. Their romantic friendship turns rapidly into physical passion which is consummated once they leave. Eva Moïnoff, the more sensual and depraved of the two, pursues numerous liaisons with women, all the while remaining physically attracted to her lover Jeanne. The two organize orgies in a flat that they have rented which becomes a veritable "brothel." While Eva seduces one and all, Jeanne, tormented by an ill-defined malaise, only survives because of her youth. Despite the advice of a doctor who urges her parents to marry her off as soon as possible, Jeanne resists their efforts and is secretly aided in this by her lover. Nevertheless, she eventually marries but continues her liaison with Eva under the nose of her complaisant husband. Having tired of sharing Jeanne's domestic discontent and her unhappiness with her husband, Eva begins to withdraw. With Jeanne's help she seduces one of Jeanne's cousins, a virtuous and naive young wife. Eva falls madly in love with her and manages to lure her away from her duties as wife and mother with tempting and fiery caresses, at least temporarily. Having lost Eva's love, Jeanne immerses herself in debauchery and becomes the mistress/protector of a music hall performer. They begin a life of "sleepless nights ... evil pleasures, mad dashes across the city in search of as-yet untasted thrills" which leads them to shady boutiques and houses of ill-repute.[46] Destroyed by her obsession, tasting any and all forbidden fruits, Jeanne ends up confined to an asylum while Eva abandons her perverse ways and gets married.

Deux Amies is a superficial, loosely-plotted, and poorly-written novel punctuated with erotic episodes. Its provocative qualities come from the use of three well-worn stereotypes: the sapphic liaison between two convent-school friends, lust for a married woman, and debauchery in Paris nightlife which results in paralysis, disease, and madness. How could bourgeois morality be damaged by the sexual excesses depicted in Maizeroy's novel, when in fact its clichéd contents are paralleled by the deficiencies of its artistic form?[47] During the trial at the Assizes Court the judges targeted certain pages they found particularly scandalous, especially the love scenes between Eva and the married cousin and between Jeanne and the music hall performer.[48] On April 27, 1885, Maizeroy was found guilty of an "offense to decency for distributing or displaying in public the book titled *Deux Amies*" and all the copies in print were seized and destroyed.[49]

DU SAUSSAY'S *JOUIR ... MOURIR* (1894)

Though shorter, Saussay's work was definitely more scandalous. His novel, published in installments from February 18 to May 13, 1894 in *Le Fin de Siècle* and illustrated by Maurice Neumont, had one chapter which vividly depicted a love scene between an aristocratic woman and a young gypsy dancer. A few days after it appeared, the writer was charged and sentenced, along with the journal's editor, Paul Perrin, to one month in jail and a fine of 3,000 francs. Soon after, the writer contributed an interesting article about his condemnation to the same journal:

> On Wednesday [May 25] the Ninth Correctional Court sentenced me along with Monsieur Paul Perrin to a one-month prison term and a three-thousand franc fine for offenses to public decency... Before the trial, I had believed with the naiveté of a man who had no experience of courtrooms...that it would be easy to prove that *Jouir... Mourir* was not immoral and especially that the chapter which was cited was of the absolutely highest morality. They had taken ten lines out of context from Chapter 17 ["In Excelsis"] and they saw a description there and most decidedly were unwilling to understand that if I had really wanted to describe lesbianism, I would have availed myself of precise and telling details – the kind that I had not wanted to use ... We praise love to the skies and condemn all the vices ... We will show the dangers that we need to avoid and the risks of passion ... No, esteemed judges, we are not pornographers. We despise filth and love only that which is beautiful.[50]

It is true that du Saussay, to guard against possible prosecution, had been careful to precede the passage which ended up being cited by the court with an imprecation against "the Almighty Vice ... that shame of humanity...wellspring of death and madness...evil passion that despoils the purity of the creature God had created with such care – Woman." In the book she was transformed by lesbian passion into a "bloodthirsty and gangrene-ridden female, locked in passion on the dungheap of ignominy and filth."[51] The imagery of this passage was no doubt a bit too extreme and the judges may not have rightly appreciated the author's tone – tinged with hellfire and brimstone – especially since du Saussay used similar flights of rhetoric to describe the carnal embraces "so otherworldly, so unreal" of the two women. Indeed, the love scene that shocked the judges was particularly purple in its prose:

> First there were kisses, embraces, bites, cries. Their bodies intertwined in the shadows, their open mouths purplish-red, as red as blood. Their arms stretched as thin as steel springs, beating against their shoulders and thighs like vines. Their nostrils, wide open, seemed to breath in the air of voluptuousness. Their eyes closed beneath taut nervous lids. Their legs bent back and their fingers tensed as if ready to strangle ... Like epileptics, the monstrous heap of their two bodies convulsed furiously.[52]

In fact, did not the prosecutions give these books, generally of poor literary quality, an influence and notoriety they didn't deserve, while the authors were transformed into misunderstood victims? It is true that one can hardly consider these novels to be apologias for sapphism. Nevertheless, at what point could these writers claim that their work was of the highest morality in order to escape the long arm of the law? Maizeroy accomplished this with the utmost hypocrisy and through the crudest literary devices when he had one of his heroines die and the other see the error of her ways at the end of *Deux Amies*. Indeed, these writers tried to justify their work as moral and to identify their lascivious descriptions of sapphic embraces as condemnations. But this was a defense the authorities would generally reject, seeing their work instead as manifestly prurient and obscene. Actually this double-edged behavior can be seen as a sign of ambivalence on the writers' part, torn between the desire to paint lesbian love as repulsive and a genuine fascination with it, as had been the case with Baudelaire.

This was also Adolphe Belot's attitude when he defended his novel *Mademoiselle Giraud, Ma Femme* (1870) on moral grounds. The book was undoubtedly one of the earliest examples of the French Decadent movement and while Belot exhibited a remarkable adroitness, he initially did not see it rewarded, since the publication of the novel in *Le Figaro* shocked a number of readers who threatened to cancel their subscriptions. When this scandalous serial novel that dealt with a love affair between two married women was published in book form that same year, it proved to be a best-seller. As he remarked a little later in the forward to the edition Dentu published in 1870, "*Mademoiselle Giraud, Ma Femme* treats a rather delicate issue but I tried hard to craft the novel's formal aspects in order to avoid ... an overly brutal description or frank detail. I would rather sin by being too vague than too precise and I believe that if by chance this book comes into youngsters' hands, its meaning will remain veiled."[53] Here again an author claims to have been motivated by elevated moral concerns. Belot believed in fact that he could stop this particular evil from spreading by denouncing its supposed cause – convent education with its passionate friendships and same-sex intimacies – and by showing its ill effects, since he understood sapphism to be a genuine and dangerous threat to marriage.[54] One cannot help but note the discreetness of the novelist's expression and his artistry. He succeeded in being explicit with mere suggestions to the reader. The word "sapphism" itself never appears in the novel and he congratulated himself for this.[55] Perhaps Belot avoided prosecution in 1870 thanks to his reserved manner of expression. As we have seen, no literary condemnation of sapphism could counterbalance a too-detailed description of it.

The courts were not alone in severely criticizing the books they banned. Even other writers attributed unhealthy influences to certain types of literature. For instance, in *La Corruption à Paris* (1888) Ali Coffignon observed that sapphism "which until now was the subject of medical studies," had fallen into novelists' hands. He wondered therefore "whether one should not in fact blame literature for the huge increase in the popularity of this vice, which is spreading through the different ranks of Parisian society." Later, Coffignon targeted "a type of naughty book, which piques women's curiosity and induces her to try sexual practices that otherwise she never would have imagined, if perversity had not been awakened in her mind."[56] Such accusations were undoubtedly based on two underlying beliefs. It was feared on the one hand, that these books, however negatively sapphism was depicted in them, could serve as a bad example to women who, men and judges thought, did not even know that such deviance could exist and then would be tempted to experience lesbian sex. On the other hand, if no representation of lesbianism existed, no lesbian would be able to put a name to her own sexuality. Similar accusations – of books' perverting influence – were even incorporated into the plots of contemporary novels, where the dormant sapphic inclination of a character would be awakened by her reading about lesbian lovers in a novel, the book in question usually offered as a gift by a deviant and vice-ridden friend.[57]

Moreover, in their own books writers took on the role of judges *vis-à-vis* the fictional lesbians who were the accused. Then, the law may have been asserting its own prerogatives when it condemned the false judges, that is, the writers who assumed the task the legal authorities shirked: to give sapphism public recognition and approbation. There was thus a power struggle between the authorities and literature. Nevertheless, these *fin-de-siècle* trials raise the following questions: does the depiction of perversion and debauchery necessarily lead to perversion and debauchery? Can representation have a moral or immoral function, a moralistic use to either tantalize or repel? Or can it only be subversive? Is representation and the artistic gesture transgressive *per se*? Indeed, these texts written by men were in many respects far less subversive than the seditious writings of lesbians like the poet Renée Vivien, who did not have the extensive popular readership many Decadent writers had.[58] As a matter of fact, men were not only totally absent from Vivien's lesbian universe and consequently never addressed or solicited as lovers or readers in her poetry; she also successfully introduced the notion of "gender trouble" whereas most Decadent writers used sapphism, however interestingly, only as an aesthetic motif or as a new spice to add to sexual intrigues.[59]

These trials attest to the extent and the nature of the intertwined relationship between the reality of sapphism and its representation. They therefore are useful in framing the question of representation differently since they provide information about a certain social reality, i.e. lesbianism, and the way it was perceived at the turn of the century. They also highlight the discrepancy that existed between sapphism as a sexual, or more precisely a social reality, and sapphism as a literary fantasy and motif.[60] They illustrate how it seemed more real and dangerous, that is, open to legal pursuit, in books than in real life. These trials also reveal the power books could have as they enunciated something unspeakable – lesbian passion and sex. They thus shed new light on the overwhelming importance given to literature and at the same time show to what extent sapphism was marginalized as a sexual taboo as well as a literary one.

In fact, the attitude of the law was very ambiguous. The state, because of its weakness and hypocrisy, was unable to regulate sexuality as long as it remained private, so it would regulate its literary representation in the guise of moral repression. Then literature would be the only space where oppression and coercion against sapphism could operate. But in the case of sapphism, literature did what trials were supposed to do: it made private matters public, exposed what went on in lesbian bedchambers where men were by definition excluded, and gave sapphism visibility. In fact, these literary trials were paradoxically initiated not to punish sapphism but to make it publicly invisible. Thus the law hoped to silence representation the way it had silenced reality.

These censored novels were neither isolated nor unique cases. Rather, they belong to a long line of books censored at the turn of the century because of their depiction of forbidden sexuality. More precisely, it was the depiction of a type of female sexuality that was considered monstrous that earned these writers their day in court. In writing these novels, authors expressed contemporary anxiety about a change in female sexuality – a fear that Eve had turned into Lilith. They also imagined and gave fictional life to a sort of global homosexual conspiracy that did not correspond to the actual social marginalization and isolation of most lesbians of the time.[61]

In addition, these novelists depicted sapphism as a sexuality characterized by debauchery and by extremes, as a risky practice for a woman's spiritual and physical well-being. Thus, these authors contributed to the vast systematic repression of homosexuality. Their writing was not very transgressive, since it reinforced the cliché equating sapphism with perversion, death and decay. Therefore, however guilty they may have been before the law, such writers silenced sapphism in their own way by distorting it. By giving literary depictions of sapphism attributes that were too perverse to actually encourage lesbians to claim it as their sexual identity, these writers aided the state's forces of repression. The law nonetheless punished such writers for their desire to play the role of defenders of creative freedom rather than grimly silent guardians of the moral order. But if Maizeroy and du Saussay challenged morality by not playing by its rules, some lesbian writers would soon go much further by challenging sexual representations and boundaries themselves.

NOTES

This essay was translated into English by Nancy Erber.

1. This is an excerpt from the opening statement made by Maître Picard, the Imperial Prosecutor, in the 1857 obscenity trial of Baudelaire's *Fleurs du Mal*. The attorneys' opening statements and summations were published in 1885 in the *Revue des Grands Procès Contemporains*.
2. The terms "sapphism" and "lesbianism" are used interchangeably throughout this essay in referring to female same-sex sexual relations. Sapphist was the term most commonly used in nineteenth-century French discourse to designate the female homosexual, though lesbian was gaining in currency by the 1890s. The older term "tribade" continued to be employed as well.
3. The migration of lesbian intellectuals to Paris continued into the 1930s. See Shari Benstock, *Women of the Left Bank: Paris 1900–1940* (Austin: University of Texas Press, 1986).
4. Jean Lorrain, "Paris Vicieux-la Marquise Hérode," *Le Courrier Français*, 2 Oct. 1887. Despite this story of an infanticide of a male child that went unpunished, it is interesting to see how turn-of-the-century writers in general appointed themselves judge and jury to condemn guilty sapphists.
5. For further discussion of French judicial treatment of male homosexuals, see the essays in this volume by William Peniston and Nancy Erber.
6. See Jean Lorrain, "Adultère!," *Modernités* (Paris: Nouvelle Librairie Parisienne E. Giraud, 1885), 83.
7. Marise Querlin, *Femmes sans Hommes* (Paris: Edition de France, 1931), 192–3.
8. The Queen Victoria anecdote may well be apocryphal. We know that a new attempt to make female homosexuality illegal failed in 1921, the MPs fearing that publicizing lesbianism would "introduce into the minds

of perfectly innocent people the most revolting thoughts." Parliamentary debates quoted by Sheila Jeffreys, *The Spinster and Her Enemies: Feminism and Sexuality, 1880–1930* (London: Pandora, 1985), 114.

9. It was prohibited to wear the clothes of the opposite sex unless one had a special certificate from the Police Prefecture. This document is reproduced in Marie-Jo Bonnet, *Un Choix Sans Equivoque* (Paris: Denoël, 1981), 195–6. The phenomenon of more and more women in the 1890s adopting trousers for cycling or strolling led "the Minister of the Interior to issue a circular (27 Oct. 1892) advising all prefectures that 'the wearing of masculine clothes by women was only tolerated for the purposes of velocipedic sport.'" See Eugen Weber, *France, Fin de Siècle* (Cambridge: Harvard University Press, 1986), 37.
10. Charles Virmaître, *Mlles Saturne* (Paris: A. Charles, 1898), 241–4.
11. The women who frequented these sorts of places were mocked in an article titled "L'autre Hérésie Sentimentale," in *Fantasio*, 1 June 1909.
12. Jules Davray, *L'Armée du Vice*, ch. 1: "Lesbos et Ses Prêtresses" (Paris: Ferreyrol, 1890), 127. Léo Taxil also protested against the law which caused "us to wallow in the filth of Roman corruption," and accompanied this critique with an astounding portrait of lesbian vice: "Ten years ago, if women clients were admitted to brothels, the police would close them down. Since 1891 they've been welcomed inside, and not even secretly. You can see private cars parked all around the houses, having dropped off theatre performers and sometimes even society ladies. There's a boulevard in the Bois de Boulogne called the Allée des Poteaux where women pick up women publicly." *La Corruption Fin-de-Siècle* (Paris: Noirot, 1891), 254.
13. This argument was shared not only by sexologists such as Havelock Ellis but also by writers who would illustrate it in their novels. See for example, Paul Adam's *Chair Molle* (1885) or Jean Lorrain's *La Maison Philibert* (1904).
14. Doctor Gallus, *Uranistes et Sapphistes* (1908), reissued (Paris: Simples Murmures, 1993), 47. Indeed, a lot of cartoons and caricatures seemed to evidence the attitude that lesbians tend to be more and more visible thanks to a certain masculine attire usually equated with sexual deviance.
15. Some documents related to that scandal are collected in *Album Masques: Colette* (Paris: Masques, 1984), 87–91. In December 1906, for instance, an article titled "La Marquise" was printed in *Fantasio* in which the Marquise de Morny was said to "despise the law of the sexes." It was mysteriously signed "Le Vitrioleur" and was illustrated with photographs showing Colette and the Marquise together and with a caricature by Sem with the caption: "An upcoming sensational debut in the *café-concert*, the Marquise 'à la Mayolaise.'" (Mayol was a famous comic male singer.) See *Fantasio*, 15 Dec. 1906. The Marquise successfully sued the newspaper for libel, but didn't get the 15,000 francs she demanded as compensation. She received only 25 francs as a derisory judgment.
16. See G. Garrigues, "Moulin Rouge," *La Vie Théâtrale* 4 (25 Jan. 1907), 26. To spare her family name from any association with the performance, the Marquise de Morny, whose nickname was Missy, used an anagram "Yssim" in the music hall's announcements.

17. See Claude Pichois, Preface, *Oeuvres de Colette*, vol. 1 (Paris: Gallimard Bib. de la Pléaide, 1984), p. xcii. Colette would play it a few weeks later under its new title, with Georges Wague, in the south of France.
18. An excerpt from the court ruling is reproduced in Patrick Waldberg, *Eros Modern Style* (Paris: Pauvert, 1964), 122, 124.
19. Querlin, *Femmes sans Hommes*, 194. Querlin's 1931 account was expanded and re-edited in 1953 in the Editions du Scorpion. Nonetheless, the remarks might seem surprising in a book about lesbians.
20. These descriptions are excerpted from an advertisement by the P. Fort Publishers, featuring their book *Scenes d'Amour Morbide* by Doctor Caufeynon (Paris, no date), directed at readers of "novels of manners and love" in Alphonse Gallais, *Mémoires d'une Fille de Joie* (1902), 7.
21. Ambroise Tardieu, *Etude Médico-légale sur les Attentats aux Moeurs*, 4th ed. (Paris: Baillière, 1862), 57.
22. The phenomenon of medical studies of "abnormal" sexuality was common in the US and Europe. Among the many works published, two have remained well-known: Krafft-Ebing's *Psychopathia Sexualis* (1886) and Havelock Ellis's *Studies in the Psychology of Sex* (1897). The Ellis book was translated into French in 1908 and regularly reissued until 1935. Other works can be cited for their contributions to sapphic fantasmagoria, such as Doctor Emile Laurent, *L'Amour Morbide* (1891), Albert Moll, *Die Conträre Sexualempfindung* (1891), Julien Chevalier, *L'Inversion Sexuelle* (1893), Cesare Lombroso and Guglielmo Ferrero, *The Criminal Woman* (1893), W.L. Howard, *Effeminate Men and Masculine Women* (1900), W.M. Tarnovski, *L'Instinct Sexuel et ses Manifestations Morbides* (1904), Wilhelm Hammer, *Die Tribade Berlins* (1906), and Edward Carpenter, *The Intermediate Sex* (1908). If we limited ourselves to one decade, 1898 to 1908, we would find that the topic of sexual inversion inspired approximately 1,000 scientific and popular studies, notes Claudine Brécourt-Villars in the preface to *Ecrire d'Amour: Anthologie de Textes Erotiques Féminins 1799–1984* (Paris: Ramsay, 1985), 27.
23. The most popular of the time were Adolphe Belot, *Mademoiselle Giraud, Ma Femme* (1870), René Maizeroy, *Deux Amies* (1885), Rachilde [Marguerite Eymery], *Madame Adonis* (1888), Catulle Mendès, *Méphistophéla* (1890), Jane de la Vaudère, *Les Demi-sexes* (1897), Francis Lepage, *Les Fausses Vierges* (1902), Charles Montfort, *Le Journal d'une Saphiste* (1902), Adrienne Saint-Agen, *Amants Féminins* (1902), and Guy de Téramond, *Impériales Voluptés* (1905).
24. Curnonsky [Edmond Sailland], "Mauvaises Lectures," *Le Courrier Français*, 25 March 1911. Curnonsky was himself the author of many scandalous novels published in the era, so the remarks must be read accordingly.
25. As Alexandre Zévaès observes, lawmakers "contravened their previous practices of scaling down the penalties stipulated in earlier laws and increased the maximum penalty for this offense." *Les Procès Littéraires au XIXe siècle* (Paris: Perrin, 1924), 225.
26. In 1901, Pougy would publish *Idylle saphique*, an autobiographical novel about her love affair with the "amazon" Barney.
27. Bonne-Amie, "Instantanées," *Le Fin de Siècle*, 6 Feb. 1892.

28. For the Fersen case, see Nancy Erber's essay in this volume.
29. *La Gazette des Tribunaux* printed court decisions.
30. The attribution of this anonymously published work is disputed by literary historians.
31. Théodore de Banville, "La Semaine Dramatique," *Le Pouvoir*, 18 Nov. 1850, reprinted in *Critiques* (Paris: Charpentier et Fasquelle, 1917), 23.
32. See the chapter titled "Les Fleurs Vénéneuses" in Zévaès, *Les Procès Littéraires*, 101–51, for a discussion of the trial.
33. *The London Review*, 4 Aug. 1866, and *The Athenaeum*, 4 Aug. 1866. When his publisher, J.B. Payne, heard that an article calling for Swinburne's prosecution for obscenity would appear in the *Times*, he withdrew the book from circulation and peremptorily notified Swinburne. See Richard Dellamora, *Masculine Desire: The Sexual Politics of Victorian Aestheticism* (Chapel Hill: University of North Carolina Press, 1990), 70.
34. A.C. Swinburne, *Notes on Poems and Reviews* (London: Hotten, 1866), 11.
35. An excerpt from the court ruling, 27 Aug. 1857.
36. On 6 May 1868, the Court of Lille ordered the destruction of *Les Amies* and condemned the Belgian publisher Poulet-Malassis to a 500 franc fine, the same penalty he had previously been assessed for publishing *Les Fleurs du Mal*.
37. Havelock Ellis had trouble discussing lesbianism even in a scientific study; the second volume of his *Studies in the Psychology of Sex* (1897) was censored before publication. Apart from Swinburne's poems, there are very few English literary works from the Victorian era that deal with lesbianism. Henry James linked sublimated lesbianism with feminism in *The Bostonians* (1886). Before that, the Irish writer Sheridan LeFanu produced, consciously or not, *the* sapphic novel of the nineteenth century, *Carmilla* (1872), where homosexuality was associated with vampirism.
38. *Les Hors-Nature* (The Unnatural Ones) was the title of an 1897 sensational novel by the writer Rachilde which featured fraternal incest.
39. Because Gustave Flaubert's writing style made *Madame Bovary* (1856) an undeniable work of art, the novel was not prosecuted even though it had caused a tremendous controversy due to its provocative themes.
40. See Jean-Jacques Lefrère and Jean-Paul Goujon, *Deux Malchanceux de la Littérature Fin-de-Siècle: Jean Larocque et Léon Genonceaux* (Paris: Editions du Lérot, 1994), 28.
41. Camille de Sainte-Croix, *Moeurs littéraires, Les Lundis de la Bataille* (Paris: Savine, 1891), 97–8, see also 266–70.
42. *Gazette des Tribunaux*, 29 March 1890.
43. In French *la chatte* (cat) is a slang term for the female genitalia, like "pussy" in English.
44. Archives of the Seine, D10 U3, no. 63, ruling recorded 12 January 1892. In both cases, the illustrator was not found guilty.
45. Zévaès, *Les Procès Littéraires*, 238.
46. René Maizeroy, *Deux Amies* (Paris: Havard, 1885), 41, 254–5.
47. Maizeroy was clearly more accomplished in his treatment of sapphism in shorter works, especially in "Les Cinq Amies" which was published in *Le Fin de Siècle* on 15 August 1891. The story ended with an infanticide, when the lesbians murder a child born to one of them.

48. It should not be assumed that the passages were read aloud in court. Instead, the page numbers alone were mentioned. In addition, the word "sapphism" never appears in the trial records.
49. See Archives of the Assizes Court – Seine, 27 April 1885, docket no. 2563.
50. Du Saussay, "Notre Condamnation," *Le Fin de Siècle*, 31 May 1894. This article echoes the one he wrote at the beginning of the serial publication of his novel: "Above all, I wished to create a pure work of art . . . If I have dared to transport the reader to the realm of frenzied passion, if I have depicted brutality and vices, it was so that the reader will be forewarned." *Le Fin de Siècle*, 1 March 1894.
51. *Jouir . . . Mourir*, in *Le Fin de Siècle*, 15 April 1894.
52. Ibid.
53. Adolphe Belot, *Mademoiselle Giraud, Ma Femme* (Paris: Dentu, 1870), preface, no page number.
54. Emile Zola defended Belot and recommended that mothers read Belot's novel "before sending their dear daughters to convent school." See the preface to the 1879 edition of *Mademoiselle Giraud, Ma Femme*, p. v. The question of boarding school/convent school friendships came to the forefront near the end of the nineteenth century, so much so that an entire book was devoted to the subject: Giulio Obici and Giovanni Marchesini, *Le Amicizie di collegio-Ricerche sulle prime manifestazioni dell'amore sessuale* (Rome, 1898).
55. See Belot, *Mademoiselle Giraud*, 169–70.
56. Ali Coffignon, *La Corruption à Paris* (Paris: Librairie illustrée, 1888), 11–12, 302. It should be noted that Coffignon seems to be guilty of the sins he accuses others of committing since his book is full of titillating details about these forbidden topics.
57. For instance, in the novel *Mademoiselle Tantale* Belot's *Mademoiselle Giraud, Ma Femme* is part of Madame Hartinges' book collection. She lends it to Miss Folkestone, whom she wishes to seduce, saying "I am Mademoiselle Giraud." Jean-Louis Dubut de Laforest, *Mademoiselle Tantale* (Paris: Dentu, 1884), 139, 142. In Rachilde's *Madame Adonis* (1888) Gautier's *Mademoiselle de Maupin* awakens the young woman Louise's unhealthy curiosity, and she soon falls prey to a female seducer.
58. For example, Vivien's poem "Litanie de la haine" in *La Vénus des Aveugles* (1904) violently attacked both motherhood and male oppression.
59. For a thorough and challenging study of "Feminism and the Subversion of Identity," see Judith Butler, *Gender Trouble* (New York: Routledge, 1990).
60. Catulle Mendès even went so far as declaring, via one of his female characters, that sapphic loves "are the bedazzled and frantic inventions of a few excessive poets, who by dint of loving feminine beauty, imagine it doubled." Catulle Mendès, *Lila et Colette* (Paris: Monnier, 1885), 57.
61. On that subject, see Francesca Canadé Sautman, "Invisible Women: Lesbian Working-Class Culture in France, 1880–1930," in Jeffrey Merrick and Bryant T. Ragan, eds., *Homosexuality in Modern France* (New York: Oxford University Press, 1996), 177–201.

8 "Don't Frighten the Horses": the Russell Divorce Case

Ann Sumner Holmes

The British aristocracy never embraced the Victorian ideals of domesticity and sexual morality with the same enthusiasm as the middle classes, whose "respectability" is a dominant theme in the social history of nineteenth-century England. The upper classes' permissive attitude toward propriety was cleverly expressed by the Edwardian actress Mrs. Patrick Campbell's famous comment: "It doesn't matter what you do in the bedroom as long as you don't do it in the street and frighten the horses."[1] According to this code, marital fidelity was not as important as the appearance of a stable marriage and happy home; scandal was more shameful than adultery. It was a rule painfully learned by the second Earl Russell and his wife. Throughout the decade of the 1890s, as their marriage publicly disintegrated, both Lord and Lady Russell encountered great hostility for their contravention of the social code. In a society that tolerated self-indulgence in private while insisting on propriety in public, the Russells became outcasts.

The marriage began on 6 February 1890, when John Francis Stanley, the second Earl Russell, married Mabel Edith Scott in St. Peter's Church, Pimlico, in London. The groom, known as Frank, was the son of Lord and Lady Amberley, both members of prominent Whig families. They were close friends of John Stuart Mill, who was godfather to their younger son, Bertrand.[2] Lord Amberley was the son of Lord John Russell, the great nineteenth-century advocate of governmental reform. The bride was the third daughter of Sir Claude Edward Scott and Lady Maria Selina Scott. Lady Scott's husband had left her years earlier, and she had sole responsibility for her daughters. The Scotts' position in respectable society was uncertain, while the Russells were politically prominent aristocrats.

After a honeymoon in Torquay, the young Russells settled in a large furnished house at 48 Eaton Square. Difficulties between the two soon arose, however, and on May 6, three months after the wedding, the young Countess left her husband and returned to her mother. After a brief reconciliation, the couple separated a second time in June and never lived together again. Beginning with a petition for judicial separation in 1890 and ending finally in divorce a decade later, the Russells' marital difficulties were highly publicized, mainly because of the charges that Lady Russell brought against her husband. Specifically, she accused him privately and publicly, both in the courtroom and in the press, of engaging in homosexual activities. At a time of increasing anxiety regarding masculinity, gender roles and homosexuality, her imputations attracted a great deal of attention. Public condemnation of homosexuality, perhaps most obviously in the trials of Oscar Wilde, was characteristic of the 1890s.[3]

What Lady Russell learned during the course of the litigation that dissolved her marriage was that it was not only her husband, accused of the same practices as Wilde, who was subject to public censure. She, too, as one who publicly made such accusations and thus caused scandal, was condemned and ostracized. Disapproval of the Countess was especially evident in the courtroom where judges were highly critical of her conduct. They were more sympathetic to Lord Russell, who appeared as a husband unjustly accused by his wife. Neither of the Russells escaped social condemnation, however, and neither was able to achieve their common goal of divorce until 1901. Judges punished both husband and wife by denying them what they wanted most – an end to their marriage.

The Russells' marital difficulties resulted not just in suits for judicial separation and divorce but also in criminal trials for libel in 1897 and for bigamy in 1901. A review of the litigation illuminates the complexities of English divorce laws in general and contemporary attitudes towards homosexuality and social propriety.

* * *

A description of the backgrounds of Lord and Lady Russell is useful in analyzing the marital difficulties in which they became entangled. Lady Amberley had died in 1874, when her son Frank was 9 years old; Lord Amberley died 18 months later in 1876. At the age of 11, Frank Russell went to live at Pembroke Lodge with his Russell grandparents, his aunt Agatha, and his uncle Rollo. Lord John Russell was 84 at the time; he died in 1878. Thus, when he was 12 years old, Frank Russell succeeded his grandfather as Earl. Lord Amberley's mother assumed parental responsibility for her grandsons Frank and Bertrand. In his autobiography, Frank Russell wrote that his grandmother "was one of the best women who ever lived," but he lamented his loss of freedom at Pembroke Lodge. He described the atmosphere there as one "of insincerities, conventions, fears, and bated breath."[4] Bertrand Russell wrote similarly that his grandmother "was a Scotch Presbyterian, Liberal in politics and religion (she became a Unitarian at the age of 70), but extremely strict in all matters of morality."[5]

Frank Russell's early education included tutors at Pembroke Lodge and a private school at Cheam. From there he went to Winchester, where he was very happy, and then to Balliol College at Oxford. He later wrote that "quite the happiest days of my whole life were my two years at Oxford."[6] Unfortunately, an incident that would haunt him for the rest of his life brought those happy days to an end. At Balliol Russell worked under the direction of Benjamin Jowett, who was at the time both Master and Vice-Chancellor. One fateful day Jowett sent for the young scholar and, according to Russell's autobiography, the master of Balliol

> told me he had been informed that I had been guilty of disgusting conduct in writing some scandalous letter, but that he thought that it was probably only a piece of thoughtlessness, and he suggested that I should go down for a month as a punishment, and come back in June to take my examination in Honour Mods. . . .

Russell was horrified and demanded to see the letter. Jowett refused to show him the document and would not schedule an inquiry. Russell then completely lost his temper and told Jowett "that he was no gentleman" and "that he was behaving in an autocratic way, indefensible even in the head of an Oxford college." Jowett said that Russell would be sent down for a year instead of a month; the young earl retorted that he would take his name off the books and "shake the dust of Oxford" off his feet.

Thus did an impetuous, quick-tempered young aristocrat end his university career. His departure from Oxford did not end speculation about the mysterious letter, however. References to the incident appear throughout the court records of the Russells' matrimonial suits during the 1890s. In 1894, during the trial for the restitution of conjugal rights, the Countess told the court that Lord Russell's grandmother, the Dowager Lady Russell, had told her that Lord Russell had been sent down from Oxford "for disgraceful behaviour with men." She also testified that the Dowager Lady Russell had said that Rollo Russell, the young Earl's uncle, had gone to Oxford after his nephew's interview with

Jowett and "advised Lord Russell to blow his brains out as he had disgraced himself so."[7] The Russells denied both of these statements. The letter itself never appeared as evidence. In an interview immediately following the first trial in December, 1891, the Countess said that she believed that the letter had been burned.[8] According to Lord Russell, Jowett later "admitted frankly that he had never seen any letter of mine, that he was by no means sure now that there ever had been such a letter, and that he was satisfied he had made a mistake."[9] Jowett later invited Russell to stay as his guest at Balliol, and he attended the Russells' wedding in 1890, indicating that he no longer condemned the young Earl.

Lord Russell's close friend George Santayana included an illuminating passage on the "Oxford incident" in his *Persons and Places*.[10] According to Santayana, before the confrontation concerning the letter, Jowett and Russell had been involved in a heated exchange with regard to Russell's friendship with the young Lionel Johnson. The two had met at Winchester, and in his autobiography Russell wrote emotionally of their friendship and "the inner spirit of Winchester as Lionel and I felt it."[11] In Santayana's account, while Lionel Johnson was still at Winchester, he had visited Russell at Balliol. The younger man missed the last train and spent the night in Russell's rooms. Jowett heard of this breach of the rules and summoned Russell for an explanation. At the interview, according to Santayana

> Jowett began by frowning and looking suspicious, and said that Johnson was *too young* to be Russell's *natural friend*. On this, instead of replying that Johnson was much older than he looked and only a year younger than himself, Russell flew into a rage, assumed a lofty tone, declared that Johnson was his intellectual and moral superior, and defied Jowett to prove anything against him.[12]

Russell's angry defiance annoyed Jowett and probably aroused his suspicions. When the master then heard of "an improper letter," instead of investigating the matter, he once again summoned Russell. Santayana believed that the implications involving Lionel Johnson made it impossible for Russell to compromise when Jowett suggested that the young Earl go down for a month. Russell responded with fury to Jowett's proposals and abandoned the University. His anger over what he perceived to be a great injustice never left him. A fortnight before Russell's death, he wrote to Santayana that Jowett's actions had been one of the great shocks of his life. He continued, "My rage and mortification at being so wronged produced a bitterness and permanently injured my character."[13]

After he left Oxford, Russell refused to return to Pembroke Lodge. He settled first in a cottage that he called "Ferishtah." After he came of age and thus had more money, he moved into a larger house known as Broom Hall. In the summer of 1889, while he was living there, he met Mabel Edith Scott. In his autobiography, Russell stated that this young woman and her mother had "a deliberate plan of campaign" to secure him as a husband.[14] Since Sir Claude Scott had left them, finances had been troublesome. Santayana wrote of Lady Scott that "she had long been a grass widow, with an uncertain income, scouring the borderland between the *monde* and the *demi-monde*.... When she learned that a young and unmarried Earl had taken a house not very far from hers, she soon found the means of making his acquaintance."[15] Whether or not the Scotts had a "plan," Russell did indeed make their acquaintance and eventually married Mabel Edith.

On 28 November 1890, less than a year after the wedding, Lady Russell petitioned for judicial separation on the ground of cruelty.[16] In her petition she stated that her husband had used insulting language to her and had treated her with contempt before the servants. Among her grievances was the claim that Earl Russell had insisted that his wife would go "every morning to put paper in the men-servants' water-closet, and to see that it was clean." She also told the court that "on or about the 6th May, 1890, at the Albermarle Hotel, Piccadilly, the said John Francis Stanley, Earl Russell, ordered your petitioner to dress him for the levee." In addition she cited instances in which her husband had "caught hold of her by the wrists and made them black and blue, forced her down on her knees, and used offensive language to her" and had "in a violent passion seized your petitioner by the shoulder, and shook her, raising a large bruise."

In the particulars of her claims, filed on 12 January 1891, the Countess included a potentially more scandalous charge:

> That in addition at 48, Eaton Square, the respondent insisted upon a man named Roberts sleeping in the house for three or four days and nights, and after the respondent had undressed going up to Roberts' bed room, remaining with him for several hours, and again in the morning. Upon the petitioner expostulating with him upon his conduct, the respondent told the petitioner to go to the devil and mind her own business.[17]

This was the charge that carried the case forward because it made any compromise impossible. While the statement is not specific, subsequent litigation made clear that implicit in the description was the allegation that Earl Russell and Mr. Roberts were involved in a homosexual relationship. In his opening speech at the trial for judicial separation, Sir Edward Clarke, who represented the Countess, admitted that the paragraph in the particulars "carries with it a very serious suggestion against Earl Russell." The Countess, however, did not base her claims on that "suggestion." Rather, Clarke argued, although the behavior described in the particulars "may have been perfectly innocent conduct on Earl Russell's part from the point of view of the serious suggestion which I said this paragraph would naturally raise, ... it was none the less great cruelty to Lady Russell."[18] What Clarke said that his client claimed in the paragraph, then, was not that her husband had been involved in a sexual relationship with Roberts but rather that he was guilty of cruelty and neglect towards her.

During the trial, the Countess contradicted that statement. When Sir Charles Russell, representing the Earl, cross examined Lady Russell in December 1891, he asked her specifically, "Did you when you introduced his name mean to make an imputation upon Mr. Roberts and upon your husband, aye or no?" The Countess replied, "Yes." Later she testified that, when Mr. Roberts had been a guest in her home, she had not thought that there was any "impropriety" because she "had never heard of such things." It was only after she had heard "things" from the Russell family that she began to be suspicious about her husband's relationship with Roberts.[19]

There was a legal problem here. The paragraph in the particulars with regard to the presence of Mr. Roberts in the Russell home did not constitute a charge of legal cruelty. The only clear accusation was that Lord Russell had been absent from his wife's presence for several hours; the remainder of the paragraph is ambiguous. Sir Charles Butt, who was the judge at the trial in December 1891, said that the paragraph should not have been included in the petition. He said that, if the matter had been presented to him, he would have said:

> Either put that into the shape of a charge, if not of criminality, of gross and filthy indecency, or I shall strike it out of these proceedings and make you pay the costs of having put it there. I do not think matters of this sort ought to rest on insinuation. Just consider the position of third persons. It ought to be, and I regret it was not so, a distinct charge of misconduct, whether criminal or not, or this ought to have been struck out.[20]

The difficulty is evident in Clarke's opening statement, when he insists that the only charge is that of cruelty. If the Countess could not prove the charge of "impropriety," the "insinuation" in the paragraph could damage her case.

With regard to the third person involved, "the man named Roberts" was Herbert Ainsley Roberts, who was a student at Caius College, Cambridge, when Russell was at Oxford. In his autobiography, Russell mentioned his friendship with Roberts during their university days, and he also identified him in a photograph of a group of young men taken at Ferishtah. In his description of the suit filed by his wife in 1890, however, he scrupulously avoided naming Roberts and referred instead to the charge involving "a man called X."[21]

Both Roberts, who at the time was the Head Mathematical Master at Bath College, and Russell testified at the trial in December 1891. The two men described their evenings together in the Russell home. They said that the Countess and Lady Scott, when she was with them, would go to bed around 10 or 11 o'clock; the men would stay up later smoking and talking in the study. Lord Russell said that he would change from his dress coat and pumps into a shooting coat and loose slippers to smoke. They would finally go to bed around one or two o'clock in the morning. Both men denied that Lord Russell had visited Roberts in his room for several hours in the middle of the night.[22]

For two men to sit smoking and talking after the women had gone to bed seemed appropriate enough. In light of the testimony of Russell and Roberts, since the Countess never produced evidence to support the insinuation in her petition, the implication of homosexual practices in the particulars appeared to be a false and scurrilous charge. With regard to the incident at Oxford, Lord Russell was questioned about the reasons why he was sent down. There had never been a formal charge or an inquiry, however, so that, in court, the Oxford incident did not support the implication that Lord Russell had been involved in homosexual relationships. If the insinuation in the particulars could not be proved, then Russell's representatives could present the Countess as a cruel and unscrupulous woman who thoughtlessly destroyed reputations.

The story of Kate Williams reinforced that image of Lady Russell. Lord Russell wrote of the Williams family in his autobiography. Mr. and Mrs. Williams had been servants in his parents' home; Mrs. Williams had evidently acted as a nurse and a foster mother to the very young Frank Russell. Her two elder children, Kathleen and Polly, were only a year or two younger than Frank, who later wrote, "In accordance with the democratic ideas of my parents they were permitted to play and go about with us on terms of complete equality." When he moved into Broom Hall, Russell said that his old nurse and her daughters became his servants there.[23]

During the trial in 1891, Lord Russell was questioned about Kate Williams. He testified that he had seduced her four years earlier, when she was 20 or 21, and that he had remained intimate with her until about two months before he became engaged. After his marriage, Kate Williams had brought an action for breach of promise against Lord Russell, and he had paid her £500 to settle the case. Russell testified that he had told his wife about the "intimacy."[24] On the last day of the trial, he told the court that Kate Williams had been living with her family "without any public reproach upon her character" until her story had been published in connection with his wife's matrimonial suit. Thus, his attorney could argue in his closing statement that "a poor young woman's reputation was ruthlessly sacrificed for the contemptible purpose of prejudice."[25]

The images of Lady Russell that appeared in the closing arguments were strikingly different. Sir Charles Russell denounced her for bringing in a charge against her husband and Mr. Roberts, claiming that its only purpose was to frighten Lord Russell into complying with her demands rather than submitting the case to court and thus publicizing her accusations. Indeed, the implication of homosexuality had become a problem for the Countess. In his closing statement on behalf of Lady Russell, Sir Edward Clarke felt compelled to address the issue by stating "expressly and distinctly, that in his view there was no ground for any such charge as that which had been so often alluded to." Clarke was shrewd enough to realize that, if the charge could not be substantiated, it would more likely evoke sympathy for the Earl, as a man unjustly accused, than for his wife. While Sir Charles Russell told the jury that Lady Russell "had been brought up as a spoiled child, not used to being thwarted," Clarke presented her as "a woman broken in spirits, nerves, and general health."[26] He wanted the jury to see the Earl as a cruel husband who had brutally destroyed the health of a delicate young woman, not as an innocent man whose malicious wife had wrongly accused him of "gross immorality and filthy indecency."

Nonetheless, Sir Charles Butt used those very words to define the charge in summarizing the case for the jury. In his closing statement he criticized Lady Russell's counsel for bringing the names of Herbert Roberts and then of Kate Williams before the jury. He said that he believed that questioning Lord Russell with regard to the latter individual "was actuated by nothing but malice." He also deplored as "another piece of malignity" the references to the Earl's career at Oxford. With regard to Lady Russell's charges of cruelty, the judge noted that other witnesses had not substantiated those accusations. He instructed the jury to disregard the charges that lacked the necessary corroboration.[27]

At the end of the judge's summary, Lady Russell's case looked weak indeed. After less than an hour of deliberation, the jury returned with the verdict that Lord Russell had not been guilty of cruelty towards his wife. The jury's decision evoked applause in the courtroom; demonstrations of approval outside the court continued for some time. Earlier during the trial, the Earl had been jeered as he left court. After the announcement of the verdict, in the streets outside the courtroom, he encountered a crowd who gave him a "warm and friendly reception." He drove away amid their cheers.[28]

His ordeal had not ended, however, for on 8 December 1891, three days after the trial had ended, an interview with Lady Russell was published in *The Hawk*.[29] There she claimed that she had letters from members of the Russell family supporting her charges with regard to Roberts and her husband. She said that she had presumed that Sir Charles Russell would call these relatives as witnesses and that she would have produced the letters at that time. She also told Augustus Moore, the editor who interviewed her, that the family doctor would not allow her mother to testify. Thus, the jury did not hear Lady Scott's "important evidence." The verdict had surprised and disappointed the Countess. The interview appeared as an effort to repeat her charges and to explain why she had been unable to produce evidence to support her accusations. The libel laws, however, prevented Moore from being specific. The interview left the impression that the Countess was bitter and frustrated but still unable to substantiate her claims. By repeating in the press what she had been unable to prove in court, she further infuriated her husband.

After the trial in 1891, the Russells legally remained married, but they continued to live apart. The charges that the Countess had publicized, as well as the Earl's personality, made a reconciliation difficult. George Santayana wrote of his friend:

> Russell as a husband, Russell in the domestic sphere, was simply impossible: excessively virtuous and incredibly tyrannical. He didn't allow her [his wife] enough money or enough liberty. He was punctilious and unforgiving about hours, about truth-telling, about debts. He objected to her friends, her clothes, and her borrowed jewels. Moreover, in their intimate relations he was exacting and annoying. She soon hated and feared him.[30]

Bertrand Russell wrote similarly in his diary that Mabel "always has to give in to Frank in every little discussion they have."[31] His brother appears as a tyrant who demanded an absolutely submissive wife. Mabel, who, according to Augustus Moore, had been spoiled and "pretty well allowed to run wild" before her marriage, could not live with such a husband.[32]

Nor could she free herself of him. In 1891 the English divorce laws were very strict, and embodied a double standard. According to the 1857 Divorce Act, adultery was the only ground for divorce, and a husband could divorce his wife for that cause alone. A wife, however, could sue successfully for divorce only if her husband's adultery had been compounded by another offense, such as cruelty or desertion.[33]

Lady Russell might have been able to obtain evidence of her husband's adultery. Santayana described a visit to Frank Russell in his new home, "Telegraph House," in 1891. There Santayana met a young woman named Martha Turner who had been a secretary at the engineering firm where Russell was a partner. She now served as his private secretary, and her mother appeared to function as a landlady or housekeeper. According to Santayana, Russell was engaged to be married to Martha Turner if his marriage could be dissolved. Meanwhile everyone was very discreet. Martha Turner and her mother occupied a room next to Russell's. Mrs. Turner was the legal tenant of Telegraph House, and Russell "was only Martha's young man who came for an occasional visit."[34] In 1895 Lady Russell testified that her husband's coachman had told her that Lord Russell had been intimate "with a lady clerk." The coachman had offered to attempt to obtain evidence of the "guilty relations" between Lord Russell and this woman.[35]

Even if the Countess could have produced evidence of her husband's adultery, however, she would have found it difficult to establish his guilt with regard to another matrimonial offense. Lady Russell had not lived with her husband since June 1890, and she had failed to prove in court that he was guilty of cruelty while they cohabited. With the approval of their families, they had agreed to live apart from one another; thus Lord Russell was not guilty of desertion. Accordingly, the Countess had little hope of obtaining a divorce. In his diary Bertrand Russell provided insight into his sister-in-law's character while describing her situation in bleak terms: "It is most fortunate, as Aunt Agatha was saying, that her nature is not a deep one; if it were, she must be almost broken-hearted by the prospect of life-long misery which is apparently all there is before her."[36]

Lord Russell also would have found it difficult to obtain a divorce. According to Santayana, Lady Scott was very careful with regard to Lady Russell's reputation in that she "chaperoned her daughter everywhere, even to hotels where the young man of the moment occupied the adjoining room."[37] Even if the Earl could have proved his wife guilty of adultery, the issue of recrimination could have been a problem. According to the 1857 Divorce Act, a plaintiff guilty of adultery, cruelty, desertion, or unreasonable delay in bringing suit could be denied a divorce. The doctrine reflected a fundamental principle underlying the English matrimonial laws. In a divorce suit, although judges could exercise discretion under certain circumstances, a respondent had to be guilty of a matrimonial offense committed against an "innocent" petitioner.[38] If Lord Russell had petitioned for divorce, his wife's solicitors would certainly have attempted to prove him guilty of adultery. Thus, Lord and Lady Russell, whose relationship was impossible to maintain, appeared to be legally bound for life.

The trial for judicial separation had ended on 5 December 1891. In January 1892, Lady Russell wrote to her husband, "Notwithstanding the cruel way you have treated me, I have made up my mind to try and live with you again."[39] Russell replied in conciliatory terms, saying that he had forgiven his wife. He did ask, however, that she repudiate the charges that she had publicly brought against him. In subsequent correspondence Lady Russell indicated that, before she would apologize for those charges, she wanted to show her husband the letters from his family that had led her to accuse him in the first place. The couple reached an impasse. He would not consider a reconciliation until she had apologized, and she would not apologize until he had met with her to discuss the documents in her possession.

The question of an allowance was at the heart of the disagreement. On 31 March 1892, Lady Russell wrote to her husband, "I think now the position resolves itself into this. Do you intend to make any provision for me in the future as regards money?" Having bluntly stated the question, she continued that "in the event of your declining to provide for me I shall be compelled to go on the stage." Her husband responded that her interview in *The Hawk* had caused him to cancel her allowance. He wrote that she must repudiate the charges that she had made in that interview before he would see her again.[40]

On 6 April 1894, the Countess petitioned for restitution of conjugal rights. This had been the remedy that the Ecclesiastical Courts had earlier offered for desertion, and the Matrimonial Causes Act of 1884 had given new meaning to the procedure. According to that statute, a decree for the restitution of conjugal rights gave the court the authority to order payment of maintenance. Additionally, the 1884 Act established the rule that a respondent who did not comply with such a decree would be deemed guilty of desertion.[41] Lady Russell thus had good reasons to petition for the remedy. Primarily, she could hope that the court would order her husband to pay her an allowance. Also, through the use of the procedure, the court could find her husband guilty of desertion, and she could then petition for a judicial separation on that ground. If the Countess could also establish proof of her husband's adultery, she would then have grounds for a divorce.

Earl Russell responded to his wife's petition on 2 May 1894 with the following answers:

> 1. That this petition has not been presented *bona fide* and for the purpose of relief, inasmuch as the petitioner had alleged and still alleges that the respondent has been guilty of the crime of sodomy.
> 2. That the petitioner has been guilty of cruelty in falsely alleging... that the respondent had been guilty of physical cruelty towards her, and also in stating on oath that she believed that the respondent had been guilty of the crime of sodomy.[42]

The offense that had been implied in 1891 was now named. Sodomy was indeed a crime in England. During the first third of the nineteenth century, more than fifty men had been executed as convicted sodomites. The well-known Labouchere Amendment to the Criminal Law Amendment Act of 1885 had established sodomy as a misdemeanor punishable by up to two years' hard labor.[43] What Lord Russell and his counsel now attempted to establish was the principle that publicly making a false accusation of such a "crime" constituted legal cruelty.

The term "homosexuality" did not enter the English vocabulary until after 1890, but the topic was very much in evidence in public discourse during the last decade of the nineteenth century. A shift in perceptions, as indicated by the Labouchere Amendment, had occurred earlier. Whereas sodomy had previously been a capital crime, in 1885 it was defined as a misdemeanor. Although, on the one hand, the Labouchere Amendment appeared to be more tolerant than earlier statutes, on the other it was more repressive in that it applied to private as well as public behavior. A new distinction was emerging between the sodomite and the homosexual; the emphasis had previously been on the act rather than the person.[44]

The trials of Oscar Wilde in 1895 later illuminated these perceptions. Wilde had fallen in love with Lord Alfred Douglas, whose father, the Marquess of Queensbury, publicly described Wilde as, in the well-known misspelling, a "somdomite." Wilde responded with a libel case. He failed in the action and was later tried, under the 1885 Act, for acts of "gross indecency" with men. The court sentenced him to the maximum penalty of two years' hard labor.

During the course of his criminal trial, Wilde described male love as "pure" and "perfect" and "intellectual," a love "such as Plato made the very basis of his philosophy, and such as you find in the sonnets of Michelangelo and Shakespeare."[45] As Linda Dowling has demonstrated, he was speaking from the tradition of Hellenism that had pervaded Oxford during Wilde's years as a student there. In Dowling's interpretation, by encouraging the study of Greek history, literature and philosophy, such university reformers as Jowett had laid the groundwork for the idealization of male love expressed by Wilde. By the early 1890s, that philhellenic tradition confronted a newer sexual realism, which emphasized a genital view of male homosexuality and was evident in the work of such writers as John Addington Symonds.

The tension between the two perceptions of male love was apparent not only in the Wilde trials but also in the work of Lord Russell's old friend, the poet Lionel Johnson. Johnson and Russell were members of a generation that had been greatly influenced by the spirit of Hellenism at Oxford. Many among that generation viewed the sexual realism of the 1890s as a threat to the Hellenic tradition. Johnson himself was direct in denouncing Symonds, calling him "an absolute Priapus."[46] Wilde was more problematic because, while in many respects he represented the older tradition of Hellenism, his trials publicized a less idealistic view of homosexuality. Russell referred to Johnson's dismay in a letter to Santayana, "This Oscar affair is awful: Alfred Douglas is a great friend of Lionel's & he is dreadfully distressed."[47] As Dowling notes, while Johnson could admire "the 'sweet sins' of Greek love portrayed in *Dorian Gray*," he was horrified by what he perceived to be the "destruction" of Lord Alfred Douglas.[48]

The Wilde trials revealed the anxiety, uncertainty, and tension surrounding homosexuality in 1895. The term had only recently become a topic for public discussion, and many observers were simply uncomprehending. Their confusion and misapprehensions frequently inspired hostility. Others, like Johnson, expressed the tension between the ideal of homoerotic Hellenism and the more graphic images of male love publicized by the trials. The verdict reflected the atmosphere of censure in 1895. While public hostility to homosexuality proved disastrous for Wilde, it was advantageous for Lord Russell.

Condemnation of homosexuality served to reinforce Russell's contention that his wife's accusations constituted legal cruelty. In 1895 his case was based not only on his wife's statements in court and in the press with regard to his relationship with Roberts. Russell's counsel also brought into evidence other references to homosexual acts. In the further particulars of his answer to her suit, Lord Russell claimed that Lady Scott, in the presence of her daughter, "told Walter Rowe that the respondent had committed an unnatural offence with a boy on board his yacht." In his questioning of Lady Russell during the trial, Lord Russell's counsel was more specific when he asked the witness if her mother had also said that Lord Russell "had put a rope round the boy's waist and towed him aft of the 'Royal' [Lord Russell's yacht] to hide his guilt."[49] Both Lady Russell and Lady Scott denied the charge in their testimony, but the idea that the two women had accused Lord Russell of the crime of sodomy in the presence of Rowe, who was the Earl's former coachman, was certainly planted in the minds of the jurors.

Lady Russell had continued to maintain that her husband's family had given her reason to believe that she should be suspicious of his past; her reference in court to the "things" that they had told her implied that they had confided in her about her husband's homosexual practices (or "malpractices" as she termed them). The doctor of Lord Russell's grandmother, the dowager Countess Russell, stated in an affidavit that she was too ill to testify, and, accordingly, both she and her daughter, Lady Agatha, were deposed at Pembroke Lodge on 16 January 1895. In their depositions the two women denied that they had told Lady Russell anything negative or scandalous about her husband's past.

The dowager Countess responded to a charge that had been brought into evidence in a letter from Mabel Russell to her husband's maternal grandmother, Lady Stanley. In the letter, dated 22 November 1890, the young Lady Russell had asked a number of questions about her husband. Among them was the inquiry, "Did he take a China boy to the upper story of his Grand Mother's house in Dover Street, which China Boy was cleverly shipped off afterwards to his own country by the Honble. Lyulph Stanley?" In the course of her testimony, the dowager Countess Russell said, "I did not tell petitioner that some scandal had arisen about her husband in Dover Street. Certainly not. I never heard of it." She was then asked, "Did you tell petitioner that respondent had concealed a Chinese boy in his room at Dover Street for some days?" and she responded: "Undoubtedly not. I never told her that the Hon.

Maude Stanley had brought the boy here. In fact she did not bring a boy here. The boy was sent to Liverpool and then to his own country, but I did not tell the petitioner so."[50] The dowager Countess may never have heard of any "scandal" with regard to her grandson's activities in Dover Street, but she evidently did know of the family's involvement in returning a Chinese boy to his own country.

The matrimonial problems of her grandson must have been extremely painful for the dowager Countess. Here were two prominent families, the Stanleys and the Russells, involved in rather unseemly litigation. The correspondence that was brought into evidence indicated that the families had been sympathetic to the young Countess until she made her charges public. They had begged her to settle the case privately, but she apparently wanted public vindication. That attitude evoked much criticism. According to an item in *Figaro* that appeared on 25 October 1894:

> There is a good deal of natural disgust in society at the suit which the Countess Russell is bringing against the Earl for the restitution of conjugal rights.... Her ladyship lost caste considerably in consequence of the divorce action, and that she should now try to compel the man against whom she sanctioned the bringing of the most abominable charges it is possible to conceive to resume cohabitation with her has certainly not raised her in the estimation of society.

Lady Russell, who had taken her charges from the courtroom to *The Hawk* in 1891, now found herself in an unfavorable light in the press. She responded by taking legal action against D.S. Hunter, the editor of *Figaro*. She appealed to the court to find Hunter guilty of contempt for prejudicing her suit and to commit him to Holloway Prison. Mr. Justice Bruce ruled that the paragraph did constitute contempt, but he did not send Hunter to prison because "newspapers are generally so well conducted in this country." Instead the editor was fined £50 and the costs of the motion.[51]

Lady Russell's behavior may have inspired "disgust in society," but did it constitute matrimonial cruelty? In his review of the proceedings, the judge, Mr. Baron Pollock, told the jurors that Lady Russell had accused her husband of "the commission of as serious a crime as a man could commit," and he lamented "that grievances of so sad, and so terrible a nature, should be aired to the public, and brought forward in public, in the columns of a newspaper."[52] After hearing Pollock's comments on the case, the jury deliberated for less than thirty minutes and returned with a verdict finding Lady Russell guilty of cruelty. Pollock then decreed a judicial separation for the couple on the ground of that offense.

In August of 1895, the Court of Appeal reversed that decision and thus established important precedents. With regard to the definition of cruelty, the judges stated, "There must be danger to life, limb, or health, bodily or mental, or a reasonable apprehension of it, to constitute legal cruelty."[53] They denied Lord Russell a judicial separation, and, on appeal the House of Lords affirmed that decision in 1897.[54] The appellate judges also denied Lady Russell's decree for the restitution of conjugal rights. Thus, they decided that Lady Russell's accusations of homosexual behavior were not serious enough to be defined as legal cruelty, but were egregious enough to serve as a defense to her petition for the restitution of conjugal rights. Neither of the Russells obtained relief, and the legal marital bond remained intact.

The decisions regarding the definition of cruelty in the Russell case are directly related to contemporary attitudes toward homosexuality. Both the Wilde and the Russell trials revealed that the idea of same-sex sexual relations inspired fear and hostility. The *Figaro* allusion to "the most abominable charges it is possible to conceive" and Pollack's reference to "the commission of as serious a crime as a man could commit" were representative of the homophobic rhetoric of the decade.

The Russell case differed from the Wilde case in that the hostility and anxiety regarding male homosexuality were directed not merely against the man accused of engaging in homosexual acts but his accuser as well. Although Lord Russell did encounter antagonism in the early days of his matrimonial litigation, by 1895 the public had begun to view him more sympathetically. As he left on the second day of the trial in 1891, Lord Russell had confronted a hostile demonstration instigated by a large crowd of "roughs" who shouted epithets and hooted at him.[55] After the verdict, which in effect pronounced him not guilty of his wife's accusations, he was greeted with cheers. Both in legal records and in the press, public references to Lord Russell after 1891 tended to portray him as an innocent man unjustly accused of "abominable" crimes by his wife, while she was denounced for continuing to make those charges. A jury and several judges found her behavior in this regard despicable enough to be defined as legal cruelty. Apparently, creating a scandal about homosexual practices was almost as serious an offense as the acts themselves.

That attitude was again apparent in 1897 in the trial of Lady Scott for criminal libel. In his autobiography Lord Russell wrote that his mother-in-law had contacted individuals who had been on the crew of his yacht, the *Royal*, and discovered that a man named Kast would attest to serious charges against his former employer. Lord Russell and his friends then received "printed libels of a most obscene and degrading character ... prefaced by a sheet signed by Lady Scott stating that she was impelled to take this action to protect her pure and holy daughter who had been so foully wronged."[56] Joining Lady Scott as defendants in the trial for criminal libel that followed were Aylott and Cockerton, two men who had assisted her in locating Kast and distributing the printed charges. Among those charges was Kast's accusation that Lord Russell had been guilty of an assault upon him at Winchester, where Kast had come from Southampton to collect a check to pay the crew's wages. Unfortunately for the defendants, Kast was unable to testify at the trial because he died in prison on 11 December 1896. Without his testimony, the counsel for the other defendants stated that they could not provide other evidence to prove the accuracy of the statements and thus could not offer the plea of justification for the libel. Hawkins then sentenced Lady Scott and the other defendants to eight months in prison.[57]

Following Lady Scott's conviction in January and the House of Lords' refusal to grant a judicial separation in July of 1897, Lord Russell devoted much of his time to political activity, especially and not surprisingly divorce law reform.[58] He also served on the London County Council from 1895 to 1904. In an election campaign in 1898, Mollie Somerville, an advocate of women's suffrage, was one of his prominent supporters. According to Santayana, she was married and the mother of two small boys. Having described her as "a fat, florid, coarse Irishwoman of forty, with black curls, friendly manners and emotional opinions," Santayana then recounts with some surprise that she eventually succeeded Martha Turner in Russell's affections.[59] Mollie Somerville was soon free to marry because her husband divorced her after she had abandoned her marriage and two sons. Lord Russell, however, was still unable to end his marriage.

Accordingly, he and Mollie Somerville set sail for the United States in July, 1899. There they established residence in Nevada, living in a house on the shores of Lake Tahoe for the six months necessary to acquire a domicile. On 15 March 1900, Lord Russell petitioned the district court of Nevada for a divorce on the ground of desertion; he was granted a decree on 14 April. On 15 April John Francis Stanley, Earl Russell, married Mollie Somerville in Reno. The new husband cabled the news of his marriage to England for publication in the *Times*. Mabel Edith Scott Russell then could petition for divorce on the grounds of her husband's adultery and, as the necessary second offense, bigamy.

As an incentive to ensure her cooperation, Lord Russell had deposited in a bank £5,000, which she could claim when a decree of divorce was granted. The newly married couple returned to England in May, 1900.[60]

On Monday, 17 June 1901, at Waterloo Station in London, Lord Russell was arrested on the charge of bigamy. Testifying at the Bow Street hearing that followed was Benjamin Franklin Curler, the judge who had performed the marriage ceremony for Lord Russell and Mollie Somerville in Reno. According to Curler, Russell's divorce was not even valid in Nevada. In that state a petitioner was required to publish notice of his intention to apply for a divorce once a week for six weeks; at the end of that time, forty more days had to elapse before a valid decree could be granted. In Lord Russell's case, the last notice had been published on 13 April 1900. Since the date on the divorce decree was April 14, the requisite forty days had not elapsed, and the decree was thus invalid.[61]

Even if the divorce had been recognized in the United States, it would not have been binding in England because English courts had consistently refused to recognize divorce decrees granted in foreign countries.[62] What Lord Russell had sought in Nevada was not a divorce that would necessarily be recognized by English courts. Instead, he wanted to provide his first wife with evidence of his commission of adultery and bigamy in order to enable her to obtain a divorce that would most definitely be valid in England.

Lord Russell found himself not a respondent in the Divorce Court but rather an accused criminal. When the grand jury indicted him for the crime of bigamy, the proceedings were sent to the House of Lords for a trial by his peers. It was quite a spectacle. The House had not tried a peer for a felony since 1841, and a Select Committee was appointed to review the Journals and to recommend proper procedure. That Committee decided that the trial should take place in the Royal Gallery, which was larger than the House of Lords chamber, and they outlined strict instructions for the distribution of 420 tickets. Only peers could collect the tickets, and they crowded into the old Palace Yard at Westminster on the day of distribution. Interest was so great that the King sent his assurances that he would provide a police force sufficient to control the crowd on the day of the trial.[63]

Despite such intense anticipation, the proceedings on 18 July 1901 were rather dull. The defense for Lord Russell was based on a technical reading of the statute making bigamy a felony.[64] As Russell's counsel argued his point in minute detail, "the general expression of the Peers changed from that of alertness and humour by distinct gradations to one of obvious perplexity, and then of profound boredom."[65] In the end, the Attorney General did not even respond to the defense argument because the Lord High Steward felt that it was unnecessary; the Government's position was based on a clear and straightforward reading of the statute. Lord Russell had little choice but to plead guilty. He made an eloquent speech to the Lords, but he was still sentenced to three months in prison for his crime.

After a decade of litigation, the Russells finally achieved their common goal. On 28 October 1901, Mabel Edith Scott Russell obtained a final divorce decree, and on 31 October, Lord Russell married Mollie Somerville a second time at the Holborn registry office. He had spent £30,000 and served a prison term in order to end his marriage. The Russells' respective matrimonial difficulties did not end in 1901. The former Countess married again in 1902, divorced her second husband in 1904, and died in 1908. Lord Russell and his second wife were divorced in 1915. He married again in 1916, separated from his third wife in 1919, and died in 1931.[66]

Lord Russell's arrest and trial for bigamy and his sentence of imprisonment are among the most intriguing events in the complex tale of the Russells' matrimonial litigation. His arrest shocked him, as well it should have, because he had no reason to believe that the Government would view as a crime what he understood to be a matrimonial offense to be considered only by the judges in the Divorce Court. In light of the strict English divorce laws, surely other individuals had adopted the same course of action as Lord Russell, and yet had achieved their ends without a public trial and term of imprisonment. Why, then, was this particular aristocrat arrested, prosecuted, and imprisoned?

Russell believed that he was punished because he was "an unbeliever and a radical," and also because Halsbury, the Lord Chancellor, "was outraged by the apparent defiance of the law by a person in my prominent position." Halsbury's statements during the trial lend credence to that perception. Although he clearly stated his sympathy with Lord Russell, "considering what misery all his domestic life must have been," he told the House that they should impose sanctions because:

> the question whether or not other persons would be tempted to do the same thing, with comparative immunity to themselves, unless there was some real punishment, – renders it impossible for me to recommend to your Lordships that the matter should be entirely passed over.[67]

Russell, then, was to be an example, indicating that the English courts would enforce the strict divorce statutes. The law in action would be the same as the "law on the books" without regard to the status of the litigants.

The term of imprisonment was something of a surprise. Many thought that the humiliation of being arrested, tried, and convicted of bigamy was punishment enough for Russell's offense. When Halsbury announced the sentence, according to the *Daily Mail*, "There was an impressive silence on this, as most of the peers had expected that Earl Russell would be dismissed with a nominal sentence of one or two days' imprisonment."[68] Once again, Halsbury and other officials certainly wanted to make the point that the courts would punish those who demonstrated disrespect for the laws in pursuing matrimonial relief.

Apart from these factors that influenced the conviction and sentence of Lord Russell, the question remains: Who instigated his arrest? It is difficult to believe that any official not in the highest levels of government would have ordered the arrest of a peer on a charge of bigamy, a crime very rarely prosecuted. Someone with great authority must have instigated the proceedings. According to the current Earl, the Russell family "always believed that the prosecution had been brought at the instance of King Edward VII in order to strengthen his own reputation for morality."[69]

Such a claim is difficult to substantiate, but it is certainly credible that Edward VII, who as Prince of Wales had been associated with scandals involving divorce and matrimonial difficulties, might have felt the need to strengthen his reputation for morality. In the 1870 Mordaunt divorce suit, for instance, the Prince himself was called to testify that there had been no improper familiarity between Lady Mordaunt and himself. In response to that scandal, Queen Victoria had written:

> The fact of the Prince of Wales's intimate acquaintance with a young married woman being publicly proclaimed, will show an amount of imprudence which cannot but damage him in the eyes of the middle and lower classes, which is most deeply to be lamented in these days when the higher classes, in their frivolous, selfish and pleasure-seeking lives, do more to increase the spirit of democracy than anything else.[70]

Three decades later, King Edward VII appeared to have become more prudent. Indeed he exemplified Mrs. Patrick Campbell's dictum to avoid scandal. The King had mistresses, but he was always discreet. Queen Alexandra ignored his affairs, and they maintained the public image of a happy royal marriage. While the King's private life might be characterized as "frivolous, selfish and pleasure-seeking," he maintained propriety in public and condemned those who did not. He found divorce especially reprehensible.[71] Such a monarch could not ignore the Russells' flagrant disregard for both the social code and the divorce laws.

George Santayana described his friend Lord Russell as a martyr who suffered ostracism, imprisonment, and ruin in the course of his matrimonial trials.[72] Russell was a martyr in that he chose to defend himself publicly when he could have addressed his marital problems in private. At the very least, he could have agreed to negotiate a monetary settlement. There was never any assurance that his wife's family would not have continued to pursue him with threats of blackmail after such an arrangement had been negotiated, but he never gave them the opportunity to settle the matter privately. He was outraged by his wife's behavior, and he was determined to defend himself at any cost. He and his family paid a high price for his stubborn refusal to relent. The cost was high because, as the case of the second Earl Russell clearly indicated, the British establishment had little tolerance for those who frighten the horses.

NOTES

1. Philip Ziegler, *Diana Cooper* (New York: Alfred A. Knopf, 1982), 4.
2. Lee Holcombe has described the careers of the Amberleys in *Wives and Property, Reform of the Married Women's Property Law in Nineteenth-Century England* (Toronto: University of Toronto Press, 1983), 132–3.
3. See e.g. Elaine Showalter, *Sexual Anarchy: Gender and Culture at the Fin de Siècle* (London: Bloomsbury, 1991).
4. Earl Russell, *My Life and Adventures* (London: Cassell and Company Ltd., 1923), 33.
5. Bertrand Russell, *The Autobiography of Bertrand Russell, 1872–1914* (Boston: Little, Brown and Company, 1951), 15.
6. Russell, *My Life and Adventures*, 104. The following account of the encounter between Lord Russell and Benjamin Jowett is derived from Russell's *My Life and Adventures*, 107.
7. House of Lords Record Office, Appeal Cases and Writs of Error (1897), vol. 467, 86–7.
8. "The Russell Case," *The Hawk*, 8 Dec. 1891, 562.
9. Russell, *My Life and Adventures*, 109.
10. George Santayana, *Persons and Places, Fragments of Autobiography*, eds. William G. Holzberger and Herman J. Saatkamp, Jr. (Cambridge, Mass.: MIT Press, 1986), 308–9.

11. Russell, *My Life and Adventures*, 90–1.
12. Santayana, *Persons and Places*, 309.
13. Ibid., 307.
14. Russell, *My Life and Adventures*, 156.
15. Santayana, *Persons and Places*, 316.
16. A copy of the petition is in volume 467, pp. 201–3, of Appeal Cases and Writs of Error (1897) in the House of Lords Record Office.
17. Ibid., 204–5.
18. Ibid., 207–8.
19. Ibid., 214, 222.
20. Ibid., 253.
21. Russell, *My Life and Adventures*, 97, 99, 113, and 164.
22. Evidence of Mr. H.A. Roberts, 237–40, and Evidence of Earl Russell, 241–50, in vol. 467, Appeal Cases and Writs of Error (1897).
23. Russell, *My Life and Adventures*, 4, 115.
24. "The Russell Matrimonial Suit," *The Standard*, 4 Dec. 1891.
25. "*Russell* v. *Russell*," *Times*, 5 Dec. 1891. In a letter to *The Standard* the solicitors of Kate Williams stated that their client denied that Lord Russell had seduced her, and they strongly objected to the use of her name in his evidence. *The Standard*, 5 Dec. 1891.
26. *The Standard*, 5 Dec. 1891, and *Times*, 5 Dec. 1891.
27. *Times*, 5 Dec. 1891.
28. *The Standard*, 3 Dec. 1891, and 5 Dec. 1891.
29. "The Russell Case," *The Hawk*, 8 Dec. 1891, 561–2.
30. Santayana, *Persons and Places*, 317–18.
31. Bertrand Russell, *The Collected Papers of Bertrand Russell*, vol. 1, *Cambridge Essays, 1888–99*, ed. Blackwell *et al.* (London: George Allen & Unwin, 1983), 48.
32. *The Hawk*, 8 Dec. 1891.
33. See Ann Sumner Holmes, "The Double Standard in the English Divorce Laws, 1857–1923," *Law & Social Inquiry* 20 (Spring 1995): 601–20.
34. Santayana, *Persons and Places*, 470.
35. Appeal Cases and Writs of Error (1897) 467: 97–8.
36. *The Collected Papers of Bertrand Russell*, 1: 52.
37. Santayana, *Persons and Places*, 470.
38. See Ann Sumner Holmes, "Hard Cases and Bad Laws: Divorce Reform in England, 1909–1937," Ph.D. diss., Vanderbilt University, 1986, 17–18.
39. Appeal Cases and Writs of Error (1897) 467: 314.
40. Ibid., 315–18.
41. C.E.P. Davies, "Matrimonial Relief in English Law," in *A Century of Family Law*, eds. R.H. Graveson and F.R. Crane (London: Sweet & Maxwell Ltd., 1957), 318.
42. Appeal Cases and Writs of Error (1897) 467: 4.
43. Jeffrey Weeks, *Sex, Politics and Society: The Regulation of Sexuality since 1800* (London: Longman, 1981), 100–2. Ironically, in light of his grandson's difficulties, Lord John Russell had moved to drop "unnatural offenses" from the list of capital crimes in 1841. According to Jeffrey Weeks, "he was forced to withdraw through lack of parliamentary support." It was not until 1861 that the death penalty for sodomy was finally removed.

44. Weeks, *Sex, Politics and Society*, 102–3.
45. Linda Dowling, *Hellenism and Homosexuality in Victorian Oxford* (Ithaca: Cornell University Press, 1994), 1.
46. Ibid., 135.
47. Gail Savage, "'...Equality from the Masculine Point of View...': the 2nd Earl Russell and Divorce Law Reform in England," *russell: the Journal of the Bertrand Russell Archives* 16 (Summer 1996), 70 n. 5.
48. Dowling, *Hellenism and Homosexuality*, 136.
49. Appeal Cases and Writs of Error (1897) 467: 13, 97.
50. Ibid., 467: 303, 25.
51. Affidavit of Countess Russell as to publication in *Figaro*, filed 7 Nov. 1894. PRO J77/534/16305.24. *Times*, 13 Nov. 1894.
52. Appeal Cases and Writs of Error (1897) 467: 356–8.
53. *Russell* v. *Russell* [1895] In the Court of Appeal. Probate Division 315 at 322.
54. See John M. Biggs, *The Concept of Matrimonial Cruelty* (London: The Athlone Press, 1962), 39–43 and C.E.P. Davies, "Matrimonial Relief in English Law," 329–30, for discussions of the significance of *Russell* v. *Russell* with regard to the legal definition of cruelty.
55. "The Russell Matrimonial Suit," *The Standard*, 3 Dec. 1891.
56. Russell, *My Life and Adventures*, 206–7.
57. "The Russell–Scott Libel Case," *Times*, 12 Dec. 1896. Record of proceedings in Central Criminal Court. *Times*, 6 Jan. 1897, 8 Jan. 1897, and 9 Jan. 1897. Santayana had been on board the *Royal* with the crew involved in these accusations, and he was present at the trial. In his notes beside Russell's account in *My Life and Adventures*, Santayana wrote, "Lady Scott when sentenced, cried: *It is all true!*" One biographer characterizes Santayana's reference as "sympathetic and approving." John McCormick, *George Santayana* (New York: Alfred A. Knopf, 1987), 78.
58. For a discussion of Russell's efforts in the area of divorce reform, see Savage, "Equality from the Masculine Point of View," 67–84.
59. Santayana, *Persons and Places*, 476–7. Santayana said that he met Mollie Somerville at Russell's home, Amberley Cottage, in 1895 (476), but Russell implied that he did not know her before the 1898 election. *My Life and Adventures*, 233. 1895, of course, was the year of his petition for judicial separation; the acknowledgment of a relationship with another woman could certainly have prejudiced his case.
60. Russell, *My Life and Adventures*, 258–9, 279. "Earl Russell's Trial," *The Daily Telegraph*, 5 July 1901.
61. "Charge of Bigamy Against Earl Russell," *The Illustrated Police News*, 29 June 1901.
62. Anthony J. Bland, "The Family and the Conflict of Laws," in *A Century of Family Law, 1857–1957*, 375.
63. House of Lords Sessional Papers, 1901, vol. VII. "Earl Russell's Trial," *Daily Mail*, 12 July 1901.
64. A transcript of the trial can be found in the Sessional Papers of the House of Lords, 1901, vol. I.
65. "Russell Trial," *The Daily Telegraph*, 19 July 1901.
66. George Edward Cokayne, *The Complete Peerage*, 13 vols., ed. Geoffrey H. White (London: The St. Catherine Press, 1949), 11: 238.

67. Russell, *My Life and Adventures*, 283–4, and House of Lords Sessional Papers, 1901, vol. I, "Proceedings on the Trial of Earl Russell," 25.
68. "Earl Russell's Sentence," *Daily Mail*, 20 July 1901.
69. Professor The Earl Russell, letter to the author, 7 March 1996.
70. Philip Magnus, *King Edward VII* (London: Penguin Books, 1979), 143.
71. Samuel Hynes, *The Edwardian Turn of Mind* (Princeton: Princeton University Press, 1968), 186.
72. Santayana, *Persons and Places*, 476.

9 Murder Most Foul: Spousal Homicides in Ontario, 1870–1915

Annalee E. Golz

In 1888, James Gowan, the chair of the Canadian Senate Divorce Committee, made a rousing speech before his peers, congratulating the nation's citizens for their steadfast dedication to the institutions of marriage and the family. Armed with statistics which compared Canada's characteristically low divorce rates with those in England and especially in the United States, he drew what was, in his view, the obvious conclusion. "Thank God," he stated, "the people of Canada know how to estimate and to value and cherish the sacred character of the matrimonial tie, the purity and sacredness of the family – they know these sentiments – attributes of the higher law – are the source and life of Christian civilization and that without them no nation can permanently prosper."[1] One year later, legal scholar John A. Gemmill, citing similar statistics, went even further, arguing that Canada showed a "cleaner record than that of any other progressive people on the face of the earth" in effectively safeguarding both the sanctity of marriage and the stability of the family unit as two foundations of the social order.[2]

While these idealistic pronouncements were designed to legitimize Canada's highly restrictive parliamentary divorce procedures, they also reflected the link many turn-of-the-century legislators and social reformers made between marital stability and the moral fabric of the country.[3] Quite in contrast, legal records and particularly criminal court records strongly suggest that marriage was by no means as stable an institution as official divorce statistics might have indicated nor as legislators would have hoped. In fact, at the local level, Ontario magistrates and judges periodically commented, with some anxiety, on certain troubling patterns. In 1912, London's police magistrate told the press that in the 19 months he had been on the bench, 300 couples had appeared before him "dissatisfied with their marital relations, and to many of them he granted separations."[4] Even more disconcerting was a statement made by one Detroit magistrate, bitterly complaining about the number of married couples from Ontario, who were flocking south of the border and clogging up the American court system with their various "domestic difficulties". If the laxness of American divorce courts, often condemned as symbols of "national depravity" and libertine republicanism, had long provided a convenient foil for expressions of national boosterism and moral smugness on the part of Canadian political and social commentators, the image of Detroit's police courts as a "clearing house" for the settlement of unhappy Ontario marriages was nothing short of alarming.[5]

That Ontario wives and husbands utilized available legal as well as informal mechanisms to "handle" a wide spectrum of marital conflicts (involving everything from non-support and desertion, adultery, and bigamy, to criminal neglect and wife abuse) is richly documented in the criminal records of the lower and higher courts of the period.[6] One crime, however, that had the greatest potential to unsettle any constructed mythologies about the state and character of marital relations in the province was that of spousal homicide.[7] It was certainly considered to be the most heinous violation of the contract of marriage and gravest transgression of the gendered obligations assigned to each spouse: the duty of husbands to fulfill their role as protectors of their wives and other dependants, and the responsibility of wives to honor their would-be masculine defenders. In addition, during the investigation and trial of a suspected domestic murderer, the character and conduct of both the accused and the victim, as well as the history and character of their often less than blissful marital relations were exposed to intense legal scrutiny, public interest, and community gossip. Nonetheless, one of the most striking features of these cases, which set them apart from other crimes involving relations between husbands and wives, was the extent to which they were constructed as relatively isolated acts, for which a plausible and definitive explanation had to be found. The compulsion to achieve this sense of closure on the part of the criminal justice system as well as local communities meant that, even though not essential for securing a conviction, certain "truths" behind the homicidal deed needed to be unraveled, be it in the form of defining a cause, establishing a motive, and/or assessing culpability. In this process of reconstruction, interpretation, and explanation, spousal murder did not generate a social critique of the unequal power relations within heterosexual marriage nor did it challenge the legitimacy of the institution itself. Rather, this crime was explained in legal and public discourse within fairly strictly defined, historically specific, and indeed relatively safe parameters. Not surprisingly, these explanations incorporated turn-of-the-century assumptions about gender, class, and race/ethnicity, but they also drew on and fueled concerns about other social and moral issues, one of the principal ones being the vice of intemperance.[8] While spousal homicide trials in general, regardless of the identified cause or motive, provided little space for sentimentality about marital relations and often exposed them at their most brutal, those linked to the "evils of drink" did reveal some of the ways legal authorities, medical practitioners, local communities, and at times, defendants themselves sought to make sense of these most foul of murders without fundamentally threatening the hegemony of that most revered of institutions – heterosexual marriage.

WHO DONE IT AND WHAT BECAME OF THEM

In the period between 1870 and 1915, at least 75 Ontario husbands and 21 wives were arrested on charges of murdering their spouses. (These figures do not include the 7 husbands who committed suicide immediately or shortly after completing their homicidal acts nor the 5 married women who were accused of conspiring with a third party to "do away" with their spouses.[9]) Once arrested, most suspected murderers/murderesses became entangled in a fairly elaborate legal process, which in the minds of judicial authorities constituted the requisite machinery of a fair and impartial system of criminal justice.

The most crucial phase, determining whether a suspect would actually be committed for a criminal trial, was the coroner's inquest, a relatively informal hearing designed to investigate all violent or otherwise "unnatural" deaths. After viewing the body and considering the evidence presented by medical "experts" and any witnesses to the alleged crime, the coroner's jury was asked to rule on the medical cause of death, whether it was indeed the result of foul play, or alternatively the consequence of disease, accident, or suicide.[10] At this stage, a number of husbands (but no wives), initially thought to be culpable for the death of their spouses, were discharged from custody. If, as occurred in the vast majority of suspected spousal homicide cases, the coroner's jury found that there was sufficient evidence to commit the accused for trial, the case had to await the next scheduled sitting of the county criminal assizes, presided over by a travelling judge, a grand jury which was responsible for forwarding a bill of indictment, and a petit jury which would weigh the evidence and render a verdict. It was during this latter phase in the judicial process, usually before a crowd of interested spectators, that the history and nature of the relationship between the accused and the deceased, what had occurred at the time of the alleged homicide, as well as statements of character were presented, contested, and at times debated by medical experts, police constables, witnesses, and of course family members. After hearing the evidence, the closing arguments of the crown and defense attorneys, and the judge's charge, the jury was asked to determine whether the defendant was guilty of premeditated murder, which carried the death penalty; of manslaughter, which took into account the absence of intent and acts of provocation and carried a maximum penalty of life imprisonment; or deserved to be acquitted, on the grounds of insanity, justifiable homicide, or because of the lack of sufficient evidence.[11] In instances when the accused was found guilty of murder and particularly when juries recommended mercy, she or he had access to one last court of appeal, that being the Governor General, who upon the advice of the Executive Council and the Minister of Justice would determine whether there were mitigating enough circumstances to commute the sentence of death to life imprisonment or to incarceration in one of the province's asylums.[12]

In the period under study, 70 husbands were formally tried at the county criminal assizes, 7 for poisoning their wives and the remaining 63 for causing their deaths through physical or other forms of violence. By contrast, of the 21 wives indicted for being directly responsible for their husbands' deaths, 12 were suspected of poisoning them, the method usually associated with female killers, and 9 of resorting to more violent methods. Furthermore, despite common turn-of-the-century assumptions that crime in general and family violence in particular were poor and working-class phenomena, a substantial proportion (42 percent) of those husbands accused of killing their wives were moderately to well to do farmers or were members of the middle or professional classes; among married women suspected of husband murder, about 46 percent were married to established farmers. In addition, if social reformers, social purity advocates, and legal authorities increasingly targeted non-Anglo men and immigrant "foreigners" for generating social disorder and for their alleged propensity to commit violent offenses, the vast majority of wife murderers were white, and most were of Anglo-Celtic heritage, the *exceptions* being two First Nations men, three men of color, one Italian, and five French-Canadians. Similarly, among those wives accused of murdering their husbands, one was Italian, two were women of color, and two were French-Canadian. The table below offers a rudimentary breakdown of convictions by gender, and what became of those accused of spousal murder during this period.

	Husbands	Wives
Hanged	17	2
Commutation	9	2
Manslaughter	24	0
Acquitted	20	17

Perhaps two of the most striking features of these statistics are first, in contrast to their male counterparts, married women accused of killing their husbands seemed to have "gotten away with murder" on a fairly routine basis, and second, that manslaughter appeared to have been a crime gendered male. But on closer inspection, the high acquittal rates among murdering wives is somewhat deceiving. While masculine chivalry and gendered mercy on the part of all-male jurors did seem to operate in some trials,[13] it should be noted that three wives were acquitted on the grounds of insanity (as were five husbands), and in the vast majority of cases, were discharged because of the lack of sufficient evidence. This at least partially reflected the difficulties and frustrations associated with convicting wives *and* husbands suspected of what judges routinely termed the "secret crime" of poisoning their victims.

VILLAINS AND VICTIMS: THE VICE OF DRINK

In an effort to understand the second statistical feature related to the gendering of the crime of manslaughter, it is necessary to explore in greater detail one of the most common explanations for marital conflicts and spousal murders at the turn of the century: the vice of intemperance. Of the 24 cases which resulted in manslaughter verdicts, 72 percent of them were directly attributed to alcohol. In effect, it was particularly during the trials of murders linked to the "evils of drink" that the character and conduct of both the accused and the victim became the subject of intense legal scrutiny, and hence the questions of intent, provocation, and culpability seemed to emerge most forcibly. Moreover, while the guilt or innocence of murderous wives tended to be perceived in binary terms, in the case of husbands, the whole issue of the possible "mitigating circumstances" under which the crime was committed did, with some notable exceptions, gain the sympathetic attention of the courts.

In 1877, after the exhaustive trial of John Williams, a brickmaker accused of beating his wife to death at his home in the village of Weston, the judge took the opportunity to comment on what he deemed to be the bitter lesson to be learned from this "wretched crime". "This case," he stated, "spoke more eloquently than a thousand temperance lectures upon the great evils arising from whiskey drinking." In concluding his charge to the jury, he outlined the difference between murder and manslaughter, adding that even though "drinking was no excuse for crime ... it was often taken into consideration as inclining the scales to mercy." After five hours of deliberation, however, the jury returned a verdict of guilty of murder with a strong recommendation to mercy, and the accused was sentenced to be executed for his offense. Despite the jury's inclination and three petitions, initiated by prominent members of the community and several members of the jury, requesting that his sentence be commuted, the death penalty was not overturned, and Williams paid the ultimate "atonement" for his crime before a crowd of prison officials, newspaper reporters, and spectators.

The potential deterrent and reformative value of this highly-publicized case was so great that, on the day after the execution, the Toronto *Globe* felt it prudent to recount and comment on the details of the case for the moral benefit of its readers. The "Weston murder," according to the reporter, was "perhaps the most impressive sermon ever preached in Canada on the subject of intemperance ... To this doubly accursed liquor, and to it alone, can be attributed the terrible fate which befell Mrs. Williams, the more terrible atonement made to the world for blood shed by her husband, and the still more terrible situation in which his innocent family are left."

In all respects, the narrative constructed around the Weston case, from the disintegration of John and Ann Williams's marital relations to his execution, contained many of the elements of a tragic melodrama, which might well have been written by one of numerous temperance organizations proliferating in Ontario in the late nineteenth century. The couple had lived seemingly on good terms for the first 18 years of their marriage, and John was said to have been a peaceable, "decent, hard-working man," well-liked by his employer and members of the small community. This amicable situation quickly deteriorated, when two years prior to the murder, their marital relations were "disturbed by the husband's intemperance." Throughout this increasingly difficult period, Ann Williams remained, by all accounts, a "true woman" of virtually flawless character. She was described as "respectable, steady, [and] inoffensive," the hardworking mother of 13 children, and a "good wife," who, despite occasionally scolding him for his drinking habits, had "borne with her husband in his excesses with exemplary patience and forbearance." She had also, according to the press, silently endured her husband's unprovoked drunken rages and increasingly "inhuman treatment", "waiting to forgive and forget, always anxious for his comfort and welfare." On the day of her murder, as explained by a neighbor, it was evident that her husband had recently assaulted her, as "her face was dreadfully beaten," and not unlike many battered wives, Ann had told her that "she expected nothing else but that he would murder her some time." Her premonitions proved correct. That evening, her husband, while drinking and carousing with two male acquaintances and after boasting all day about the recent "licking" he had given his wife, angrily swore that "he would kill her the next time." The next morning Ann was found dead, her death, according to the coroner, having been caused by a severe head injury and a ruptured liver.

While John Williams's "inordinate use of drink" transformed an otherwise peaceable, inoffensive husband into an "unnatural" instrument of brutality, and was identified as the principal cause of Ann's death, the two other men present at the Williams's house on that fateful night were also widely condemned for their complicity in the tragedy. After spending the day of the murder on a "hunt for whiskey," it was said that these two men, Stones and Chapman, had thoughtlessly supplied Williams with "a half-gallon jar of whiskey," knowing "full well" how it might affect him. This act, which the press found "incomprehensible," was equalled by the reprehensible and callous indifference the two men displayed when Williams openly threatened to murder his wife, doing nothing "to protect Mrs. Williams from the drunken fury of her husband." And finally, during the night when one of the Williams children repeatedly asked the two men to intervene because his father was "licking" his mother, they both refused, stating that the couple had been "quarrelling the night before, and it would not amount to anything." For this inaction, Stones was arrested as an accessory to the murder on "account of his apathy and neglect to interfere when he knew that something was wrong." Although his case never came to trial, both Stones and Chapman came to symbolize the other evil consequences of intemperance: working-class idleness and more seriously, men's failure to assume their obligations to protect defenseless women.

While Stones and Chapman had doubly transgressed the codes of acceptable masculine behavior and hence were denounced by the judge for contributing to Ann's death, in the final act of this temperance drama, John Williams was ultimately redeemed in the eyes of the press and much of the community. Even though he had, after his arrest, consistently denied knowing (or remembering) anything about the matter, insisting that he was "as innocent as the Child unborn," it was during the last days of his incarceration and after all hopes for a reprieve were dashed, that he underwent his final metamorphosis on the eve of his execution. Under the guidance of a local minister, Williams composed a stirring public confession which contained all the elements necessary to draw accolades and to create a sense of closure. Assuring the public that "no man" was "more prepared to die" than he was and that he was deeply grateful for the fairness with which he had been treated by the court, he stressed that his greatest hope was that "his terrible fate would exercise a deterrent influence on others given to the use of drink." He attributed his downfall to two factors, which reflected and confirmed late nineteenth-century notions about the underlying causes of criminal and intemperate behavior. By running away from home at an early age and severing all ties with his parents, his life had been devoid of proper parental authority and moral guidance. From that moment on, as he went on to point out, he had "neglected God too," having seldom "darkened a church door" and spending his Sundays "idling and fooling his time away". With this emotive final statement, addressed to his children, friends, and the general public, Williams's identity as a brutal drunken husband capable of a gruesome murder was quickly supplanted by that of a "most unfortunate man," with many officials expressing keen regret that "the law was irrevocable."[14]

The Williams case was atypical, not for its excessive moralizing about the evil consequences of intemperance, but because of the severity of the sentence imposed. Of the more than 27 wife killings directly linked to alcohol in the period between 1870 and 1915, only two other husbands, James Carrutter, a respectable farmer from the township of Essa, and Thomas Kane, a Toronto plasterer, were sent to the gallows. In the former case, Carrutter confessed to whipping his wife to death, directly attributing his murderous violence "to drink alone," and like Williams, admonishing others to beware of "that curse" while awaiting his execution.[15] But the explanations surrounding Kane's homicidal deed, the way in which he was constructed in the press, and the dynamics of his murder trial differed significantly from those of the other two condemned wife killers. During the Williams trial, for example, press reporters had frequently commented that the accused did not have the physical appearance of a murderer, since his features did not suggest a "strong animal or treacherous nature," but rather that of a respectable-looking and ordinary man of average mental caliber and physical vigor.[16] By contrast, from the moment the badly beaten body of Mary Kane was discovered in the couple's "wretched hovel" in 1889, the public renditions of this "unparalleled atrocity" contained few elements of tragedy and Kane himself was described in virtually subhuman terms. As a destitute laborer, he came to symbolize and confirm late nineteenth-century assumptions not only about the interconnection between intemperance and "poverty, squalor and vice," but also about how a latent brute animalism characteristic of the male members of the "lower orders" could be unleashed through the inordinate consumption of alcohol. In providing detailed descriptions and sketches of the scene of the crime, for example, Toronto press reporters commented on how the scantily-furnished apartment and the absence of domestic amenities clearly indicated that all of Kane's meager wages had gone to the purchase of whiskey. The crime itself was portrayed as a "cruel and callous butchery", the result of the "hideous and fiendish brutality of an enraged animal." What made this murder particularly revolting to the public was the fact that after committing the "hideous" deed, Kane had lain down on a lounge beside his dead wife's battered and bloody body, and after sleeping away his "drunken orgy," he had, with an "appalling coolness," attempted to conceal the evidence and then spent the day in another "drinking bout" with friends.

Given the degree of outrage and sensationalism this case generated and the certainty with which the Toronto *Globe* predicted that Kane would "atone for his cruel and callous butchery on the gallows," once the trial began, the selection of a reasonably impartial jury proved to be a difficult and protracted process, so onerous in fact that at one point a search for more potential jurors had to be conducted on nearby streets. That Kane's conviction was more or less a foregone conclusion, despite his claims of innocence, was further attested by the fact that during the proceedings, which spanned no more than a few hours, no defense witnesses were called. The jury, after a short period of deliberation, returned a verdict of guilty with a recommendation to mercy on the grounds that "the prisoner was under the influence of liquor when the crime, was committed," but this verdict was quickly denounced in one letter-to-the-editor as both "disgraceful" and as a dangerous precedent. The Minister of Justice and the Executive Council seemed to agree, arguing in a written statement that clemency would not be granted because "they did not consider being under the influence of alcohol as a sufficient excuse for such a crime." When taken to the gallows and much to the disappointment of the reporters and spectators, Kane refused to confess to the crime, nor did he offer an eloquent speech of remorse and repentance. This display of stoic fearlessness confirmed what many had suspected about his character: a "careless indifference that betokened callousness of the worst kind."[17]

With the notable exception of these three married men, the majority of husbands, whose wife killings were directly linked to intemperance, were convicted of manslaughter, and received sentences ranging from two to ten years. What this suggests is that despite the fairly consistent hardline rhetoric of legal authorities and the harsh punishments handed down in selected cases, judges and juries (as well as abusive husbands themselves) seemed to share the view that, particularly in instances of beating or other violent deaths, drunkenness signified a "loss of control" and hence obliterated the "intent" to kill. More generally, manslaughter verdicts also allowed judges to exercise considerable discretion when sentencing prisoners to terms of imprisonment, sentences which often depended on the recommendations of the jury or on the circumstances under which the offense was committed.

One factor that did tend to tip the scales of justice was the fact that not all married women were of such an exemplary character as Ann Williams. Particularly when wives were also prone to drunkenness, defense attorneys had sufficient ammunition to argue that the death had been the result of a drunken row between two equals, or to make a strong case for provocation. After all, as social commentators and temperance advocates were apt to point out, "drunkenness among the women" was "ten times worse than in men, because it causes them to lose their maternal instinct and feeling, and they become thoroughly degraded."[18] Hence unlike the dynamics of wife battering or attempted murder trials, in which abused wives attempted to defend their character and to convince magistrates that they were undeserving of their husbands' cruelty, the strength of the prosecution's case in wife murder trials often relied on statements of good character provided by family members, acquaintances, and neighbors. In some instances, however, such positive endorsements were not forthcoming. This was particularly evident when the deceased was known within her community to be a woman of intemperate and disorderly habits. In fact, in a number of situations, the death of wives might have been prevented had neighbors been more inclined to maintain a watchful eye or to intervene during marital "disputes." For example, in 1883, when Margaret Edgar, the wife of a Hamilton laborer, died of exposure after her husband had beaten her and driven her out of the house in the depths of winter, her nearest neighbors were quick to point out that she had a bad reputation for being "addicted to liquor," and as a mark of her social marginalization, that they had rarely if ever visited her at her home. On the day in question, a number of them had heard the couple quarreling, which was cited as a frequent occurrence, and at least one neighbor had seen Mr. Edgar push his scantily-clad wife down the front steps and lock her out of the house. But given the social and moral distancing strongly implied in their testimonies, no one seemed at all predisposed to assist her or to offer her refuge. Rather, as they themselves admitted, the next thing they had heard was that her half-frozen body had been discovered lying behind a neighbor's rain barrel.[19]

That there was "nothing worse" than having a drunken, quarrelsome, and neglectful wife was also a complaint that many abusive and murdering husbands voiced in the courtroom when attempting to explain their crimes or when speaking in their own defense. In these cases, juries and judges were confronted with the tension between a husband's obligation to act as a male protector and his real or self-perceived prerogative to chastise his wife for her alleged failings. In instances when physical "punishment" resulted in death, manslaughter verdicts seemed to incorporate this very tension, devolving some of the responsibility onto husbands and their weakness for alcohol, but much of it onto the actual effects of drunkenness and/or onto wives themselves. As one judge explicitly stated, in summing up the evidence in the 1882 murder trial of James Bibby, a laborer accused of killing his intemperate wife, "in a case where a man came home, found his wife drunk, and in moment of temper [fatally] struck her ... a jury would be likely to look leniently upon the sad occurrence." In this instance, the jury agreed, finding the prisoner guilty of manslaughter but recommending as lenient a sentence as possible.[20]

While this judicial logic was a common one, particularly when charges were reduced from murder to manslaughter, the general character of the deceased could also sway government officials in the direction of mercy, or could prompt juries to opt for an acquittal. In 1870, Arthur Pierce's death sentence was commuted to life imprisonment on the grounds that, even though the evidence showed that he had beaten his wife to death while under the influence of alcohol, the prisoner "when he commenced his prolonged and brutal beating and kicking, did not have it in his mind at that time, to take the life of his wife." The other argument which worked in his favor was the claim that his wife "was as bad as the man," being of "a depraved and brutal nature."[21] Dan Whales, a hotel keeper from the town of Mitchell, was pardoned by the

Minister of Justice in 1896 after serving several years of his life sentence for killing his wife, on the grounds that his wife had "a very bad temper and had incited her husband to the murderous deed."[22]

While the verdicts and sentences in alcohol-related wife murders could be determined by a number of factors, it was nonetheless the case that intemperance emerged as one of the most pervasive social and legal explanations for wife killings, particularly in cases of beating and other violent deaths. In fact, when legal authorities speculated about the possible motives behind a suspected wife murder, alcohol frequently emerged as the predominant cause. In a letter written by the Carleton County Crown Attorney to the Deputy Attorney General in 1915, informing him about the upcoming trial of Noe Piché, an oiler charged with beating his wife to death, he listed several possible motives for this murder, including everything from his rumoured intimacy with another woman to the insurance policy he held on his wife's life. But in concluding his letter, he rejected all of these various theories, stating that "the attack on her was probably due to the brutality of the husband when under the influence of liquor, rather than to a premeditated assault upon her with the object of causing her death."[23]

Certainly the prevalence of the intemperance argument emerged out of turn-of-the-century and predominantly Anglo-Protestant middle-class concerns and campaigns around the innumerable social ills associated with alcohol, including everything from ill-health and insanity, poverty and idleness, to the commission of all types of violent and non-violent crimes. Moreover, it was this vice that was directly implicated for causing husbands, and particularly those of the poor and working classes, to neglect or abandon their duty as breadwinners, to "forget" their marriage vows and to beat their wives, and to lose all semblance of masculine respectability. In 1884, when sentencing Robert Edgar, a laborer, to five years' hard labor for the manslaughter of his wife, the judge took the opportunity to lecture the prisoner on what he considered to be some of the fundamentals of true manhood. While he began by suggesting that "a man who will beat his wife must have lost all self-respect and all feelings of a man," the judge quickly went on to add that the prisoner "had been brought to beating his wife through drink; in fact drink was really what had led to her death." These circumstances dictated that "it would not do to be too lenient, as it would only be holding out an inducement to other men to follow in his footsteps." In concluding his statement, the judge expressed the hope that "the main lesson" of this crime would not be lost: "that temperance was an essential to true manhood."[24]

If intemperance became the most common and in many respects the most comfortable explanation for family disharmony, marital strife, and domestic violence, it followed logically that greater state regulation of the liquor traffic or its eventual eradication, campaigns which gained momentum in this period, would resolve most if not all social and domestic ills, up to and including the problems of non-support, child neglect, wife battering, and indeed most wife murders. What this meant was that social and legal attention was diverted away from the unequal distribution of economic resources and hierarchical relations of power that structured relations between husbands and wives. The focus on intemperance also did not fundamentally challenge the self-perceived prerogative of some husbands to use physical violence to assert their marital authority and to enforce wifely obedience and submission.

The connection between intemperance and wife killings also fed into ethnic and racial prejudices directed against various marginalized groups, including "hot-blooded foreigners" like Italians[25] and First Nations peoples. In the case of Aboriginal peoples, for example, the so-called protective and paternalistic provisions of the 1876 Indian Act made it a separate criminal offense to sell alcohol to Natives, while social reformers and home missionaries routinely portrayed First Nations men as treating their "women as mere drudges."[26] Contrary to these presuppositions, only one case of suspected wife murder by a First Nations man that was directly linked to an alcohol-related beating death appeared in the Ontario court records between 1830 and 1920.[27] When the news broke that Jonas Froman, an Onondaga Native and the proprietor of a small grocery store on a reserve near Brantford, had killed his wife while under the influence of alcohol, however, newspaper headlines seemed to imply that this was a relatively common occurrence: "A Brantford 'Brave' Kills His Wife ... Whiskey Again to Blame." Besides blaming alcohol, newspaper accounts also attributed this "fiendish" crime to his "heathenism," as a form of "judgement" on the accused since he had, a few weeks prior to the murder, been one of the chiefs in the band council who had refused to allow a Protestant minister to preach on the reserve. After Mr. Froman's trial, when the verdict of manslaughter was returned and he was sentenced to ten years' imprisonment, the press announced that a remarkable discovery had been made: that the prisoner was actually of mixed ancestry. During the American Revolutionary War, his white father had been abandoned by his parents while still an infant, and had been raised by a Loyalist Onondaga couple, who had actively supported the British cause. This hitherto unmentioned chronicle of his "romantic ancestry" certainly transformed him from the "vicious brave" of earlier accounts to the rather "fine looking and intelligent man" who had been spared from the gallows. It also seemed to have offered the public a thinly veiled justification for the lenience of his sentence,[28] a fate which was not shared by the other First Nations man and most men of color accused and convicted of wife murder.[29]

In a number of murder trials, however, the issue of intemperance emerged under rather different circumstances. During the 1870s two working-class women, Elizabeth Workman and Catherine Sabourin, were arrested and tried for killing their drunken and/or abusive husbands.[30] The outcome of these trials differed markedly: Mrs. Workman was hanged for her offense while Mrs. Sabourin was acquitted on the grounds of self-defense. In 1872, when Elizabeth Workman, a washerwoman, was arrested and tried for beating her husband to death with a piece of wood as he lay in bed, there was little operating in her favor. Unable to afford a lawyer, she was eventually represented by an inexperienced defense attorney, who only had a few hours to prepare the case and who seemed to harbor strong class prejudices against his client. In commenting on the case, he wrote that the Workmans were clearly of "a very low class," and even though Mr. Workman was known in Mooretown as a "drunken brutal cruel husband," he was convinced the murder was the result of other factors: "a licentious loose life had weakened or destroyed all fine domestic feelings on the part of husband and wife. Coarse language and blows were common." The actual evidence presented at the trial, however, suggested a rather different story. Witnesses described Elizabeth Workman as a "quiet, industrious, hardworking woman," who had for years been subjected to the drunken and "tyrannical violence" of her husband. She had also been routinely coerced into giving her meager wages to him so he could purchase more alcohol. Despite evidence of her otherwise good character, the history of habitual abuse, and the fact that the Crown was unable to prove that she had acted with "murderous intent," the jury, after a brief trial, returned a verdict of guilty with a strong recommendation to mercy and she was sentenced to be hanged.

Shortly after her conviction, however, both the trial itself and the severity of Mrs. Workman's sentence began to generate considerable criticism. Her growing number of supporters, which included the *Sarnia Observer*, leveled the harshest critique at the presiding judge, who in his charge to the jury, had expressed the unequivocal "opinion that their verdict would have to be murder or nothing." Similarly, during sentencing, the judge had been equally emphatic when he warned the prisoner that, despite the jury's unanimous and strong recommendation of mercy, he held out little hope for commutation. In the end, he was proven correct. The efforts of a locally-organized clemency campaign, which included numerous petitions on her behalf and a trip to Ottawa by two Lambton County councillors who personally argued her case, proved to be futile. In attempting to convince the government that Mrs. Workman was worthy of "sympathy and leniency," her supporters certainly did not go so far as to suggest that this was a case of justifiable homicide; rather they simply pointed out that she was a woman of generally good character, that there was no indication that the murder had been premeditated, and that the mitigating circumstances or undue provocation under which the crime was committed should be taken into consideration. The Executive Council, however, declined to interfere in the case on the grounds that they "failed to perceive such mitigating circumstances in the case as might give reason for the exercise of clemency." Given the degree of sympathy Mrs. Workman's case had generated within the local community, her execution was very poorly attended; nonetheless, it did send a particularly bitter message to those battered wives who might retaliate against their abusive husbands, rather than merely enduring the violence or simply calling the police.[31]

Seven years later, Catherine Sabourin, the wife of a poor laborer and mother of six children, was also arrested and tried for murdering her husband, by striking him several times with an axe during a "drunken brawl." While the circumstances of the crime did not differ substantively from that of Elizabeth Workman, her murder trial took a dramatically different direction. Initially, Mrs. Sabourin, dubbed the "green-eyed monster," drew little sympathy from the inhabitants of the village of Billings Bridge nor from the Ottawa newspaper reporters. After conducting extensive interviews of village locals and the children of the couple who had witnessed the "fatal row," the press constructed a history of the Sabourin's volatile marital relations and of the crime. Neighbors were quick to point out that both Octave and Catherine Sabourin not only had a "bad reputation" for their addiction to alcohol, but also for "terrorizing the community" with their increasingly violent marital wars. At times, these battles had erupted over very "trivial" matters but most often had been fueled by Mrs. Sabourin's scandalous and "passionate fondness" for attending every dance in the vicinity which had met with the disapproval and reprobation of her husband. Consequently, for years, as the Ottawa *Citizen* put it, they had "blackened and bruised each other, sometimes the man coming out victorious, and other times his wife." More recently, as one daughter told the reporter, it had become increasingly evident that "one of the two would have to be sacrificed," and "it was just a matter of courage and strength who that one would be." The climax to this constant and escalating marital warfare, according to the children, had occurred during a "drunken brawl": Mr. Sabourin had thrown his wife to the floor and had attempted to choke her; then after insisting that "one of us must die to-night" had proceeded to attack her (rather symbolically) with a whiskey bottle; Mrs. Sabourin, who had armed herself with an axe, responded by "butchering" her husband, striking him several times, and thereafter for two days hesitated to call a physician as he lay dying of head injuries. While the accused later told a neighbor that she was "very sorry" for what she had done, she explained that she had been "mad with drink" and would not have grabbed the axe had her husband not "vexed her." Given the gruesome details of this "final act in the bloody drama," one Ottawa reporter typically concluded that this case would prove to be "one of the most powerful temperance lectures on record."

At Catherine Sabourin's subsequent trial on a charge of willful murder, the main issue considered by the court was whether she had intentionally killed her husband, had been unduly provoked, or had acted in self-defense. Mrs. Sabourin's defense attorney asked the jury to "disabuse their minds of any prejudice caused by sensational newspaper reports" and consider her the repeated victim of his intemperance. It was this which had turned a previously sober and respectable woman into one with a "strong appetite" for alcohol and had precipitated Mr. Sabourin's "barbarous" and "cannibalistic" acts of verbal and physical violence. "With such terrible brutality as this," he thundered, "did not the poor woman have a terrible life?" At the conclusion of the trial, the presiding judge asked the jury to consider whether "the killing was done after provocation or in self-defence," a choice which virtually ruled out the possibility of a verdict of "vengeful" murder. After a short deliberation, the jury returned a unanimous verdict of not guilty and Mrs. Sabourin was immediately discharged from custody.[32] What requires explanation, however, is why a basically respectable woman like Elizabeth Workman was executed for killing her abusive drunken husband and Catherine Sabourin, a woman of "questionable" character, was exonerated. Certainly, in the latter instance, the defendant benefited from the rhetorical abilities of her lawyer who developed a convincing and heartrending argument for acquittal; and also from a relatively sympathetic judge, who had stated in his charge to the jury that "the husband's conduct, as related, surpassed anything in barbarity he had ever heard of." More generally, the period between Mrs. Workman's hanging and Mrs. Sabourin's acquittal also witnessed the growing involvement of women in the temperance movement, either in mixed-gender lodges like the Sons of Temperance, or in the highly influential and popular Woman's Christian Temperance Union, which was established in Ontario in 1874 and became a province-wide organization in 1877. Although there is no historical evidence to suggest that the local chapter of the WCTU, for example, was in any way directly involved in Mrs. Sabourin's case, nor that this exceedingly conservative evangelical organization would have condoned her violent actions, one of the principal foci of its various campaigns was to expose the "atrocious" consequences of intemperance on family relations, and particularly the "suffering" it caused innocent wives and children.[33] Comprised principally of Anglo-Protestant middle-class women, the WCTU's perspective on the "victimization" of family dependants by brutish drunken husbands/fathers was certainly premised on highly questionable classist, racist, and ethnocentric assumptions directed against native-born and immigrant working-class men, who were consistently constructed as the primary offenders.[34] At the same time, the WCTU's gender analysis did, as Kathryn Harvey has suggested in another context, create a space for the public naming of wife-battering as a crime,[35] and contributed to a climate in which specific (and largely unsuccessful) legislative and legal changes designed to protect married women were enacted beginning in the late nineteenth century.[36]

THE PREMISE OF THE TEMPERANCE DRAMA

Although intemperance was not the only explanation which emerged out of incidents of spousal murder – sexual betrayal, material greed, and insanity being others – it did emerge as a particularly potent and prevalent one at the turn of the century. This was at least partially because the "vice of drink" condensed various Anglo-Protestant middle-class anxieties associated with industrialization, urbanization, the shifting racial/ethnic composition of the province due to steadily increasing non-Anglo-Celtic immigration rates, and the general breakdown of marriage and familial relations. Within this context, the connection between spousal murder and the inordinate consumption of alcohol as constructed by legal officials, newspaper reporters, temperance advocates, and defendants themselves not only confirmed and fueled these anxieties, but also displaced one identified cause of domestic violence as peripheral to the patriarchal institutions of marriage and the family, and the exercise of husbandly and fatherly authority. Consequently, intemperance was largely perceived as a tragic and disruptive invasion into otherwise harmonious and sacrosanct marital and familial relations, and was considered to be one of the principal sources of male violence and female depravity.

For these reasons, those spousal homicide trials in which drunkenness was a factor not only resembled temperance dramas as played out in the courtroom, but also became part of a broader moral and social critique of the liquor traffic, rather than an indictment of family violence and its rootedness in the unequal relations of power between husbands and wives. This focus accounted for certain ambiguities associated with the prosecution of alcohol-related murders. In the case of husbands, the relative frequency with which manslaughter verdicts were handed down reflected the tensions between the strong rejection of intemperance as an "excuse" for murderous violence and the more empathetic consideration of the effects alcohol had on otherwise "good" albeit morally weak men or the mitigating circumstances under which the crime was committed. These tensions also overlapped with the perception that drunkenness and violence were more likely to occur among the socially marginalized, be it the poor and working classes, First Nations peoples, or immigrants. In the case of murdered and murderous wives, on the other hand, the close association between female intemperance and wifely degradation shaped the way in which they were constructed in the courts in death and were dealt with by the criminal justice system in life. Public and legal assessments of their character determined whether wives were perceived as culpable for their own deaths, were constructed as dangerous, axe-wielding, and vengeful women, or were considered the undeserving and suffering victims of their husbands' vice and depravity.

While the courtroom became a site in which the conduct and character of the accused and the victim became the subject of intense legal and community scrutiny, in the end, the connection between intemperance and spousal murders ultimately left two myths unchallenged: first that strong drink not male dominance was the chief cause of domestic violence; and second, that one of the main benefits of the institution of heterosexual marriage was that it served at least for "good" wives as the primary source of their physical and economic protection.

NOTES

1. Canada, *Senate Debates*, 28 Feb. 1888, 58–9.
2. John A. Gemmill, *The Practice of the Parliament of Canada Upon Bills of Divorce* (Toronto: Carswell & Co., 1889), 52.
3. Between 1870 and 1915, 173 Ontario couples managed to obtain divorces through the passage of private bills through parliament. See *Canada Yearbook 1921* (Ottawa 1922), 825. For contemporary histories of Canada's divorce laws and procedures, and their relationship to issues of national morality, see Constance Backhouse, "'Pure Patriarchy': Nineteenth Century Canadian Marriage," *McGill Law Journal* 31 (1986): 266–71 and *Petticoats and Prejudice: Women and Law in Nineteenth-Century Canada* (Toronto: Women's Press, 1991), 167–99; James Snell, *In the Shadow of the Law: Divorce in Canada, 1900–1939* (Toronto: University of Toronto Press, 1991) and "'The White Life For Two': The Defence of Marriage and Sexual Morality in Canada, 1890-–1914," *Histoire sociale/Social History* 16 (May 1983): 111–28.
4. Toronto *Globe*, 9 Nov. 1912.
5. Toronto *Globe*, 15 Aug. 1912.
6. This is based on a sample of criminal cases gleaned from the Ontario court records of 42 countries and representing four levels of the judicial system: the Police or Magistrates Court, the County Court Judges' Criminal Court, the Court of General Sessions, and the High Court of Justice or the Criminal Assizes.
7. Although spousal murders have not been the subject of detailed historical analysis in Canada and especially in Ontario, see Erin Breault, "Educating Women About the Law: Violence Against Wives in Ontario, 1850–1920," (MA thesis, University of Toronto, 1986), 47–70; E. Stoddard, "Conflicting Images: the Murderess and the English Canadian Mind, 1870–1915," (MA thesis, Dalhousie University, 1991); Karen Dubinsky and Franca Iacovetta, "Murder, Womanly Virtue and Motherhood: the Case of Angelina Napolitano, 1911–22," *Canadian Historical Review* 72 (1991): 505–31; J.A. Sharpe, "Domestic Homicide in Early Modern England," *The Historical Journal* 24 (March 1981): 29–48; Mary S. Hartmann, *Victorian Murderesses* (New York: Schocken Books, 1977); Ann Jones, *Women Who Kill* (Boston: Beacon Press, 1996).
8. Two other prevalent explanations for spousal murders revolved around the issue of sexual transgression on the part of the accused or the victim as well as the highly contentious question of insanity. For the sake of brevity, however, these very important themes cannot be explored in this article.
9. These cases are part of a larger sample of 129 wife and 33 husband murders which surfaced in the Ontario criminal records and newspapers between 1830 and 1920.
10. For an excellent study of coroner's inquests in cases of suicide, see Susan J. Johnston, "Twice Slain: Female Sex-Trade Workers and Suicide in British Columbia, 1870–1920," *Journal of the Canadian Historical Association* (1994): 147–66.
11. For legal definitions of murder, manslaughter, and recognized grounds for acquittal, see G.W. Burbidge, *A Digest of Criminal Law of Canada*

(Toronto, 1890), 216–19; S.R. Clarke, *A Treatise on Criminal Law as Applicable to the Dominion of Canada* (Toronto, 1872), 252–62.

12. For an excellent discussion of this process, see Carolyn Strange, "Stories of Their Lives: the Historian and the Capital Case File," *On the Case: Social History and Case Files Research*, eds. Franca Iacovetta and Wendy Mitchinson (Toronto: University of Toronto Press, forthcoming).
13. For a discussion of chivalric justice, see Carolyn Strange, "Wounded Womanhood and Dead Men: Chivalry and the Trials of Clara Ford and Carrie Davies," *Gender Conflicts: New Essays in Women's History*, eds. Franca Iacovetta and Mariana Valverde (Toronto: University of Toronto Press, 1992), 149–88.
14. See (1877) *Queen* v. *John Williams*, AO, RG 22–392, York County CAI, Box 208 (1877–8); NAC, RG 13, CCF, vol. 1415, no. 119A; Toronto *Globe*, 24 Sept., 30 Oct., 31 Oct., 1 Dec. 1877.
15. (1873) *Queen* v. *James Carrutter*, NAC, RG 13, CCF, vol. 1410, no. 65A; Toronto *Globe*, 21 April, 12 June 1873.
16. See e.g. Toronto *Globe*, 30 Oct. 1877.
17. (1890) *Queen* v. *Thomas Kane*, AO, RG 22–392, York County CAI, Box 249 (1890); Toronto *Globe*, 18 Nov., 19 Nov. 1889; 15 Jan., 16 Jan., 29 Jan., 10 Feb., 13 Feb. 1890.
18. This statement was made by J.J. Kelso, the Superintendent of the Children's Aid Society in Toronto, and was included in the Reverend Joseph McLeod's majority report after the hearings of the Royal Commission on the Liquor Traffic held between 1891 and 1895. Canada, *Royal Commission on the Liquor Traffic* (Queen's Printer, 1895), 529.
19. (1884) *Queen* v. *Robert Edgar*, AO, RG 22–392, Wentworth County CAI, Box 177 (1884); Toronto *Globe*, 7 Dec., 12 Dec., 20 Dec. 1883; 11 Jan. 1884.
20. Toronto *Globe*, 17 Aug., 29 Aug., 1 Sept., 5 Sept., 6 Sept., 7 Sept., 10 Oct., 13 Oct., 14 Oct. 1882.
21. (1870) *Queen* v. *Arthur Pierce*, NAC, RG 13, CCF, vol. 1408, no. 31A; *London Free Press*, 23 June 1870; *Dumfries Reformer*, 14 Dec. 1870.
22. *Stratford Evening Herald*, 6 April 1896.
23. AO, RG 4–32, Ontario Attorney General Files, 1915–#21. See also (1915) *King* v. *Noe Piché*, AO, RG 22–392, Carleton County CAI, Box 25 (1914–19).
24. Toronto *Globe*, 11 Jan. 1884.
25. See e.g. (1900) *Queen* v. *Frank Werke, alias Oreco*, AO, RG 22–392, Welland County CAI, Box 166 (1895–1918); *Welland Tribune*, 1 Dec., 5 Dec., 25 May, 1 June 1900.
26. See e.g. J.R. Miller, *Skyscrapers Hide the Heavens: a History of Indian–White Relations in Canada* (Toronto: University of Toronto Press, 1989); John L. Tobias, "Protection, Civilization, Assimilation: an Outline History of Canada's Indian Policy," *Historical Perspectives on Law and Society in Canada*, eds. Tina Loo and Lorna R. McLean (Toronto: Copp Clark Longman, 1994), 290–305; Mariana Valverde, *The Age of Light, Soap, and Water: Moral Reform in English Canada, 1885–1925* (Toronto: McClelland & Stewart, 1991), 114–16.
27. It is also possible that if and when domestic crimes were committed and evaded the prying eyes of the local Indian agent, they were handled internally

according to Aboriginal systems of law. Although this has remained an unexamined topic in Canadian and especially Ontario legal and feminist history, Hamar Foster does examine the treatment of First Nations peoples under the laws of European colonizers in British Columbia. See Hamar Foster, "'The Queen's Law Is Better Than Yours': International Homicide in Early British Columbia," *Crime and Criminal Justice.* eds. Jim Phillips, Tina Loo, and Susan Lewthwaite (Toronto: University of Toronto Press, 1994), 41–111.

28. (1881–82) *Queen* v. *Jonas Froman*, AO, RG 22–392, Brant County CAI, Box 8 (1882–1903); Toronto *Globe*, 5 Sept., 6 Sept., 7 Sept., 13 Oct. 1881; 12 April 1882.
29. With the possible exception of Jonas Froman, harsher standards were generally applied to First Nations men and men of color who were accused of killing their wives, than was the case with their white counterparts. In the criminal trials which resulted in the execution of the defendant, both Henry White, a Black man from Elmira convicted of murdering his wife in 1875, and Benjamin Carrier, an Onondaga Native similarly convicted in 1880, might well have been found guilty of manslaughter or had their sentences commuted according to the criteria which guided similar cases involving white men. Anderson Veney, a Black man who was also hanged for wife murder in 1893, clearly displayed symptoms of insanity both prior to and at his trial, but both the judge and the jury agreed that he had not been insane at the time he committed the crime. Hiram Richardson, also a Black man, was the only wife killer who was sentenced to life imprisonment on a manslaughter charge. It should also be noted that the motive attributed to all of these murders was sexual jealousy. See (1875) *Queen* v. *Henry White*, NAC, RG 13, CCF, vol. 1414, no. 100A and Toronto *Globe*, 14 Aug., 6 Nov., 12 Nov., 24 Dec. 1875; (1880) *Queen* v. *Benjamin Carrier*, AO, RG 22–392, Brant County CAI, Box 7 (1863–81) and NAC, RG 13, CCF, vol. 1417, no. 141A; (1893) *Queen* v. *Anderson Veney*, AO, RG 22–392, Essex County CAI, Box 36 (1892–4); (1893) *Queen* v. *Hiram Richardson*, AO, RG 22–392, Kent County CAI, Box 66 (1892–4).
30. I have not included Angelina Napolitano's case in my discussion here, since it has already been the subject of a detailed study. See Dubinsky and Iacovetta, "Murder, Womanly Virtue, and Motherhood: the Case of Angelina Napolitano, 1911–1922."
31. (1873) *Queen* v. *Elizabeth Workman*, NAC, RG 13, CCF, vol. 1410, no. 64A; *Sarnia Observer*, 22 April 1873; Toronto *Globe*, 20 June 1873. See also Neil Boyd, *The Last Dance: Murder in Canada* (Scarborough: Prentice-Hall Canada, 1986), 82–3.
32. (1880) *Queen* v. *Catharine Sabourin*, AO, RG 22–392, Carleton County CAI, Box 16 (1863; 1876–80); Ottawa *Daily Citizen*, 31 Jan., 2 Feb., 3 Feb., 24 April 1880.
33. See e.g. Wendy Mitchinson, "The WCTU: 'For God, Home and Native Land': a Study in Nineteenth-Century Feminism," *A Not Unreasonable Claim: Women and Reform in Canada, 1880s–1920s*, ed. Linda Kealey (Toronto: Women's Educational Press, 1979): 151–67; Lynne Marks, *Revivals and Roller Rinks: Religion, Leisure, and Identity in Late-Nineteenth-*

Century Small-Town Ontario (Toronto: University of Toronto Press, 1996), 81–106.

34. See Mariana Valverde, "'When the Mother of the Race Is Free': Race, Reproduction, and Sexuality in First-Wave Feminism," *Gender Conflicts*, 3–26.
35. Kathryn Harvey, "Amazons and Victims: Resisting Wife-Abuse in Working-Class Montreal, 1869–1879," *Journal of the Canadian Historical Association* (1991), 138.
36. These legislative and legal changes included: the passage of the Ontario Deserted Wives' Maintenance Act in 1888, whereby working-class women in particular were granted the option to petition the lower courts for weekly maintenance on the grounds of desertion, non-support, and cruelty; and the 1909 amendment to the Canadian Criminal Code, which introduced whipping as a discretionary punishment for husbands convicted of assaulting their wives and causing them bodily harm. See Annalee Golz, "'If a man's wife does not obey him, what can he do?': Marital Breakdown and Wife Abuse in Late Nineteenth- and Early Twentieth-Century Ontario," *Law, State and Society: Essays in Modern Legal History*, eds. Susan Binnie and Louis Knafla (Toronto: University of Toronto Press, 1995): 323–50.

10 Queer Follies: Effeminacy and Aestheticism in *fin-de-siècle* France, the Case of Baron d'Adelsward Fersen and Count de Warren

Nancy Erber

READ ALL ABOUT IT

> "What books, which companions, which neuroses or mental aberations provoked these shameful practices and the attention of the police?" (*Le Matin*, 11 July 1903)

On July 10, 1903, the daily newspaper *Le Matin* reported a "big scandal" in the French capital. The headline on page two was promising. It read "Satanic Masses," followed in smaller type by the tantalizing nuggets: "Orgies and Saturnalia," and "Monsieur d'Ardouzet [*sic*] Arrested Last Night." That same day another daily, *Le Figaro*, relegated the story to its crime news column deep inside the paper, but it was equally quick to underline salacious aspects of the case with the headline: "A Parisian Scandal." A newspaper well-known for its conservative politics, *Le Figaro* noted coyly that the suspects, "Count de W." and "Baron d'A.," were "from excellent families." What offense were these crime reporters buzzing about? This item, which was buried on page four of *Le Journal* on the day of the arrests, sketched out the story.

> Some time ago, two young men ... rented an apartment between the Avenue Friedland and the Avenue MacMahon for an annual rent of 8,000 francs. The two tenants, Baron d'A. and Count W., had numerous

visitors but soon the visitors themselves attracted the neighbors' attention, and the neighbors reported their suspicions to the Parquet. Police agent Baule, from the Surêté, began an active surveillance of the apartment. Boys from the ages of 12 to 15 were seen; after the schoolday was over, they came and spent many hours in this meeting place established by W. and his friend, d'A. In cognizance of these facts, Monsieur de Vallès, the investigating magistrate, along with Hamard, the chief of the Surêté, and Bloc, his deputy, arrived at the apartment near the Etoile in the evening and arrested Monsieur d'A. They also seized a number of erotic objects and some suggestive correspondance. The police are on the look-out for Count W.[1]

By the following day, all the Paris dailies had picked up on "the scandal at the bachelor pad" as *Le Journal* called it. Others dubbed it "the scandal on the Avenue Friedland" and by citing the location of the offense in the elegant neighborhood near the Etoile, these headlines telegraphed that money, caste, and class were involved. In short order, the accused men's identities were publicly revealed: "Baron d'A" was the 23-year-old Baron Jacques d'Adelsward Fersen, and the missing "Count W." the 22-year-old Count Albert Hamelin de Warren. For the next three months, the investigation occupied a choice spot on the front pages of Paris newspapers.[2]

From the very beginning press reports suggested that the activities which caught the eye of the police were homosexually oriented. For example, when *Le Matin* first broke the news of the arrests it reported that a manservant of "unmentionable sexual morality" had been charged with attempted blackmail. "Monsieur d'Ardouzet" (Jacques d'Adelsward Fersen) was identified as his target.[3] Other Paris dailies used similarly oblique but easily decoded language. *Le Journal* called the investigation a "very delicate affair," while *Le Matin* promised "stomach-turning accounts" of what it termed "sadists' exploits." *Le Matin* described the gatherings as "orgiastic bacanalias" and *Le Figaro* reported that the men had staged "detestable spectacles" and "restorations of ancient saturnalias" in their apartments. Fersen was called "the high priest of the cult" and his apartment on the avenue Friedland a "temple." When the news broke that many of the guests at the afternoon parties were schoolboys, the reporters' references to decadent Rome and golden age Greece drew on well-established associations to pederasty. "More than forty children corrupted," trumpeted one headline.[4]

Allegations that the men and their guests had engaged in Satanic rituals were frequent too in the earliest press coverage as reporters struggled to piece together stories from neighbors' accounts and their own observations of the police and the investigating magistrate ("juge d'instruction") at work. In fact, two daily newspapers used and re-used the titillating headline "Black Masses" on their front-page stories. *Gil Blas*, a newspaper with a well-established bent toward the artistic and satiric, quickly published a lengthy article on the topic by the contemporary writer Jules Bois. It explored the purported links between homosexuality and Satanism, or as Bois phrased it "unnatural acts" and the "inverting ... religion of the Devil." However, by the time of the trial in November, the press's initial excitement over these possibly heretical acts had died down and journalists writing about the case acknowledged their error with phrases like "the alleged Black Masses." Nevertheless, the association of sexual transgression with occult practices is highly suggestive, condensing several currents in turn-of-the-century French culture, including some decadent writers' fascination with transgressive religious practices and deviant sexuality.[5]

Was it sorcery or sexual misconduct that first attracted the attention of the police? In fact, Jacques d'Adelsward Fersen and Albert Hamelin de Warren were arrested and eventually tried on morals charges: public lewdness ("outrages publics à la pudeur") and the corruption of minors ("excitation des mineurs à la débauche"). At their well-publicized trial in November 1903 the two claimed in their defense that they had done no more than hold poetry readings and stage reenactments of scenes from the literature of classical antiquity for an intimate circle of friends. Yet, in staging these *tableaux vivants*, it seemed that the men's aestheticism had gone too far in blurring the boundaries between art and life.

Contemporary anxiety over the presumed corrupting influence of literature and the perceived danger to the republic of an aristocratic class seemingly exempt from the social contract converged in their case.[6] And, there is no doubt that editors and journalists kept the Fersen and de Warren affair alive throughout the long months of investigation because, then as now, sex sells newspapers. Summoning a panoply of commentators in their ongoing coverage of the case, various newspapers enlisted experts on Satanism, contemporary literature, psychology, and sexual aberration to weigh in with their views. The men's family background, military service record, education and affective history provided material for more columns of newsprint. By examining that news coverage today we have an opportunity not only to review the incoherent and fungible state of the new science of sexology, whose tenets were popularized by some of the writers involved. We can also catch glimpses of the emergent rhetorical power of the concept of sexual deviance in the pro-natalist political discourse of the age.[7]

When considering the press's and the judicial system's approach to the Fersen and de Warren affair, it is important to remember that homosexual acts *per se* were not criminalized in the French legal code. Although the code was silent on same-sex acts, the French press was not. To cite one of the most salient examples, the trials of Oscar Wilde in London in 1895 sparked lengthy debates and much editorial comment in Paris.[8] In addition, a decade earlier, Count Eugène de Germiny's arrest in Paris on a charge of public indecency also caught the press's attention. And throughout the *fin-de-siècle*, accounts of arrests on charges of public indecency or other incidents involving homosexual men surfaced briefly in the press, where aspects of the subculture and commerce of male homosexuality had the status of an open secret.[9]

As recent studies have shown, accounts of crimes of passion and the subsequent criminal trials were a staple of the press during the era and journalists often infused their coverage with the drama of a *feuilleton*.[10] Still, the glare of press attention traditionally accorded to instances of sexual misconduct was heightened in Fersen and de Warren's case because the accused men were presumed homosexuals *and* of noble birth. This gave journalists across the political spectrum an opportunity not only to investigate the social implications of sexual non-conformity. It also enabled those of a populist slant to scrutinize contemporary judicial methods and take a position on the persistence or non-existence of class privilege in the criminal justice system of the Third Republic.[11]

Katherine Fisher Taylor pointed out the importance of the pre-trial investigation period when she observed that "jurists have described the French system and its history in terms of an inquisitorial model versus an accusatorial one."[12] The weeks- or months-long *instruction* during which an examining magistrate questioned the accused, interviewed witnesses, and assembled evidence allowed time and opportunity for leaks to a curious public. In addition to the journalists and editors who kept the story alive in the Paris press, the tale of Fersen and de Warren had other authors, of course. Counter-narratives were developed by relatives of the accused who also used the newspapers at times to intervene in the public construction of the case. Most visible in this regard were the men's mothers, who sent letters and made statements to the press. Their attempts to present another side did not always accord with journalists' views of the case or with each other's.

Certainly, the press coverage itself was not entirely monochromatic. While on the whole journalists adopted a censorious stance toward the events (as in *Le Figaro*'s description of the men's parties as "detestable"), not all toed the line. For instance, when the story was still fresh, *Gil Blas* offered some comic relief; its light-hearted commentary contrasted with the tone of moral condemnation which colored much of the press's initial reaction:

> Two young Parisian *gentlemen* who hungered for novelty hosted a series of children's parties at their home. This attracted the attention of the police. It seems that they were introducing the little schoolboys of our *lycées* to the sort of homework that had only a distant relation to the kind the Education Ministry is recommending. In addition, a certain number of ladies and gentlemen joined in these juvenile pastimes, which certainly must have flattered the children, who always long for adult attention ... The principal of the *lycée Carnot* has assured us that in order to protect his charges from being accosted by "shady women" at the end of the school day, he himself patrols the sidewalk outside the establishment. Alas! He hadn't reckoned on "shady men."[13]

Another, *Le Courrier Français*, also deviated momentarily from the newspapers' chorus of moral indignation. It printed a sixteen-stanza comic poem about the case, which was called simply "Black Masses." "The perpetrators," the author observed, "weren't very naughty. Satan was disappointed. He didn't get his money's worth ... Now [the police prefect] Lepine is persecuting them ... If it were up to me, I'd punish these childish deeds by making them copy [Sade's] *Justine* 100 times over." Mocking "benighted inverts" who "don't know how to make love to a woman," these verses demonstrate, as Christopher Robinson has observed, that "public opinion in the [era] was a mixture of contempt and hostility toward male homosexuality."[14]

Unlike Oscar Wilde's trials eight years earlier, the prosecution of Fersen and de Warren attracted few advocates among Paris *literati*.[15] It inspired no defense committees and generated little public debate over personal and artistic freedom. Nevertheless, Fersen was indebted to Wilde, who was both a literary forebear and a model for a certain unconventional approach to life. Like Wilde, Fersen was a dandy and an aesthete and the newspapers would make much of his personal appearance – the flowing locks, fastidious manners, and extensive wardrobe – as well as the exotic furnishings of his apartment. His public statements, circulated in the press, reinforced the image. For instance, when asked at the time of his arrest to state his profession, it was widely reported that he proclaimed with a theatrical flourish that he was "oppressed by literature."[16] And his writing both published and unpublished would, like Wilde's, undergo scrutiny by state prosecutors and the press in search of incriminating lavender undertones.

Yet there were crucial differences between this turn-of-the-century aesthete and his forebears. While the English aesthetes (and their predecessors, the French Romantics) aped and subversively mocked the anachronistic upper-class refinements they adopted, Fersen claimed this manner of living as his birthright. Because of this – his class position and his literary avocation – two popular stereotypes merged in the figure of Jacques d'Adelsward Fersen. On the one hand, he was presented in press reports as an idle and morally corrupt aristocrat. But since he presented himself so emphatically as a writer and reader of contemporary literature, he also served as a public example of the unhealthy influence of modern art. Little wonder that few of his colleagues in literary Paris rallied to the cause! Jean Lorrain, a prolific author of satirical novels as well as decadent, openly homoerotic poetry, commented on the case in his roman à clef *Pelléastres* (1903). The narrator conveyed little sympathy for the men's plight and disposed of their case with this sardonic comment: "Literary poison! We read about it every day in the newspapers, which blow up even the most trivial incidents and give them earth-shattering proportions. This is how an outrageous headline like 'Black Masses' came about, glorifying the petty goings-on in bachelor flats, the little queers' night out on the Avenue Friedland [and] citing it as proof of how strong the contamination is. The Press spread this deluded tale because it knew how it would stir up its readers." But Lorrain later returned to the topic in his role as a gossipy newspaper columnist and offered a public defense of Fersen (whom he had once met and, he claimed, intensely disliked). Published as the men's trial date drew near, his two essays in *Le Journal* debunked the press's initial hysteria about the alleged Satanic practices and described Fersen as a pretentious young man with an intense desire to taste the flowers of evil celebrated by Baudelaire, and thus a legitimate offspring of the national culture. As for his allegiance to Satanism, Lorrain argued: "First of all, Mister Jacques d'Adelsward is a Protestant. Since the Black Mass is a parody of Catholic rites, it would have no appeal for this young snob, who was much more interested in color-coordinating the shades of his neckties with the gems adorning his fingers."[17]

Meanwhile, other writers kept their distance and made no public comment. For instance, Pierre Louÿs, the best-selling author of *Chansons de Bilitis* (1895) and *Aphrodite, Moeurs Antiques* (1896), two Sapphic-themed works, condemned Fersen in private and observed unsympathetically in a letter to his brother: "His vice disgusted both Chrysis and Bilitis [the lesbian heroines of Louÿs' work]. They didn't hesitate to condemn it and they are not prudes. If [Fersen] had listened to them, he wouldn't be in the jam he is now."[18]

Many in the press presented Fersen to the public as Lorrain had – as an effeminate man.[19] For instance, a "prose sketch" in an article titled "The Degenerates" complemented the numerous illustrations the dailies published of the foppish young gentleman. Its solemn introduction made its intent clear: to demonstrate a congruence between the inner and outer man. "We have chosen to reproduce a 'verbal portrait' of Jacques d'Adelsward provided by one of his friends in order to show the true psychological nature of the decadent baron-poet . . . He has a magnificent head of hair, blond, lightly tinted with henna. His fingers are loaded down with rings – at least 2,000 francs worth of gems. He wears loud, attention-getting waistcoats and is never seen without a box of rice face-powder in his pocket. In short, a very elegant get-up, but a little on the eccentric and compromising side."[20] When Fersen's queer aesthetics and effeminate personal style are placed in the context of the French politics of reproduction and the nationalist-masculinist fervor of the turn of the century, it becomes evident that his public persona posed multiple challenges to his observers. It compounded – or confounded – artistic allegiance, sexual preference and class affiliation. This view reemerged in sensationalized form in a pornographic novel titled *The Memoirs of Baron Jacques: Sinful Rutting of the Decadent Nobility* which was published in 1904. It presented a pair of insouciant young sinners, "Baron d'A" and "Louis." Early on "Baron d'A" confesses in a direct address to the reader that he believed himself to be above the law: "I fear that Louis, my beloved companion, my comrade-in-arms, is leading me down a slippery slope. But the hell with it, we're rich. The law only picks on the poor. Besides, my apartment is quite discreet . . . "[21] The contemporary press, with few exceptions, portrayed Fersen as equally arrogant.

The substance of the afternoon and evening parties hosted by Fersen and de Warren continued to pique the press's curiosity, and during the months preceding the trial, the newspapers continued to publish accounts of the parties themselves and the people who attended them. Tantalizing information surfaced about highly-connected guests – or, alternately, Catholic priests – spied at the scene. "The neighbors say that twenty to thirty people at a time attended the parties on the Avenue Friedland," explained *Le Figaro*. "Names have been mentioned which we cannot repeat, but one thing is unfortunately certain. The parties attracted children." As to the afternoon gatherings, *Le Journal* reported that "rumor has it that . . . several men of the cloth are implicated in this dirty business... The boys who visited the bachelor flat during the afternoons... were between eight and fifteen years old. The 'priests' offered them cake, champagne, flowers, ribbons and perfume. If something came up and these strange rites couldn't be celebrated in the 'temple' on the Avenue Friedland, Jacques d'Adelsward and his friends would take long drives through the Bois de Boulogne ... The children, who had been given cakes and sometimes a little money, would go home peacefully and say nothing to [their] parents about it."[22]

Needless to say, Fersen's lawyer Maître Demange protested the quantity and content of the press coverage, observing that "journalists' imaginations have been running wild [and] much has been exagerrated."[23] Yet the press's airing of the details of Fersen and de Warren's alleged improprieties was not mere scandal-mongering; instead, it served a higher purpose. Specifically, it was a reminder to the reading public of an unhappy fact – the existence of male homosexual commerce in the capital. Still, a public-spirited concern with moral order and national hygiene motivated journalists and editors to delve into such a "delicate subject," as it was frequently called.[24] For instance, an article in *Le Matin* referred obliquely to "certain taverns where an unmentionable business takes place" while *Le Journal* noted forthrightly that "ephebes who used to frequent the *Scarabée d'or* tavern on the rue de Dunkerque" were being questioned in the investigation. Yet another article alluded to well-established cruising spots in the city, observing that "young men with clean-shaven faces, dressed in workers' blouses and cloth caps, the type you find every night on the main streets between the *faubourg Montmartre* and the *place de l'Opéra* ... were also welcome at the avenue Friedland." *Gil Blas* commented sardonically that the investigation had "uncovered some surprising facts," namely, that male prostitution, like its female counterpart, existed as an organized, albeit illegal enterprise in the capital. It also quoted "a professional ephebe" who downplayed the shocking rumors circulating about Fersen and de Warren's parties. "We put on pink robes. Sometimes we took them off. Nothing more."[25]

WHO WAS THAT MAN?

> "I often saw [de Warren] on the Champs-Elysées playing with children, making sand castles." (A family friend quoted in *Le Journal*, 12 July 1903)

Baron Jacques d'Adelsward Fersen was the first to be arrested, on July 10. His friend, Count Albert Hamelin de Warren, had left for America two weeks earlier – “fled,” according to most newspaper accounts; “gone to attend his elder brother’s wedding,” explained his mother.[26] Because of his absence, it should not be surprising that when journalists did pay attention to de Warren, he usually received less than flattering attention. For instance, early in the police investigation *Le Figaro* stated flatly that Fersen “appears to be less guilty than his co-indictee Count de Warren.” In a similar vein, another article reported on the incriminating evidence found in that shady character’s apartment. “The Marquis [*sic*] de Warren’s apartment is decorated in dark colors, much more somber than Jacques d’Adelsward’s. Investigators discovered human skulls and other ritual objects associated with Satanism there, and also a very suggestive collection of letters and obscene photographs.”[27]

In contrast, *Le Figaro* described Fersen in sympathetic terms as “a tall and handsome lad, [who] has an advanced degree in literature, [is] a poet, [has] an enormous fortune and intends to make a career as a diplomat . . . ” Still, Fersen did not always fare so well in the hands of journalists, since his elevated social position marked him as suspect. For instance, the first impression (later amended) conveyed by a writer for *Le Matin* highlighted Fersen’s anti-republican connections, describing him as “a fervent Catholic and a royalist who’s equally involved in politics and literature” and a man whose mother had “donated 200,000 francs to found a royalist publication.” Along the same lines, *Le Journal* printed an anecdote about Fersen’s arrest in which each line of dialog evoked a man who had led a privileged existence:

> When the officer arrived at the baron’s apartment, Fersen was in evening dress . . . “You would be better off wearing something a little more modest,” advised Monsieur Hamard, “since you are going to the *Santé*.” “The *Santé*? What is that?” “A prison.” “A prison?” the baron cried in a terrified voice. “You’re not going to subject me to that repulsive promiscuity? I’d rather go to a clinic! Perhaps you’re right. I’d better change my clothes.”

The article reported that Jacques d’Adelsward then opened a closet which contained more than 200 neckties in a variety of styles and colors, countless pairs of shoes and a disorderly pile of silk dressing gowns, shirts with lace-edged sleeves and peplums of different shades. Finally he took out a dark-colored suit and imperiously asked the officer if he could enjoy the privacy of his dressing room while changing his clothes.[28]

After the news of the arrests, reporters quickly delved into the men’s family and personal history. Readers learned that Albert Hamelin de

Warren was a young man who had had to make his own way in the world despite his aristocratic name and title. In fact, his elder brother had only recently obtained from the Pope "the title of Duke, which would bring a newfound prestige to the name de Warren." And since the family had little money, the eldest brother had set off for the United States with Albert in tow in search of a wealthy Yankee bride "to regild his coat of arms," as one journalist noted acerbically. In contrast, Jacques d'Adelsward Fersen had foreign roots and monarchist antecedents. His most famous, or infamous, ancestor was Count Axel de Fersen, who had fought with the French forces during the American War of Independence and served as aide-de-camp to General Rochambeau. Axel de Fersen was perhaps best known as the purported lover of Marie Antoinette, and served the counter-revolutionary cause by making several fruitless attempts to aid the royal family's flight. In addition to his ancestor's historic treachery, newspapers noted the premature and unexplained deaths of two of Jacques' closest male relatives. His paternal uncle, a painter, "killed himself accidentally" and his own father had drowned while on a yachting trip to the Far East. One article also pointed out that Fersen was the product of a mixed marriage: Protestant and Catholic. Students of degeneration theory would find all these tidbits highly suggestive.[29]

On July 13 *Le Matin* reported a rumor that Fersen's family had requested a psychiatric examination for him. "For the record, we noted in yesterday's edition that there might be a question of a very particular type of neurosis in this case."[30] That newspaper was not alone in its approach; journalists offered numerous diagnoses of the accused men and, when focused on Fersen, catalogued myriad examples of his aberrant, mainly gender deviant, behavior. Although their terminology differed (often within the same article), newspapermen often concurred on one central point – that the men's "repulsive behavior," while abnormal, could be explained as the result of a mental disturbance or dysfunction. For example, a journalist at *Le Figaro* noted sympathetically: "This phenomenon is less rare than we think, a highly intelligent and cultivated mind which is unbalanced in a certain area." Even *Le Matin*, consistently among the most hostile in its coverage, allowed that Fersen "deserved to be pitied" because he had "a sick mind," was "unbalanced" and was "a pathological case."[31]

The press's focus on what they termed the men's "psychology" or "special mental state" is indicative of "the obsessively entertained problematic of sexual 'perversion' or, more broadly, 'decadence'" that pervaded turn-of-the-century thought, culminating in a "sudden, radical condensation of sexual categories," as Eve Kosofsky Sedgwick has observed.[32] Reflecting the divergence of opinion among physicians of the time, journalists not only ascribed the men's presumed sexual orientation and transgressive behavior to a mental affliction, they also made their upbringing a central topic of investigation. They found, not surprisingly, that both had been exposed to unhealthy practices and seedy companions in the morally corrupt atmosphere of contemporary Paris. De Warren, it was reported, had suffered from typhoid fever in his youth and thus, a family friend confided, he still enjoyed playing with children. In Fersen's case, as a child he was "fascinated by gems and gaudy costume jewelry, caught up in fantasies of the loveplay of gods and goddesses. He had no interest in trafficking with [female] prostitutes [and was] still so much a mama's boy that his mother was a welcome guest in his bachelor apartment." Even those closest to him had long been concerned about his character or, more specifically, his masculinity.[33]

LITERARY CORRUPTION

> "[Fersen] has a passion for literature, especially ultra modern literature." (*Le Journal*, 11 July 1903)

By the time of his arrest at the age of 23, Fersen had already published several slim volumes of verse and prose: *Poèmes de l'enfance, Chansons légères* (1901), *Ebauches et débauches* (1901), *Notre-Dame des mers mortes* (1902) and *Hymnaire d'Adonis* (1902). An additional volume, *Les Cortèges qui sont passés* (1903), was published while he awaited trial. In general, when the press wrote about Fersen, the man and the writer, it alternated between condemning literature as a cause or seeing it as yet another symptom of his troubles. As a result, both the books he read and the ones he wrote came under press scrutiny. Soon after his arrest, newspapermen began to examine his literary production. Excerpts from a homoerotic poem ("Charming in your Eton collar, in my mind's eye I see you on the tennis court") as well as a prose meditation on death ("I wish to be buried in the village cemetary") were printed in *Le Journal*. *Le Matin* illustrated its probe of "the Baron's psychology" with an excerpt from his latest collection of verse, a volume which contained more than one "apologia for unnatural love," the article noted. One melancholy but "thought-provoking stanza" began: "Women have disappointed my amorous ardor/Near them I've found nothing but disdain and pain/My dream of reaching them has been shattered/ There's nothing left but to flee and fear them/or to offer my heart to other pleasures." The verse buttressed a contemporary view of male homosexuals as misogynists and failed heterosexuals.[34]

Gil Blas joined the fray with "A Study of the Case File," the cleverly worded title making it clear that Fersen's work was being read for diagnostic purposes. The article quoted extensively from the young man's recently published novel, *Notre-Dame des mers mortes*, and concluded that its main character was a thinly disguised self-portrait of the author. "Having lost his elder brother when he was quite young [the main character] was sent to boarding school, where for ten long years ... his hunger for light and open spaces heightened his sense of beauty ... All the motherly kisses and caresses of which his years in boarding school had deprived him became, in his imagination, lost love, the desire for love ... Soon, everyone noticed his highly refined tastes ... "[35]

In addition to examining Fersen's own work, journalists also explored his contact with literature, pointing, for example, to an "unhealthy childhood" in which "he abandoned himself passionately to the reading of erotic literature." One character sketch of Fersen was titled "The Story of a Neurotic" (*Le Roman d'un Névrosé*), cleverly suggesting an association between mental pathology and modern literature. It was illustrated with a sketch of the nattily attired young baron, wearing a cinched-in waistcoat and clutching a walking stick. In another article an acquaintance of Fersen explained that unwholesome books and bad company had indeed gotten him into trouble. "Because he frequented some people who were bad influences, he decided to put into practice what he had read in the classics or in ultramodern books. He called these 'pagan spectacles'."[36] If one wanted to name names, a writer for *Gil Blas* was ready. Pierre Mortier observed that Fersen "adored Verlaine, Baudelaire and Nerval ... Symbolist poets, Decadent poets, bizarre poets ... " And he found that two recent best-sellers had an especially powerful influence on his thinking: Jules Bois' study *Satanisme et Magie* (1895) and Jean Lorrain's novel, *Monsieur de Phocas* (1901), a portrait of the artist as hyper-aesthete.[37]

When Fersen, his family, and attorneys began to marshal arguments in his defense, the young man's association with art and artifice was one they chose to emphasize. *Gil Blas* humorously drew attention to this strategy by calling the scandalous *tableaux vivants* "literary evenings" as if the men's private entertainments were nothing out of the ordinary. *Le Matin* sardonically observed that Fersen fended off his accusers "by singing the same refrain over and over: 'poetry, art, literature, beauty'." At least one guest at the men's *soirées* supported this line of defense and his statement, allegedly given to the investigating magistrate, made its way into the daily press. The man, variously identified as "a poet named Esbach" or "a composer named Desbach," was said to have told Judge de Vallès: "I was at one of the shows that Jacques d'Adelsward organized. It had a very special mystical quality and fine artistic touches. I saw nothing in the least bit scandalous or which could be considered offensive to [conventional] morality." He went on to elaborate that "the *tableaux* were fantastical, but not at all improper. For instance, one day Monsieur d'Adelsward stood beside a bed on which a young man lay draped in a shawl. D'Adelsward recited Baudelaire's "La Mort des Amants" while other young men dressed in togas and sandals, swathed in clouds of incense, played flutes or scattered flowers. 'None of this,' [Desbach] declared, 'was in the least offensive.'"[38]

Satirists and cartoonists exploited many elements of the case, poking fun at Fersen's aesthetic pretensions and at the possible involvement of clergy in this salacious affair. A cartoon printed in *L'Assiette au Beurre* showed two priests reading a newspaper titled "Sublime Ignorance," and remarking: "It says here that the government has just closed down a chapel on the Avenue Friedland where young folks were celebrating black masses." "No doubt those were funeral masses in honor of the Holy Father. Oh, those good boys!"[39] During an era when the state was wresting control of education and property from the Catholic church, the cartoon suggested calculated ignorance on the curés' part. Another illustrated journal, *Le Canard Sauvage*, dedicated an entire issue to the case and, since its contributors were mainly avant-garde writers and popular cartoonists, the issue demonstrated a blatant lack of respect toward everyone involved in the case. Cartoonist Hermann-Paul contributed a sketch of two suave dandies dressed in evening clothes and posing in a fashionable slouch. It was captioned simply "Choir Boys." A sketch by Paul Iribe depicted a beringed and corsetted dandy imploring his lawyer: "You must stop this medical examination. Doctors don't understand poetry, you know!" And Roubille contributed a cartoon of a well-dressed man rejecting the advances of a female prostitute in the Bois de Boulogne. He protested, affronted: "She takes me for one of those vulgar persons who are attracted to women."[40]

THE TRIAL: SENTIMENTAL EDUCATIONS

> "Very unhealthy literature!" (Judge Bondoux, quoted in *Le Journal*, 29 Nov. 1903)

The trial began on November 28 and lasted two days. The public was not admitted, but newspapers reported that the courtroom was "packed with robes" as attorneys came to listen to the testimony. A reporter for *Le Journal* joked that the "cloakrooms at the Court have rarely been busier" as curious onlookers crowded in. The dailies gave the story front-page coverage. The courtroom reporter for *Le Matin* opened his account with a generous dose of venom: "The Black Masses ... in truth this pathetic and downright filthy case doesn't live up to its name ... there's nothing Satanic or superhuman about these two ... and their aesthetic *tableaux vivants*, the clouds of incense, see-through robes, fine pastries and human skulls are really no more artistic than the revolting taste of a pansy hairdresser."[41]

The press coverage was enlivened by hand-sketched portraits of the presiding judge, Bondoux, and of the accused men. The nattily-attired Fersen was pictured in a fashionable slouch; the more somber de Warren was shown gripping the courtroom railing in a rigid, defensive posture. In general, the written accounts also played up the contrast between them; they treated Fersen gently while excoriating de Warren. For instance, *Le Journal*'s court reporter described Fersen as a "smooth talker... defending himself with great finesse and a solid grasp of points of law." De Warren, on the other hand, was "so incoherent that his attorney was heard to say that he regretted not having ordered a psychiatric examination for his client."[42]

The presiding judge led the accused men, as was customary, through a brief recitation of their life stories. Here too the newspaper accounts accentuated the men's differences. De Warren's time at the bar was briefer and his story was on the whole "less interesting," opined *Le Matin*. But "at least he got a few laughs from the audience" when he attempted to explain his role in the affair, *Le Journal* noted. Fersen's performance got higher marks. "His testimony was delivered with absolute precision and unflappable poise. The words were well chosen, his sentences elegantly phrased, his voice well modulated ... all in all, an admirable presentation." Fersen was called to the bar first and, prompted by Judge Bondoux, he began by recounting the travails of his youth. After his father's death he did not respond well, he said, to the program of "virile education" his family proposed. At boarding school, the other pupils called him "a girl" and when a schoolmate took him to a brothel, his revulsion earned him the nickname "stupid kid." It was at school that he was introduced to the work of the authors he most admired: Virgil, Plato, Theocritus, Baudelaire, Verlaine. "Very unhealthy literature!" Bondoux interjected.[43]

Fersen's testimony made it clear that art played a role in his downfall. He explained to the judge that a chance encounter with de Warren at a Mardi Gras ball developed into a friendship because of his attraction to the "very artistic" milieu in which de Warren lived. As for the amateur theatricals held in his own apartment, Fersen testified that he "wanted to put on stage what [he] had read in Baudelaire." Perhaps "it was an inappropriate venue for literature," he conceded, but never, he insisted, were obscene acts committed publicly there. He specifically rejected the role of a corrupter of youth and denied that he had ever enticed schoolboys to come to the entertainments in his home. "I drove to the *lycée Carnot* five or six times to pick up boys I already knew... Once I accompanied de Warren to meet a mutual friend [there]." When the judge asked him if he had exposed the boys to "erotic poetry" and "obscene photographs," Fersen replied acidly: "Yes, I often gave readings of Verlaine and Baudelaire, but this wouldn't teach them anything they didn't already know." As for his collection of photographs (presumably artful homoerotic studies like the ones produced by his contemporary von Gloeden): "I considered them artistic. That's why I displayed them openly in my home."[44]

A number of schoolboys testified for the prosecution, but most newspaper accounts discreetly limited themselves to simply noting their presence and hinting at their identities. One court reporter used it as an occasion to lament the boys' twice-sullied innocence and the shame brought upon their families: "We understand that it would be difficult, in fact impossible, to spare these poor lads and their fathers the pain and humiliation of making this public confession before the judge. But it's absolutely revolting to listen to these twelve and fourteen year-old youths lisp out their accusations and incriminate themselves at the same time ... "[45]

In its turn, the defense attempted to counter the prosecution's one-sided picture of the accused men's character by introducing evidence of their heterosexuality. Fersen highlighted significant encounters with young women when he recounted his life story. First, there was "the girl" who was his first true love. He identified her with novelistic flair as "a gypsy girl with ebony tresses, whom I met in Venice." Then as Fersen confided to the court, came the days when he sowed his wild oats before becoming engaged to "a virginal young lady." "I threw myself into the search for artificial paradises and aesthetic pleasures which I know now are shameful, nothing more than the basest slime. But suddenly I saw the light, the truth, and I made one last effort. I hoped that true love could save me, and in fact I loved a young lady silently, from afar... Little by little hope grew in me. I was almost certain of salvation when all at once my fate was sealed." The moving story of his all-too-brief courtship, one reporter noted, "had a profound and immediate effect on the audience."[46]

In a similar vein, a friend of de Warren attempted to bolster his defense by testifying to his heterosexual exploits. He stated, to Judge Bondoux's evident disbelief, that de Warren had had many mistresses. The judge's dismissive retort gave his attorney, Henri Robert, the opportunity for one of his famed clever replies. As *Le Journal* reported: "Judge Bondoux then turned to ask [de Warren]: 'How did you support these mistresses since you have said that you were broke?' 'With my love,' he replied heatedly. Mister Henri Robert interjected with a sigh: 'Your Honor, you know at the age of twenty, one does not have to pay for one's mistresses' favors; it is only as one gets on in years . . . '"[47] The interchange was featured in all the dailies' accounts, which also noted the courtroom audience's appreciative laughter at the attorney's display of quick wit.

Fersen's sexuality was the focus of scrutiny in Dr. Vallon's testimony. A specialist in mental disorders, he was one of the team of three experts, Mottet, Magnan, and Vallon, asked to assess Fersen's mental state. Presenting their joint conclusions at the trial, Vallon testified that although Fersen exhibited "hereditary defects," they believed he was not "a sexual invert." Reviewing the patient's family history, Vallon noted the presence of "very distinct hereditary defects. One of his grandmothers was committed to an asylum . . . his father also had spent time in an asylum before his marriage. One of his uncles was an epileptic. He should have been brought up under the most stringent moral supervision in order to counteract these hereditary influences, but he was not." One of the ways in which contemporary specialists in legal medicine and criminology participated in the shaping of judicial practice was by evaluating the degree of an accused person's responsibility for criminal acts. Vallon delivered this opinion: "we cannot say that [Fersen] was not responsible. In fact, he has expressed remorse and should have been ashamed a lot sooner. But, we ought to recognize his diminished responsibility because of certain hereditary factors. This merits a certain indulgence."[48]

The second and final hearing on December 3 was given over to the attorneys' summations. The state prosecutor Lescouvé earned compliments from the press for his closing statement, which was "high-minded, well-modulated, and admirably organized." He argued that the men were guilty of both charges and urged that they be penalized in order to set an example. "If our laws no longer permit us to punish the sin, as they did in the Middle Ages, we can still punish the wrong-doers, so that this will not happen again." However, he did call rhetorically for justice tempered with mercy. There was, Lescouvé concluded, another culprit on trial here: "salacious authors who corrupted [Fersen's] mind and perverted his senses."[49]

Unlike the prosecutor's speech, the defense attorneys' closing arguments were summarized sketchily. Reporters noted unenthusiastically that Demange, Fersen's attorney, had given a "lengthy rebuttal" of the prosecution's case in which he argued that the evidence presented was insufficient for conviction. But Henri Robert, de Warren's attorney, gave the expected "fiery oration" in which he minimized the significance of the men's actions – their "petty pleasures" as he called them – and asserted dramatically that the two "were just little fish caught up in the machinery of the state. The big fish has gotten away." As Robert's speech drew to a close, Fersen was said to have exclaimed campily: "Oh, how charming! It's just like being at the theater!"[50]

The judge returned his verdict after an hour's deliberation. The men were convicted of only one charge, the corruption of minors. Bondoux noted in his decision that after all, the acts the men were charged with had not occurred in public. The two were sentenced to six months in prison, a 50-franc fine, and the loss of civil rights in family councils for five years. Having already served six months in pre-trial detention, Fersen was released. De Warren's attorney announced immediately that he intended to appeal his sentence.

There is no record of an appeal and no trace in the public record of de Warren's life after his release. However, Fersen's name soon reappeared in the pages of Paris newspapers, which discreetly reported a suitably romantic suicide attempt on his part. He was discovered unconscious at the gateway to Mademoiselle Maupeiou's (his ex-fiancée's) country villa, a bullet having grazed his temple. After his recovery he went into voluntary and rather public exile in Capri, where he reigned with his young Neapolitan lover Nino Cesarini over the elegant house and grounds of his property the *Villa Lysis* with its custom-built opium den. And he never disappeared entirely from Paris's literary horizon either; he continued to publish a stream of homophilic poetry and prose which was loyally and favorably reviewed for years in small avant-garde journals like the *Mercure de France*. He even returned to the capital briefly in 1908 to found and edit the first homophile literary journal, *Akademos*, which he subsidized through twelve issues. In 1923 he died on his estate in Italy of heart disease, his condition aggravated by years of opium addiction. He was buried, at his request, dressed in pink robes.

Although Fersen and de Warren's case is largely forgotten today, the "Pink Masses Affair," as Jean Lorrain dismissively called it, captured a fundamental tension in the ideological status of homosexuality in the era. Thus, it merits our continued attention.[51] The range and discordance of the newspapers' construction of the case and its principal actors reveals something of the evolving categorization of sexual normality and abnormality at the turn of the century. Homosexuality was categorized simultaneously as a freely chosen vice and an involuntary mental affliction. It was diagnosed as a hereditary condition, understood to be the legacy of degenerate ancestors, and viewed as a social condition, the effect of a corrupting society. Clearly, newspaper stories about the case expressed on a popular level the unresolved contradictions of medical and social commentators' views.[52] The conduct of the trial and its outcome, the tenor of the expert witnesses' testimony and the accused men's personal statements give us yet another glimpse into the dynamic forces at work in the contemporary social regulation of sexuality. When proponents of the "moral order" at the *fin-de-siècle* were attempting to set France on the road to moral and heterosexual responsibility, Fersen and de Warren's queer follies served as a brief reminder that licence still flourished in the land.

NOTES

The research for this essay was generously supported by a PSC-CUNY Award.

1. *Le Matin*, 10 July 1903; *Le Figaro*, 10 July 1903; *Le Journal*, 10 July 1903. All translations, unless otherwise indicated, are my own. It should be noted that Albert Hamelin de Warren, "Count W." in this item, precipitously set sail for the United States on June 26 and returned to Paris in the fall of 1903.
2. The choice of a sobriquet for ongoing cases in news headlines was a common practice at the time. See *Le Journal*, 11 July 1903; *Gil Blas*, 12 July 1903. By July 12, all daily papers had published the men's names fully and accurately. While Jacques d'Adelsward Fersen's name has been rendered in many variations throughout the years, note that in the text of this essay I have chosen to refer to him as "Fersen" since this is the surname he used throughout his adult life. See James Money, *Capri, Island of Pleasure* (London: Hamish Hamilton, 1986), 88ff for an account of his name choice and post-conviction years.

3. *Le Matin*, 10 July 1903. It should be noted that in the French legal code, private acts of same-sex intercourse were not penalized, provided both consenting parties were above the legal age, which had been set at thirteen in 1836. Among many recent analyses of the evolution of the French code and legal terminology concerning homosexuality, see Michael David Sibalis's "The Regulation of Male Homosexuality in Revolutionary and Napoleonic France, 1789–1815," in *Homosexuality in Modern France*, Jeffrey Merrick and Bryant T. Ragan, eds. (New York: Oxford University Press, 1996): 80–101. For a nuanced discussion of changes in the popular and medico-juridical discourse of homosexuality, see Vernon A. Rosario, "Pointy Penises, Fashion Crimes and Hysterical Mollies: the Pederasts' Inversions," 146–176 in the same volume. For a discussion of police harassment and surveillance of male homosexual activity in the *belle époque*, see Peniston, this volume.
4. *Le Matin*, *Le Journal*, and *Le Figaro*, 11 July 1903. A discourse that presumed a shared understanding of the superiority of the present day's 'moral order' and cited the 'moral degeneracy' of particular ancient civilizations was commonplace in the era. For instance, Krafft-Ebing observed in the introduction to the influential *Psychopathia Sexualis*: "We are certainly far beyond sodomitic idolatry, the public life, legislation and religious exercises of ancient Greece, not to speak of the worship of Phallus and Priapus in vogue among the Athenians and Babylonians, or the Bacchanalian feasts of the Romans and the privileged position held by courtesans of those days." Like others, he linked the survival of the state to strict regulation of private morality and warned against incipient "periods of civic and moral decline," whose symptoms included gender confusion. "The episodes of moral decay always coincide with the progression of effeminacy, lewdness and luxuriance of the nations." R. von Krafft-Ebing, *Psychopathia Sexualis*, trans. F.J. Rebman (New York, 1930), 6. For a wide-ranging discussion of the association between the Mediterranean and male homosexuality in contemporary art and literature, see Robert Aldrich, *The Seduction of the Mediterranean: Writing, Art and Homosexual Fantasy* (London: Routledge, 1993). See Robert Nye's two substantive studies on the political effects of *fin-de-siècle* concerns with moral order and disorder, *Crime, Madness and Politics in Modern France: the Medical Concept of National Decline* (Princeton: Princeton University Press, 1984) and *Masculinity and Male Codes of Honor in Modern France* (New York: Oxford University Press, 1993).
5. *Le Matin*, 11 July and 12 July 1903; *Le Journal*, 11 July 1903; *Gil Blas*, 12 July 1903; *Le Journal*, 29 Nov. 1903. The author Jules Bois caused a stir with the sensational exposé *Satanism et Magie* (1895), which examined a contemporary resurgence of Satanism, but the novelist Joris-Karl Huysmans, whose novel *A Rebours* (1884) functioned as a sort of would-be decadents' Bible or handbook, was the key figure in literary Paris to turn his attention to it, in particular in his novel *Là-Bas* (1888). For a comprehensive study of literary decadence, see Jennifer Birkett, *The Sins of the Fathers: Decadence in France, 1870–1914* (London: Quartet Books, 1986). Useful insights on the movement, its precursors and inheritors can also be found in Arnould de Liederkerke, *La Belle Epoque de l'Opium*

(Paris: Editions de la Différence, 1984), and, in the context of homosexual writers and themes, Christopher Robinson, *A Scandal in the Ink: Male and Female Homosexuality in Twentieth Century French Literature* (London: Cassell, 1995).

6. See Annie Stora-Lamarre, *L'Enfer de la Troisième République: Censeurs et Pornographes 1880–1914* (Paris: Imago, 1990). Like the case of the Count de Germiny discussed by Peniston in this volume, it should be noted that the arrest and condemnation of upper-class men like Fersen contrasted with actions of the criminal justice system of the Ancien Régime, when nobles were relatively safe from prosecution for sexual or moral infractions. See Maurice Lever, *Les Bûchers de Sodome: Histoire des 'Infâmes'* (Paris: Fayard, 1985).
7. For a nuanced discussion of the multiple associations of homosexuality in Western Europe in this period, see Eve Kosofsky Sedgwick, *Epistomology of the Closet* (Berkeley: University of California Press, 1990), esp. ch. 1.
8. For a wide-ranging analysis of the English press coverage of the trials see Ed Cohen, *Talk on the Wilde Side: Toward a Genealogy of Discourse on Male Sexuality* (New York: Routledge, 1993). Wilde's extensive literary and social relations in France are discussed in Richard Ellmann, *Oscar Wilde* (New York: Alfred A. Knopf, 1988) and Jacques Langlade, *Oscar Wilde, Ecrivain Français* (Paris: Stock, 1975). For a discussion of the trials' coverage in the French press see Nancy Erber, "The French Trials of Oscar Wilde," *Journal of the History of Sexuality* 6 (April 1996): 549–88.
9. On the usage of *germiny* and *germinism*, see Claude Courouve, *Vocabulaire de l'Homosexualité Masculine* (Paris: Payot, 1985), 17. Examples of other cases in the contemporary press include an item titled "Behind the Polo Stands" which reported the arrest of two men for public indecency in the Bois de Boulogne, printed in *Le Journal*, 4 Aug. 1903. Readers in 1903 also learned of the suicide of General MacDonald in Paris, en route to England from his post in Ceylon because of a homosexual scandal, and of a Parisian dentist's murder of his male lover.
10. For studies of crime, criminology, contemporary social questions, and the press that span the era, see Ruth Harris, *Murder and Madness: Medicine, Law and Society in the fin-de-siècle* (Oxford: Clarendon Press, 1989), and Edward Berenson, *The Trial of Madame Caillaux* (Berkeley: University of California Press, 1992).
11. For a discussion of procedures and pitfalls of the justice system, see Benjamin F. Martin, *Crime and Criminal Justice under the Third Republic: the Shame of Marianne* (Baton Rouge: Louisiana State University Press, 1990). A discussion of the role of the French police can be found in Jennifer Davis, "Urban Policing and Its Objects: Comparative Themes in England and France in the Second Half of the Nineteenth Century," *Policing Western Europe: Politics, Professionalism and Public Order, 1850–1940*, Clive Emsley and Barbara Weinberger, eds. (New York: Greenwood Press, 1991).
12. Katherine Fisher Taylor, *In the Theatre of Criminal Justice* (Princeton: Princeton University Press, 1993), 6. Her point is that the trial itself contains many elements of spectacle.

13. *Gil Blas*, 11 July 1903. Despite the lighthearted tone, the article was titled "Cette Répugnante Aventure."
14. *Le Courrier Français*, 19 July 1903. Raoul Ponchon's *gazette rimée* was a regular feature and could be counted on to poke fun at news scandals and the dominant "moral order." For a discussion of contemporary hostility to male homosexuals, see Robinson, *Scandal in the Ink*, 7. The comic verses underline what Robert Nye observed in *Masculinity*, that (middle- and upper-class male) homosexuals in France had little to fear from the criminal code but needed to concern themselves with "judgments from fellow citizens about the quality of [their] masculinity." See 107ff.
15. It should also be kept in mind that this was the epoch of the Dreyfus affair. For discussions of the two, see Jacques Langlade, *La Mésentente Cordiale: Wilde–Dreyfus* (Paris: Julliard, 1994).
16. See *Le Journal*, 13 July 1903. The earliest news accounts erroneously identified him as a student of law or diplomacy, something which Fersen, who identified himself as an artist, wanted to correct.
17. Jean Lorrain, *Pelléastres*, quoted in *Cahiers Gai-Kitsch-Camp* 21 (1993), 21. His columns appeared in *Le Journal*, 2 and 3 August 1903. As Robinson observed in *Scandal in the Ink*, "the Romantic motif of the artist as social and moral outcast, particularly in its Baudelairian form of the artist condemned to explore evil in order to transmute it into beauty, was characteristic of the turn-of-the-century Decadent movement" (p. 40).
18. In Jean-Paul Goujon, *Pierre Louÿs, une Vie Secrète* (Paris: Seghers, 1988), 84.
19. In this respect I see Fersen's cultivation of his persona and the press's reception/dissemination of it, as an example of Wilde's legacy to cultural practices in France. In his very useful study *The Wilde Century: Effeminacy, Oscar Wilde and the Queer Moment* (New York: Columbia University Press, 1994), Alan Sinfield points out that in Britain "the [Wilde] trials helped to produce a major shift in perceptions of the scope of same-sex passion. At that point, the entire vaguely disconcerting nexus of effeminacy, leisure, idleness, immorality, luxury, insouciance, decadence and aestheticism which Wilde was perceived as instantiating, was transformed into a brilliantly precise image" (p. 3).
20. *Le Journal*, 13 July 1903. See Robert Nye's telling observation of the misogyny embedded in *fin-de-siècle* contempt for the effeminate male in "Michel Foucault's Sexuality and the History of Homosexuality in France," *Homosexuality in Modern France*, 225–41.
21. The novel is attributed to Alphonse Gallais. Originally published in 1904, it was reprinted in *Cahiers Gai-Kitsch-Camp* 21 (1993): 87–131. For discussions of the political and cultural meanings of the pornographic novel in France, see *The Invention of Pornography: Obscenity and the Origins of Modernity, 1500–1800*, ed. Lynn Hunt (New York: Zone, 1993).
22. *Le Figaro*, 11 July 1903, and *Le Journal*, 11 July 1903.
23. *Le Matin*, 17 July 1903.
24. Clearly, the context was contemporary scientific and legislative debates over female prostitution and state regulation of sexuality. For relevant and wide-ranging discussions, see Alain Corbin, *Les Filles de Noce: Misère Sexuelle et Prostitution aux 19e et 20e Siècles* (Paris: Aubier Montaigne,

1978) and Jill Harsin, *Policing Prostitution in 19th Century Paris* (Princeton: Princeton University Press, 1985). The publishing world at the *fin-de-siècle* also witnessed a remarkable increase in sensational exposés of lesbianism and lesbian prostitution in Paris. See Catherine van Cassalaer, *Lot's Wife: Lesbian Paris, 1890–1914* (Liverpool: Janus Press, 1986).

25. *Le Matin*, 11 July 1903; *Le Journal*, 11 and 12 July 1903; *Gil Blas*, 12 and 19 July 1903. In *Gil Blas*' punning phrase, "un traite des blancs" or "white male slavery," took place in Paris.
26. On 14 July 1903 *Le Journal* reported that de Warren's family had announced they had received a telegram from him. He was traveling in the US, passing through New York, Chicago, and Philadelphia, and was expected home in three months.
27. *Le Journal* and *Le Figaro*, 11 July 1903.
28. *Le Figaro*, 11 July 1903; *Le Matin*, 13 July 1903; *Le Journal*, 11 July 1903.
29. The family histories excerpted here for both men appeared in *Le Matin*, 12 July 1903. A similar article on Fersen was printed in *Le Journal* on 13 July 1903. See Lynn Hunt, *The Family Romance of the French Revolution* (Berkeley: University of California Press, 1992) for a finely argued analysis of the socio-political context of sexual slanders involving Marie-Antoinette and the court.
30. *Le Matin*, 13 July 1903. When the doctors' report was presented at the trial and reported in the press, Fersen's mother, the Baroness d'Adelsward Fersen, sent a letter to *Le Journal* disputing not only their findings of a 'degenerate heredity' but also protesting the newspaper's interpretation. See *Le Journal*, 30 Nov. 1903.
31. *Le Figaro*, 12 July 1903; *Le Matin*, 15 July 1903.
32. Sedgwick, *Epistomology of the Closet*, 9.
33. *Le Matin*, 11 July 1903; *Le Journal*, 11 and 13 July 1903.
34. *Le Journal*, 13 and 14 July 1903; *Le Matin*, 12 and 15 July 1903.
35. *Gil Blas*, 12 July 1903.
36. *Le Journal*, 13 July 1903.
37. *Gil Blas*, 12 July 1903.
38. *Gil Blas*, 18 and 19 July, 2 Aug. 1903; *Le Matin*, 17 July 1903.
39. *L'Assiette au Beurre*, 25 July 1903.
40. *Le Canard Sauvage*, 26 July 1903.
41. *Le Journal* and *Le Matin*, 29 Nov. 1903.
42. *Le Journal* and *Gil Blas*, 29 Nov. 1903. The hostility expressed here toward de Warren, the social climber, echoes the tensions that Vernon Rosario isolated in his analysis of French nineteenth-century sexologists' writings on male homosexuals who "disrupted public morals by their gender and class deception." See *Homosexuality in Modern France*, 152.
43. *Le Matin*, *Le Journal*, and *Gil Blas*, 29 Nov. 1903. The article in *Le Matin* called attention to the emphasis put on Fersen's formative years by dubbing the hearing "boarding schools on trial" in a reference to the contemporary debates over a perceived association between single-sex education and homosexuality.
44. *Le Journal*, 29 Nov. 1903.
45. *Le Matin*, 29 Nov. 1903. The writer went on to argue that the boys' exposure to the testimony gave them an inappropriate sexual education.

46. *Le Journal* and *Le Matin*, 29 Nov. 1903. As noted earlier, Fersen was engaged at the time of his arrest to Blanche de Maupeiou, the daughter of a wealthy Protestant industrialist. For an imaginative reconstruction of Fersen's life, see Roger Peyrefitte's novel *L'Exilé de Capri* (Paris: Ernest Flammarion, 1959).
47. *Le Journal*, 29 Nov. 1903.
48. *Le Journal*, 29 Nov. 1903. The Baroness d'Adelsward immediately protested the doctors' findings and newspapers' uncritical reporting of it in a letter to the editor. For a discussion of contemporary theories of hereditarianism and the "neuropathic family," see Ian Dowbiggin, *Inheriting Madness: Professionalization and Psychiatric Knowledge in Nineteenth Century France* (Berkeley: University of California Press, 1991).
49. *Le Journal*, 4 Dec. 1903.
50. *Le Journal*, 4 Dec. 1903. Robert's dramatic assertion that the selective nature of the evidence introduced by the prosecution shielded highly-placed people implicated in the investigation is reminiscent of the rumors surrounding other homosexual scandals, such as "the Cleveland Street scandal" and Oscar Wilde's trials. Fersen's remark was reported in *Gil Blas*, 4 Dec. 1903.
51. The case did live on for a while in the annals of sexual history. For instance, it appears in Georges-Anquetil's *Satan Conduit le Bal* (1925) as the scandalous instance of a young blue-blood "celebrated in the best Paris salons, but [also] a snob corrupted by the pernicious influence of Oscar Wilde and Baudelaire." See *Cahiers Gai-Kitsch-Camp* (1993), 46.
52. Vernon A. Rosario calls this succinctly a "hybrid ontology/pathology" in his essay "The Pederasts' Inversions" in *Homosexuality in Modern France*.

11 A New Man for a New Century: Dr. Crippen and the Principles of Masculinity

Julie English Early

In London, 23 November 1910, the American Dr. Hawley Harvey Crippen was hanged for the murder of his wife, Cora. In October Crippen's trial had lasted five days, but the case itself commanded newspaper attention for nearly six months. Further, it has not only earned Crippen a place at Madame Tussaud's, but also prompted an array of fictionalized retellings, and has figured in retrospective accounts of sensational British crimes for over 80 years.[1] Even with numbers of new entrants to the field, Crippen continues to jostle among a select few contenders for the title of Britain's second most famous murderer.

Despite many dramatic elements, the case played out the most commonplace story of the love triangle gone disastrously wrong. Yet if the plot was familiar, contemporary interest was nonetheless riveted to its steady pace of sensational disclosure. Newspaper coverage of the "North London Cellar Murder" began with the discovery of partial remains presumed to be the missing Cora Crippen; continued through the trans-Atlantic pursuit of the fleeing suspects and their dramatic "Capture by Wireless"; speculated on the adulterous relations of Crippen and his shorthand-typist, Ethel Le Neve; sought detail of the checkered pasts of the principals; shuddered with relish at the grisly forensic detail of the trial; and kept a subdued death watch until Crippen's execution. Crippen was convicted of poisoning his wife with hyoscine, then mutilating her body: beheading it, dismembering it, removing her sexual organs, and burying the fileted remains of her torso in his coal cellar. The state of the remains spoke for a particularly methodical viciousness consonant with other details underscoring Crippen's cold self-interest: his pressed financial circumstances that could be alleviated with his wife's property; his quick installation of his mistress, Le Neve, in the house to live over the remains; and, as a suggestion of abnormality "naturally" reflecting depravity, his flight to Canada with Le Neve cross-dressed as his son. Set behind the closed doors of a seemingly benign if dreary suburb, the case offered adultery, sexual violence, and cross-dressing, all underwritten by greed, and Crippen's questionable professional life of medical quackery conducted at the margins of the law.

In this light, an early *New York Times* article headlined "Explaining the Keenness of Interest" (30 July 1910) would seem superfluous.[2] Yet the author, writing while the trans-Atlantic chase was still proceeding, reflected reporters' pervasive ambivalence about whether to value the extraordinary or the ordinary in the drama. Remarkably, by the close of six months of newspaper attention – and Crippen's conviction – the image of a cold-blooded murderer and mutilator failed to take hold, either in the rapidly shifting perspectives of the popular press, in legal professionals' commentaries, or, for that matter, in the robust latter-day genre of true-crime coffeetable books. Rather, Crippen's unique appeal among murderers is reflected in the title, for example, of Tom Cullen's reconstruction of the case, *Crippen: the Mild Murderer* (1977).

Arguably, the most remarkable feature of the case is the transformation of Crippen from the vicious mad-dog killer and likely sexual degenerate of early police and newspaper speculation to the principled, honorable, and beleaguered little man whose necessary execution was met with rueful regret.[3] However, just as remarkable is how compelling this construction of the banal and the benign appears to have been. While crowds at well publicized criminal trials are often large, even in this the Crippen case excelled: newspapers ran photographs of thousands choking the streets outside the Old Bailey lining up for passes to the trial, which were issued for half-days only in order to accommodate the extraordinary interest.[4] In 1910, the Crippen case could reasonably have been added to a string of public shocks taken as anxious or, in some cases, deplorable signs of the times. The year had already offered the death of King Edward VII, the death of Charles Stewart Rolls in a dramatic aviation test accident, the revelation of Arthur Munby's secret marriage and erotic obsessions, and the street dramas of labor strikes and massive suffrage marches.[5] With events that could be framed as somberly epoch-making or as signs of dangerously experimental technologies or of moral depravity or as disturbing disintegrations of social stability, the narrativizing of the Crippen case is remarkable precisely for what appears a nearly perverse effort to normalize its most sensational elements. The *New York Times* writer's desire to explain "the Keenness of Interest" is, retrospectively, even more pertinent.

No doubt the rather ordinary love triangle was a timeless story, yet in the Crippen case, the fable had been updated with features speaking to a disturbed cultural moment. Embedded in the case were the most timely, up-to-the-minute elements of anxious modernity in a complex city: new technologies, urban anonymities, and disturbances at the boundaries of class and gender. The circumstances of the principals particularly crystallized multifaceted problems of class and "knowability"; in the characterization of its central figure, Dr. Crippen, it also offered a "solution" of principled masculinity that would quiet an array of anxieties about the city, class, technology, and most important, gender and sexuality. Crippen considered in isolation was something of a cipher. But if we view him, as contemporaries did, in relation to the women in his life, we can discern the attempts to normalize the case. These normalizing efforts were distinct features of a culture that increasingly and anxiously seemed out of control. Paramount to this effort would be a redefinition of masculinity. As an antidote to the problems of the modern world, a definitive sense of principled masculinity would, however, require updating and reaffirming knowable constructions of Victorian womanhood to define the resultant new man who must cope – often unhappily – with them. The beleaguered little man constructed from Crippen would, in fact, bear a striking similarity to Modernism's characteristic anti-hero. Against all odds, the narrative that would coalesce was a strangely moral tale of the sad little man pushed to the point where he might discover his own deep wells of character. T.S. Eliot in homage to this version (with a nascent resemblance to his own J. Alfred Prufrock) appeared at a costume party as Crippen; Raymond Chandler would later sigh, "You can't help liking this guy somehow."[6]

"SOME INEXPLICABLE SYMPATHY"[7]

Crippen never confessed, never explained. He granted no interviews, and left as a record only his letters to Ethel Le Neve, sold by her to the newspapers, and his trial testimony, rife with confused lies and stonewalling denials. Crippen was a blank slate to be written on, and not only the contemporary press, but the substantial numbers of memoirists with the least brush with the case would do so – with affection.

Crippen's chief prosecutor, Sir Richard Muir, secured the verdict that put Crippen to death, yet Muir thought him "not the ordinary type of man one would expect to commit murder and then to cut up the body." According to Muir's biographer, "A quieter and more inoffensive-looking little creature it would have been impossible to find."[8] Sir Travers Humphreys, also on the prosecution team, gave an even more apologetic view: "He made a bad mistake and paid the penalty…, but in another country he would I feel sure have been given the benefit of 'extenuating circumstances.'"[9] Crippen's solicitor's clerk would recall, "of all the criminals we ever defended, there was never one who so compelled my sympathy as Crippen."[10] In court, Ethel Le Neve's defense counsel, F.E. Smith, depicted Crippen as an evil seducer, yet privately he memorialized him as "a brave man, and a true lover"[11]; Smith's biographer adds, Crippen "died at least in the very odour of chivalry."[12] Famed barrister Sir Edward Marshall Hall, only a bystander to the case, confessed "I too always felt some inexplicable sympathy for him." Crippen's nemesis, Scotland Yard Chief Inspector Dew who tracked him to Canada, thought "there was something almost likeable about the mild little fellow." The Governor of Pentonville Prison found him "a very mild inoffensive little man who never gave anyone any trouble."[13] According to the prison duty book, the warders, too, "looked upon him not only with respect, but with something like affection."[14]

With surprising unanimity, the defense, the prosecution, the police, prison officials, and commentators express an avuncular fondness for "the little man" who, against all odds, became a Mr. Pooter of crime.[15] In this version, the hapless little Dr. Crippen was an unfortunate who – in his fashion – nonetheless embodied timeless qualities of honor, forbearance, devotion, diligence, and gentlemanly discretion. Filson Young's 1920 introduction to the trial transcript codifies the version of Crippen that prevailed: "the very crime itself brought out in him high human qualities." However, pathologist Bernard Spilsbury's biographers point, perhaps unwittingly, to the most fundamental paradox: Crippen "comes to life … by his very lack of conspicuous qualities."[16]

Indeed, the affection that memoirists express is to a great extent based on absence: Crippen was inoffensive, said almost nothing, and made no trouble. His pleasant but empty demeanor of good manners caused no discomfort. In this version of Crippen, gone is the medical charlatan, the predatory patent-medicine con man with at least one business associate well-known to Scotland Yard's fraud squad. Gone is the adulterer and the attendant speculations on sexual degeneracy. Gone is the man of peculiarly little affect with virtually no intimates and no comprehension that anyone might have been concerned with his wife's welfare. The "inexplicable sympathy" for Crippen is explicable, not in relation to Crippen himself, but only through his relations to his mistress, Ethel Le Neve, and to his wife, Cora. This version of Crippen emerges to reflect a broader desire, in unsettled and unsettling times, to construct masculinity by determining its correct relation to appropriate and inappropriate femininity. With tempting details in the case to confound easy class and gender typologies, it would require a determined effort to define appropriate femininity by constructing first, the dutiful innocence of Ethel Le Neve, and second, the sluttish vulgarity of Cora Crippen.

"A MADDENING CLIENT"[17]

Although Ethel Le Neve was sought with Crippen on suspicion of murder and mutilation, she was charged at the Bow Street Magistrates' Court only as an accessory after the fact. In a one-day trial at the Old Bailey (25 October) following Crippen's conviction, Le Neve was found not guilty of criminal knowledge which, the prosecution maintained, had prompted her to disguise herself as a boy for nearly a month while fleeing with Crippen to begin a new life in Canada.

Like Crippen's character, Ethel Le Neve's is constructed in multiple narratives: of her family and acquaintances in the newspapers, in Crippen's letters, in her defense counsel's narrative, and in her autobiography written for the *Daily Chronicle* after her acquittal. Less of a blank slate than the silent Crippen, Le Neve, with an array of blots on her record, posed something of a challenge to the ultimately successful defense strategy which offered her as an example of innocent young womanhood. In presenting Le Neve's case, her defense chose not to address specific points of her behavior, but overrode them to construct a broader innocence of type. Further, her counsel, F.E. Smith, placed Le Neve within a larger cultural narrative that would implicate the jury in his client's fate, rather than separate them from her. Nonetheless, remaking the independent working woman to construct her as everyman's daughter required deft moves to naturalize and neutralize what was regarded by many as a particularly threatening new type.

As one of the new breed of women office workers, Le Neve's circumstances easily fit features highlighted in works of cultural grumbling such as those included in G.K. Chesterton's timely *What's Wrong with the World* (1910). The shorthand-typist Le Neve ventured beyond clearly defined lower-class factory work or domestic service to the somewhat indistinct mixing of classes in the office. In the 1890s when clerical work began to open to women, it had seemed suitable for middle-class women, yet low wages and reservations about gentility "in business" soon made clerical work primarily a top tier for self-improving working-class women.[18] However, with class distinctions less clear than in retail clerking or waitressing – two areas offering greater employment for women – the relation of the clerk-typist to the men of the office, especially the manager, could blur distinctions of the private and the public. These are precisely the terms in which Chesterton's objection is framed:

> Modern women defend their office with all the fierceness of domesticity. They fight for desk and typewriter as for the hearth and home, and develop a sort of wolfish wifehood on behalf of the invisible head of the firm. That is why they do office work so well; and that is why they ought not to do it.[19]

Although Chesterton suggests that the office worker may be a dupe complicit in suspect business practices, the "wolfish wifehood" of the too loyal employee also clearly threatens the sanctity of middle-class domestic peace.

If the young woman office worker could be decried on Chesterton's conservative grounds of misdirected hyper-femininity that threatens domestic class boundaries, she could equally be deplored on the grounds of a presumed alliance with suffrage causes. The notable suffrage marches of 1909–10 organized marchers under occupational banners, including contingents of office workers. Further, feminist playwrights often found working conditions of the burgeoning ranks of women retail and office clerks ripe for exposure.[20] Thus, the portrait of the working woman was tinged with the potential immorality of the available woman, if not the abnormality of the mannish one.

In Le Neve's case, professional and private circumstances had afforded an unusual degree of freedom. Unlike women workers in large sex-segregated offices, she moved daily in a mixed office, and lived in lodgings without restrictions on her movements – a freedom she exercised. Crippen and Le Neve "kept company" for seven years, and had begun sexual relations almost four years before the murder with afternoon trysts in rooms rented by the hour. For more public moments, their business relations offered a cover – they dined frequently enough at Frascati's to have a favorite table. And the night after the murder, Le Neve, according to Crippen's testimony, stayed with him for the first time at his home, 39 Hilldrop Crescent. Over the next few weeks until she moved in, she returned to her own lodgings only to pick up a few things. As a 1930s retrospective of the Edwardian decade observed, "[y]oung women found opportunities of self-realization such as they had never known before, and corresponding facilities for going astray."[21] Contemporary with the Crippen case, reviewers of H.G. Wells's *Ann Veronica* (1910) were outraged by a heroine prepared to live with her lover and have his child without marriage. In a statement widely reprinted in the newspapers, Le Neve's landlady, Mrs. Emily Jackson, gave an account of nursing Le Neve following a miscarriage a little more than a year before the murder. Mrs. Jackson, who expressed motherly feelings for Le Neve, counseled only that Ethel's involvement with a married man might lead to unhappiness – a prediction qualitatively different from the "unhappiness" of the Victorian tale mixing the fallen woman, abandonment, foundling hospitals, and desperate prostitution. After a brief recuperation, the modern Miss Le Neve returned to work.

If Le Neve's independence as a "pink-collar worker" could raise vague alarms, they would only be exacerbated by her clearly distant relations with her family. In Le Neve's case, the history of a good daughter whose family had championed her self-improvement was not readily available. She had left behind her birth name of Neave to invent her own romanticization of it, had pastoralized her provincial East Anglian origins, and had severed connections from the gritty Camden Town neighborhood where she had been raised after the family's move to London. After briefly living with her married sister, she moved to lodgings at a much improved Hampstead address.[22] For readers of her autobiography, she underscores respectability: "She, I may say, was the only landlady I ever had."[23] However, at the point of crisis, Le Neve's parents appeared to have reservations: Walter Neave, in an appeal to his missing daughter, notably fails to express certainty of her innocence, or fear for her in the clutches of a man sought for murder; on 17 July, the *Daily Mail* published his "open letter" urging Ethel "to give yourself up," warning that "[e]very hour that you stay away you are making the situation terribly worse for yourself." On the pair's arrest in Canada, her parents cabled her to "tell all you know to the authorities."[24]

Le Neve's defense team decided that that would not be wise. Ethel did not testify, nor did the defense present any evidence, but instead relied solely on F.E. Smith's closing statement which was a narrative of character. Smith would construct Le Neve as a type derived not from a "different" working-class ethos, but, he reminded the jury, from the happenstance of family fortunes: "ten or eleven years ago, at the age of sixteen or seventeen, an age which I hardly need to remind you young girls in happier circumstances are going to a finishing governess, it became necessary for her to earn her own living as a typist." Ethel's transformation to everyman's middle-class daughter – albeit disadvantaged – proceeded as Smith described the perils to a young woman entering the public world. What chance would she have, "a schoolgirl aged seventeen, an age when most of you would be shielding your daughters in happy homes from the world?" Crippen "was the one really important figure looming so largely in her life." Against that influence, Smith asked the all-male jury "to think of the seven years, and how they were spent, and contrast them with the lives that you give to your daughters; seven years of drab and dreary toil by day as a typist; by night a gloomy lodging-house, and this in the very dawn of womanhood!"[25] Understandably susceptible, and (under other circumstances) admirably loyal to authority, she was herself a victim, not only of Crippen, but of parental failures of fortune that the middle and lower-middle class jury members, too, could experience to place even their own daughters at risk. In short, Le Neve was less a threatening or assertive climber than the product of social forces encroaching on a (mythologized) happy home.

In an anecdotal account, however, Smith was said to have taken in private a line quite different from that contained in his address to the jury. He told the Lord Chief Justice that Le Neve had not testified in her own behalf because "he knew what she would say."[26] Unlike her defense counsel, Le Neve did not see the virtue of continued silence. Her newspaper autobiography begins and ends with her reasons for telling all: as she rebuilds her life, she wishes to be free of any onus that might attach to her – despite the "not guilty" verdict – from misinterpretation of specific incidents. Her explanations, she trusts, will "[soften] the harsh judgments of my critics."[27] But with multiple narratives beyond that of the courtroom in play, Le Neve's autobiography must necessarily have a diffuse agenda. It is, as Smith anticipated, an uneven performance. Throughout, her self-portrait strives for the sentiments that the young woman he described might have; perhaps not surprisingly it reveals peculiar blind spots about what might qualify as normal or abnormal. The temptations to explain were legion; succumbing to them produced, not a coherent portrait, but an oddly *ad hoc* self-construction responding to shifting demands.

Somewhat imprecisely following Smith's lead to construct "our daughter," Le Neve recalls a Norfolk childhood of tree-climbing, catapult-shooting, and "tomboy pranks" to suggest a modern androgynous youth fascinated by trains and engines. The *joie de vivre* of the strapping New Young Miss sets up (and explains) a cruel irony: "[l]ittle did I imagine then that I was fitting myself to play the part of a boy in real life";[28] at the same time, however, her "naturalization" does much to undo Smith's careful portrait of a fragile and dutiful daughter.

In the trial Smith strategically reduced Le Neve to a "typist"; in her own story the claim for greater importance as "Dr. Crippen's private secretary" was irresistible. Crippen's marginal business dealings had commanded newspaper attention, but business fraud, even as it reflected on character, was too complex and tangential an issue to figure in either trial. Yet readers of the newspapers could not remain unaware that her ten years with Crippen had spanned two press inquiries into company fraud, his private entrepreneurial ventures from convenience addresses marketing preparations such as the suggestively named "Amorette," and his unqualified practice of dentistry. Le Neve's attempts (unevenly) to shade her background, and (unwisely) to assert her responsibilities in business preface the more delicate tasks of explaining, first, her intimate relationship to Crippen, and second, her cross-dressed flight with him from police inquiries. Her language of calm sympathy and support place the relationship in an appropriately modest key: their "friendship deepened almost inevitably" as its elements of "gratitude," "obligation," and "infinite patience" became "real love". He was "the only person in the world to whom I could go for help and comfort"; she was his respite from "angry words," and scenes of "a stormy character" that left him "unhappy at home." Mutual mildness, not passion, drew them together.[29]

Just as the tenor of their relationship was subdued, so too, she would have the reader understand, was their very conventional domesticity. The crucial sequence of events in Crippen's and Le Neve's version is this: Cora was last seen alive late on the night of 31 January. On 2 February, Crippen told Cora's friends that she had been called suddenly to America on business, but he told Le Neve that his wife had left him. That night, according to Crippen's testimony, Le Neve slept for the first time at his home (she modifies the haste: "As far as I remember ... the second week in February"). On 20 February, less than three weeks after Cora had been "called away," Ethel accompanied Crippen to the Music Hall Guild's annual fund-raising gala; they sat with Cora's friends and Ethel wore Cora's jewels – which regrettably "attracted so much attention." (She protests, "all I wore ... was the 'rising sun' brooch.") Their reception was, she thought, unreasonably chilly – and unfair because "neither of us was very anxious to go," but the thrifty Dr. Crippen had bought tickets that must not be wasted.[30]

Despite what might appear an unseemly promptitude in taking her place in Crippen's home, Le Neve would attempt to cloak an unattractive blush of materialistic entitlement with middle-class virtues as she understood them. While Smith created the image of our middle-class daughter, Le Neve promoted one of our middle-class wife, a prudent (if precipitous) suburban wife managing the household for Crippen's comfort and managing herself as a credit to him. At 39 Hilldrop Crescent, she quickly embarked on tidying – and appropriating. Several pieces of furniture were sent to storage. She asked readers to understand her dismay: the house "was furnished in a higgledy-piggledy way. . . . The only thing in the house which I liked was the ebony piano." Not only was there "scarcely anything which matched" but the "extraordinary litter" made it "almost impossible to keep it as tidy as I should like." The state of the household was a tremendous challenge, "however, I made the best of things as I found them." The efficient office-wife that Chesterton had imagined prudently counseled closing off some of the rooms ("I economised in the household work as much as possible").[31] In her domesticity with Crippen, Le Neve demonstrated an appropriate, responsible respect for tasteful and prudent materialism, and in the couple's union, presented a calm mingling of disembodied mild souls whose physical coupling few would be tempted to imagine. If passion had been successfully erased, to an even greater extent perversion was unimaginable.

As one symptom of the "normalizing" impulses throughout the case, the cross-dressing, after initial reports, did not suggest deviant sexuality; the father–son subterfuge stood instead – despite testimony of lunch-hour trysts in cheap hotels and a miscarriage – for an immature, child-like, even absent sexuality for the "tiny" pair.[32] When they were still missing, character sketches by acquaintances had tipped toward "irregularity." Crippen was "not a man's man," one ventured; he was, for example, fond of dressing as a woman in home costume entertainments. Le Neve's father thought that Crippen was probably "masquerading as an old woman. His gait, his effeminate mannerisms, and his gentle manner all combine to make such a make-up easy for him." He was also certain that Crippen would be wearing goggles to disguise his remarkable bulging eyes and would have fled to France (where presumably a man dressed as an old woman wearing goggles would excite little notice). Early in the case, however, a Scotland Yard spokesman set the tone for how sniggering suggestions of deviance would be managed. Responding to early reports of Ethel's disguise aboard the *Montrose*, the "unnamed official" gave out perhaps the most peculiar bit of popular wisdom in the case. To calm speculation, he offered a solemn if improbable reminder: "It is," he advised, "by no means an uncommon practice for young women in long-distance liners to pass as boys in order not to lose, by confinement in the female quarters, the company of a father or brother."[33]

Ethel's version of their flight takes a more ebullient, but no less respectable and innocent tack. She explained that she was persuaded by Crippen to flee only to allow "scandal" to die down. The previous day he admitted to police that he had lied to Cora's friends and to Le Neve when he announced that Cora had died in America about two months after leaving him (or being called away on business – his story to her friends). To his knowledge, he now insisted, she was still alive. Thus, Ethel faced the scandal of living with a married man, not a widower (just, however, as she had in the two months before Cora's supposed death). In these bizarre contortions, the absence of a rationale for the boy-disguise is submerged beneath the sheer fun of the "merry joke," and "the excitement of adventure." After the channel crossing, she recalls awakening "fresh and cheerful . . . full of high spirits." A visit to a Rotterdam barber to improve on Crippen's inexpert job is especially merry: "When I came out with a poll as closely cropped as Jack Sheppard, we both burst out laughing." "They were very happy days": as perfect tourists, they enjoy all that Brussels offers, but soon wished for new sights. On a whim, "in a quite accidental way," they book passage to Quebec for yet more adventure: "I was quite easy and free from care as I followed Dr. Crippen on to the deck of the *Montrose*."[34]

Until the shock of their arrest, it had been nearly a month of mirth. However, "[w]hat followed is a long and dreadful nightmare." Only after her acquittal can she now, in her autobiography, convey the high spirits of the two chums together, the amusement of the "boyish escapade."[35] The irrepressible child on a lark, on the one hand, sharply countered Smith's portrait of somber and dutiful compliance with Crippen's desperate plan. On the other, it cashed in Le Neve's own narrative plant of a free-spirited, gender-bending childhood. Yet the incoherence of the two stories mattered little; both versions removed images of vigorous, desirous adult sexuality to a comfortable distance that dovetailed nicely with a socially-sanctioned distaste for addressing potential irregularity, or at bottom, adult sexuality at all. After all, the man who had concocted "Amorette" might well understand the need it was marketed to fulfill.

Le Neve's letters to Crippen were buried with him at his request. However, his letters to her were reprinted in the newspapers, and each is touchingly framed by words of longing before settling down to respond to her queries. The main business of each letter is business. The only personal request Crippen made of Ethel was that she take his first or middle name, Hawley or Harvey, as a remembrance. On the day Crippen was hanged, Le Neve was in Southhampton boarding a ship for Canada under the name "Miss Allen." Crippen had named her his beneficiary in the will he wrote two days before his execution. And, leaving little to chance, she promptly dropped a friendly note to Crippen's solicitor to remind him of it. She later filed a claim for Cora Crippen's property as well.[36]

"EXTENUATING CIRCUMSTANCES"

Ethel Le Neve was cast as the neat, trim, loyal, sensitive (yet fun-loving) innocent largely through an audience's act of will and desire to make a cast of characters meaningful through a reassuring typological mapping. The portrait of Cora Crippen that emerged was that of Le Neve's opposite. Legally, the victim's name was Cora Crippen. Born in Brooklyn, Kunigunde Mackamotzki had early on simplified her first name to Cora. She was, however, known in press accounts almost universally by her stage name, Belle Elmore. In his testimony, Crippen never used her name at all: she was the woman, this woman, that woman. Shortly after the Crippens' move to London (in 1897, he was sent to establish an office for the American company Munyon's Remedies), Cora began exploring opportunities for a career in the music halls. They lived in a series of rooms in faintly raffish streets in Bloomsbury. In her early efforts, under Crippen's aegis as the "Bright Lights Company," she was billed as Macka Motzki. Even as (the non-ethnic) Belle Elmore, she had limited success: some bookings in London, and out of town tours. At the time of the murder, she had not performed in some years, instead devoting her considerable energies to the Music Hall Ladies' Guild in support of needy performers, retirees, or their survivors.

The Guild met each week at Albion House, the Oxford Street building where down the hall Crippen had offices both for the Yale Tooth Specialists, and Munyon's Remedies. On 2 February, Crippen had notified the Guild that Belle had been called away suddenly on personal business and would be unable to fulfill her duties as treasurer. In the middle of March, he began relaying them news of an illness that continued to worsen. On 26 March, her obituary appeared in the stage tradesheet, the *Era*.

In the very gray area of the status accorded music hall performers, the women of the Guild represented achievement and respectability. Some were still performing; some were wives of well-known performers; others had retired in comfort after successful careers. They all counted Belle Elmore a friend. When Crippen informed them that Belle had been called away, they regretted they had not seen her off with flowers at the station. As the weeks went on, they were concerned that, so unlike her, Belle had not written. Most disconcerting, in less than three weeks, Crippen and Le Neve attended the Guild gala – with Belle's distinctive rising-sun brooch pinned on Ethel's bosom.[37]

With news of Belle's death in California, they were distraught, and they expressed the wish to send a wreath at least for the grave. Crippen's account of his wife's demise, however, was not only vague, but incoherent. Clearly, having thought through only the broadest outline of his story, he invented contradictory details in apparent surprise at being pressed for them with the result that within a week, the Guild women went to Scotland Yard to ask for an investigation. There, Inspector Dew put them off: He temporized that Crippen's wife may have left him; Crippen's details may have been confused in his shock; or he may just be reticent to tell "his business to the world."[38]

The Guild women refused to accept the dismissal. They searched for any confirmation of Crippen's story, checking shipping lines, inquiring of County officials in California, even enlisting an amateur detective. Guild members touring in America pursued inquiries there. They wrote to Crippen's son (she had died staying with him, Crippen improvised, and provided a Los Angeles address); however, they soon learned that Crippen's son had married, moved, and the couple had just lost their first child – all events unknown to Crippen.[39] When after two months they received a response, they learned that he had not seen Cora. Their second visit to Scotland Yard was fronted by a Guild member's husband, John Nash, who used a social acquaintance with the executive head of the CID to get attention at the top. As a result, Chief Inspector Dew was told to follow up.[40] Dew interviewed Crippen on Friday, 8 July, and left largely satisfied with his account: his wife had left him; she was to his knowledge still alive; and he had lied to save face. However, when Dew returned in a few days to clarify a few minor points, he found that Crippen and Le Neve had fled. A subsequent search of house and garden turned up the filleted torso buried in the coal cellar. International bulletins immediately followed. Without the Guild women's persistence there would have been no inquiry; without John Nash's connections, the women would continue to have been ignored; without Crippen's panicky flight, the case would have been closed. Clearly, Belle had friends.[41]

Guild members all gave warm testimonials to the newspapers about their friend; reporters quickly tracked down others for comment as well. Tradesmen in her neighborhood found Mrs. Crippen friendly, "a very charming woman . . . a very well dressed lady . . . very quiet." The milkman found Mrs. Crippen "very pleasant . . . always very nice . . . and about the last woman I should ever think would be murdered." Her family in Brooklyn shared letters indicating a warm-hearted, affectionate nature. Crippen's partner in the Yale Tooth Specialists spoke of her "charming manners," and added, "what passes my understanding is how Crippen could have thrown her over in favour of his typist."[42] Hunting for photographs, the newspapermen found a variety of costumed publicity shots, and they found one Adeline Harrison who would eagerly share her impressions of Belle Elmore at great length.

Mrs. Harrison was variously identified as a friend and neighbor. She was neither. She had, however, known Belle Elmore for twelve or thirteen years; she had been hired to help write an act for her when Belle first arrived in London. Mrs. Harrison's story is more than anecdotal recollection: it is, like later overviews of the case, a fully imagined narrative, a "docu-novelette" of the character of the relations among the three principals and how they developed. As a portrait of Belle Elmore, it is also a virulent account that would displace the numbers of warm remembrances.[43] In Mrs. Harrison's view, Belle was a vulgar and domineering slattern. She had no talent, no taste, and was fat, greedy, self-indulgent, and capricious. She pinched pennies for the household and spent extravagantly on clothing and entertainment. She slept late, and (incontrovertible evidence of her character) she was a vile housekeeper. Mrs. Harrison detailed with relish the setting of domestic squalor. At 39 Hilldrop Crescent the grimy windows were always kept tightly closed; lights were seldom on throughout the house. "They lived practically in the kitchen, which was generally in a state of dirt and disorder... dirty crockery, edibles, collars of the doctor's, false curls of her own, hairpins, brushes, letters, a gold jewelled purse, and other articles." In the next sentence she completes the kitchen scene: an untidy female cat "was scratching wildly at a window in a vain attempt to attract the attention of a passing Don Juan."[44]

Even without Mrs. Harrison's pointed segue, the equivalence of household squalor with sluttish sexuality was a recognizable code. In Edwardian studies, housekeeping had become an icon of morality in social investigators' probes of East End life. Point by point, Belle fit the pattern: wasteful, more concerned with personal adornment than wholesome nutrition, careless of her things, untidy, and most damning of all, a late sleeper. It is telling that Mrs. Harrison's thumbnail sketch of Ethel Le Neve's attractions highlighted everything that she found lacking in Belle: "the quiet, ladylike, unassuming typewriter, always to time, neat in appearance, methodical, obedient." In Mrs. Harrison's view, it was no contest.

One's public face, however, could be deceptive; careless observers might overlook telling signs. Only the home would tell, and while an East End interior might be predictable, the uniform suburban facade might hide a middle-class imposter. At the least, the brick rows could mask increasingly fine middle- class gradations. Discerning the truth, as Sims had suggested, required imaginative entry into the home to identify the telltale markers of taste and values that would peel one thin tier off another.[45]

Curiously, in Crippen's trial the image of a sluttish Belle became useful to both defense and prosecution; a self-indulgent and immoral woman was exactly the sort, as Crippen's defense maintained, to disappear with another man who would give her greater luxury. The prosecution, too, benefited from a general picture of a woman who wanted murdering; although their witnesses spoke well of her, the image remained of the sort of woman one liked if one liked that sort of woman. Yet unlike Crippen's well-documented adultery, there was no evidence of Belle's sexual promiscuity. The most that Crippen could suggest was her relationship with Bruce Miller, the music hall performer whom she had not seen in six years. Much was made of his letters – newsy letters with no compromising content apart from the much debated significance of their close, "love and kisses to Brown Eyes." Miller traveled from Chicago to deny flatly any "illicit relationship." To the direct question, "Were you her lover, sir?" he answered, "I was not."[46] The only other suggestion of sexual promiscuity came, again, from Crippen – reaching even further back in time. When he had met his wife in Brooklyn nineteen years before, he testified, she was living alone, but she was "under the protection" of an older man.

Belle's illicit sexuality was "established" not by evidence, but by suggestion, and even that was thin. But the generic type could be suggested in other ways; if the purportedly free and easy morality of the 'music hall class' couldn't be precisely grounded by fact, the generality of class could be conveyed in ethnicity. Cora's sister, Mrs. Theresa Hunn, had come from Brooklyn to testify to Crippen's lies to the family about Cora's death, but on the stand had to respond to unusual interest in the family itself. Having clearly stated that she was Cora's full sister, Mrs. Hunn had further to clarify the simple fact in three separate responses: "I am the sister of Belle Elmore … Her maiden name was Cora Mackamotzki." "I am a full sister of Belle Elmore. My father's name is Mackamotzki." "Mackamotzki was my sister's maiden name." And, at last, what was wanted: "My father was a Pole."[47]

Other opportunities to suggest Belle's type came more directly with important physical evidence. Thrown into the coal-cellar grave with the filleted torso were several Hinde curlers still wrapped with hair – dark brown at the roots and blond at the ends. Many testified to Belle's great care with grooming and especially that she "was very particular about her hair"; thus her close friend Clara Martinetti said she had "noticed when her hair was a little untidy from taking her hat off that it was darker at the roots." Mrs. Harrison, however, was ready with Belle's private rather than public appearance. When her hair was still down in the morning before she had dressed, the dark roots were very noticeable, and, she added, she knew Belle had made poor Crippen bleach her hair.[48]

As much as the supposed character of the victim was gratuitously interwoven into the trial, in its points of law, the five-day trial was not a trial of character. Fully three days were given over to forensic evidence to prove the remains showed poisoning by hyoscine and, most important, that the remains were those of Cora Crippen. Of critical importance was whether a mark on a scrap of skin was an ovariotomy scar, or simply a fold mark. Crippen recalled that when they first met "she had had some miscarriage or something of that kind."[49] With the removal of her ovaries before she was twenty – her sister testified to having seen a "fresh scar" a few months after her marriage to Crippen – a highly speculative pall was cast by what such "female trouble" might have meant.[50] The medical evidence was, however, so badly managed, and in its detail, so hopelessly confusing to the jury, that Lord Chief Justice Alverstone's summing up framed the case in terms the jury could more readily grasp. In his charge to the Crippen jury, they must first, he stressed, understand the character of the principals, particularly, that of the victim.

While Alverstone reminded the jury that "this is not a Court of morals, this is a Court of law," he nonetheless pronounced a view of both victim and accused: "The fact that Mrs. Crippen, or Belle Elmore, was an immoral woman at some time, the fact that the man confessedly is a very immoral man" is not, however, the issue. He warned, for example, that Crippen's relationship to Le Neve and his lies to Belle's friends should only be considered as they bear directly on the case. But of clearly greater moment, "Now, what was the character of the woman?" Alverstone answers himself: "a woman who had had a past." Thus "a woman making very warm friendships, very popular, very vivacious" appeared not to have the good taste of appropriate reticence, and relished adornment, particularly "jewellery such as a person in that class of life would be fond of." "She was in a position that many women in that rank of life would aspire to have." Alverstone then reviewed evidence connecting Crippen to the remains; and finally, whether the remains were those of Cora Crippen: he sorted through the pathologists' evidence but also called attention to the curlers wrapped with bleached hair, and remnants of a woman's undervest, "a woman's vest with lace on the arms . . . which, of course, you know only adorns the garments of women who like that sort of adornment."[51]

In his Charge to the Jury, Alverstone transformed testimony of a warm, affectionate woman inconvenient to an adulterous husband to suggest a slatternly termagant who was understandably (if not, under law, excusably) murdered. What Alverstone expressed with at least some restraint, Filson Young's influential narrative made explicit. In Young's story, the salient points for understanding the crime came entirely from Belle's background and purported character. Her Eastern European lineage marked her vulgarity, her appetites, her morality, and her delusions. Her "exceptional liveliness" was only loud vulgarity. The Music Hall Guild appealed "to the impulsive kindness of heart which is characteristic of people of her type." With no talent or charm, she sought attention with clothes and jewels to secure "her little social triumphs among her friends" who apparently shared her "florid taste." Her public display attempted to mask the private "squalid existence described by Mrs. Harrison." However, her "inordinate vanity" soon turned ugly with shows of "violent temper" toward her peaceful, indulgent husband. He found "something like repose" with Le Neve, the "quiet, reserved, attractive girl." Belle's public vulgarity was trial enough, but far worse, it signaled a private vulgarity of appetite: "Mrs. Crippen's former manner of life and her popularity with a certain class of men must have familiarized her with ways in which she could be easily independent of her husband." Indeed, "We must remember what she had been and what she was . . . her vanity, her extravagance, her shrewishness had long worn out" the little man who "was not a robust man . . . She, on the other hand, was robust and animal. Her vitality was of that loud, aggressive, and physical kind that seems to exhaust the atmosphere round it." What could a man pushed to the brink do? In extremity, Crippen followed his nature when he bought hyoscine: " – always considerate, you see, even in the weapon he used to kill his wife. He had decided it would be better that she should cease to exist; and his ingenuity and consideration combined hit upon the most merciful and the safest poison he could have used."[52]

"THE VERY ODOUR OF CHIVALRY"

At the heart of the Crippen case is the effort to redefine middle-class masculinity through the determined classing of feminine sexuality. Peculiarly, Crippen becomes the more heroic as his sexual appetites and performance are reduced to an appropriately modest level. Disembodied and etherealized, a nobler passion merged abstractions of love and honor to replace vulgar desire. Belle's purported sexual rapacity was symptomatic of her class and ethnicity. Far less demanding of the middle-class man was Ethel, the appropriately nervous and debilitated typewriter, poised to rise from rather sordid origins because she – the androgynous child delighting in the lark of dressing as a boy – had never been infected by voluptuous distortions of real femininity. She also understood the higher values of property. Unlike Belle, a woman of undiscriminating excess, Ethel saw the principles of tasteful selection. Thus Le Neve had not invaded their middle-class domesticity; Cora Crippen – as Belle Elmore – had forfeited it. With middle-class values, as her autobiography approximated them, and with Mrs. Harrison's catalog of Belle's dereliction, Ethel was an entitled usurper. She had learned the restraint and self-congratulation of the middle-class connoisseur to distinguish herself from the lower-class gourmand. In sex as in goods, less is more.

Belle and Ethel, whether appalling or suitable, were finally object lessons of the difficult demands women, of whatever variety, placed on men: they inappropriately insisted on mattering in the delicate balance between masculine sexuality and gentlemanly manliness – a balance more comfortably managed as an abstraction. If for men, the public and the private were posited as legitimately coherent, in the Crippen case, they had been placed disastrously at odds. A man's uncomplicated symmetry between public and private realities was skewed by the two Belles, a private slut and a public matron, but equally by two Ethels, the bustling private hausfrau and the weary public drudge. The stoic man of honor who maintained a gentleman's silence had cruelly been placed by circumstances in a tragic dilemma: women's "natural" aptitude for performativity ultimately disrupts the continuity of the private and the public. Crippen's crime, to replace Belle with the "real" Ethel, was an act to restore the fiction of the continuity.

The players, Cora and Ethel, had quarreled over Crippen's sexuality: one woman found herself doomed to little; another more appropriately was content with little. Indeed, a good part of the narrative task was the assertion of how much is enough. In the most exaggerated version,

Crippen was "the victim of a double demand to which the poor little man's frail physique and advancing years rendered him unequal."[53] Under assault, masculinity was reasserted and reclaimed, not as measured by women's demands, but by equating vulgar physical desire with the lower class, and spiritualizing middle-class love to equate its disembodied "truth" with virtue.

In the Crippen case, the spiritualized manliness of the beleaguered New Man was a patently defensive restoration; Crippen's gesture was seen as a strike at the unnatural enfeeblement of men cowed by women's demands. Only the undemanding woman permitted men, unfettered, to define abstractions of manliness; and better yet, provided occasions for gestures of protective, honorable, manly sacrifice. The defensive construction of Crippen, however, would soon take on aggressive confidence in Modernist representations vaunting the beleaguered but (at heart) valiant antihero. In 1910, the construction of Crippen was a start.

NOTES

1. Novels based on the Crippen case appear with some regularity. See Catherine Meadows' *Dr. Moon* (1934); Ernest Raymond's *We, the Accused* (1935); Ursula Bloom's *The Girl Who Loved Crippen* (1954); Richard Gordon's *A Question of Guilt* (1981); Peter Lovesey's *The False Inspector Dew* (1982). In addition to numbers of memoirs, book-length retellings include Max Constantine-Quinn's *Doctor Crippen* (1935); Michael Gilbert's *Dr. Crippen* (1953); Tom Cullen's *Crippen: the Mild Murderer* (1977). The case appears regularly in popular compendia of famous crimes, beginning with the reprint of the trial transcript in the British Notable Trials series (1920); Filson Young's introduction has been reprinted in John Mortimer's collection, *Famous Trials* (1984). Michael Hardwick includes Crippen in *Doctors on Trial* (1961); Alan Dershowitz has revisited the case with an introduction and notes to a special edition of a trial reprint (1991). Crippen and LeNeve earn an improbable place in George Melly's *Great Lovers* (1981). The case has inspired a number of plays; the first, a one-act, "Tracked by Wireless," opened in London the same day as Crippen's trial. More ambitiously, a musical comedy, *Belle, or the Ballad of Dr. Crippen* opened in 1961, but closed in six weeks. In pre-*Sweeney Todd* days, reviewers found it in bad taste. In 1962, a film, *Dr. Crippen*, was released, starring Donald Pleasance, Coral Browne, and Samantha Eggar.
2. Newspaper accounts referenced, unless otherwise indicated, are reproduced in Jonathan Goodman's compilation, *The Crippen File* (London: Allison and Busby, 1985).

3. See Tom Cullen, *Crippen: the Mild Murderer* (London: Bodley Head, 1977), 185.
4. *Daily Graphic*, 19 Oct. 1910.
5. King Edward VII died on 6 May 1910; Charles Rolls (partner to Royce) had been the first Englishman to fly round trip without touching down to France, and at an aeronautical exhibition at Bournemouth was the first Englishman killed in a flying accident. Arthur Munby's secret master–slave marriage to maid-of-all-work Hannah Cullwick was exposed following publication of his will. In the first week of July 1910, the newspapers were filled with the scandal. A week later Crippen and Le Neve hit the headlines; the discovery of the remains in the coal cellar was reported 14 July 1910. Labor unrest in 1910 was severe with strikes among dockworkers, coalminers, ironworkers, on the railways, and in the textile trades. From April through July, increasingly heated Home Rule debates in Parliament reflected violent confrontations in Ireland. On 18 June, an estimated 10,000–15,000 women marched in support of a suffrage bill introduced four days before; on 23 July, following the second reading of the bill, 12,000–20,000 marched and gathered in Hyde Park. See Hannah Cullwick, *The Diaries of Hannah Cullwick, Victorian Maidservant*, ed. and intro. Liz Stanley (London: Virago, 1985), 6–7; Sir George Clark, *The Illustrated History of Britain* (New York: British Heritage Press, 1983), 257; and Lisa Tickner, *The Spectacle of Women: Imagery of the Suffrage Campaign, 1907–1914* (Chicago: University of Chicago Press, 1988), 112–19.
6. Peter Ackroyd, *T.S. Eliot: a Life* (New York: Simon, 1984), 143, and Goodman, *Crippen File*, 197.
7. Sir Edward Marshall Hall quoted in Cullen, *Crippen: the Mild Murderer*, 143.
8. Sidney Theodore Felstead, *Sir Richard Muir: a Memoir of a Public Prosecutor* (London: John Lane, 1927), 116, 117.
9. Sir Travers Humphreys, *Criminal Days* (London: Hodder and Stoughton, 1946), 113.
10. Quoted in *The People*, 23 April 1933.
11. Edward Marjoribanks, *The Life of Sir Edward Marshall Hall* (London: Gollancz, 1934), 279.
12. Frederick W.F. Smith, 2nd Earl Birkenhead, *F.E.: the Life of F.E. Smith, First Earl of Birkenhead* (London: Eyre and Spottiswoode, 1959), 101.
13. Cullen, *Crippen: the Mild Murderer*, 143, 178, and Goodman, *The Crippen File*, 8.
14. Filson Young, ed., *The Trial of Hawley Harvey Crippen*. Notable British Trials Series (London: Hodge, 1920), p. xxxii.
15. George and Weedon Grossmith's *Diary of a Nobody* first ran in *Punch* and was then published separately in 1892. With affectionate condescension their 'diary' enshrined Mr. Pooter as the quintessential North London lower middle-class clerk. Like Crippen, he lived in Holloway.
16. Young, *Trial*, p. xxxiii; Douglas G. Browne and E.V. Tullett, *Bernard Spilsbury: His Life and Cases* (Harmondsworth: Penguin, 1955), 39.
17. Birkenhead, *Life of F.E. Smith*, 102.
18. See e.g. Wells' *Ann Veronica* (1909) in which Ann flees a suburb to find work in London but discovers she would need clerical training – and

would earn an unliveable wage. Gissing's earlier *Odd Women* (1893) concerns, in part, a clerical training school for the daughters of educated people.

19. G.K. Chesterton, *What's Wrong with the World* (New York: Dodd, 1910), 166–7.
20. Elizabeth Baker's *Chains* (1909) concerns the stresses of lower middle-class marriage and women's retail clerking as an unsatisfactory alternative; *Miss Tassey* (1910) focuses on a woman who has been fired at age 45 as too old for 'counter-work'; *Lois* (*c.* 1920) concerns women in a typing pool; *Miss Robinson* (1918) is the story of an MP's private secretary. Elizabeth Robins is best known for *Votes for Women* (1907); Cicely Hamilton's *Diana of Dobson's* (1908) is set among women clerks living in a retail shop's dormitory. For discussions of Edwardian feminist theatre, see Vivien Gardner and Susan Rutherford, *The New Woman and Her Sisters: Feminism and Theatre, 1850–1914* (Ann Arbor: University of Michigan Press, 1992).
21. G.P. Gooch, *Edwardian England* (London: Ernest Benn, 1933), 28.
22. In the color-coded maps in Booth's *Life and Labour of the People in London* (1902–4), the streets of Hampstead are virtually all red-lined to indicate unmixed "well-to-do"; Le Neve lodged on Constantine Road, one of the few streets marked "Poverty and Comfort (mixed)" (Third Series: *Religious Influences: London North of the Thames: the Outer Ring* [volume 1]).
23. Ethel Clara Le Neve, *Ethel Le Neve: Her Life Story with the True Account of Their Flight and Her Friendship for Dr. Crippen* (London: Cowes, 1910), 10.
24. *News of the World*, 7 Aug. 1910.
25. Young, *Trial*, 201, 202.
26. Birkenhead, *Life of F.E. Smith*, 105.
27. Le Neve, *Life Story*, 6.
28. Ibid., 6.
29. Ibid., 8, 9–12.
30. Ibid., 21, 23–4.
31. Ibid., 20–2.
32. The diminution of both Crippen and Le Neve is persistent in newspaper reports where they are "tiny," "pathetic," "pitiful." Crippen was in fact relatively short – 5'5", but Le Neve was a few inches taller, not particularly tiny for a woman. Nor did she have a child-like body; her hips quickly split the seam of her boy's trousers, and their Belgian hotelier quickly saw through her disguise precisely because of her too-curvaceous body. Similarly, Smith's image of the "young, inexperienced girl" shaded the fact that Le Neve was then 27.
33. *Daily Express*, 15 July 1910; *Daily Mail*, 18 and 25 July 1910.
34. Le Neve, *Life Story*, 46–52.
35. Ibid., 54–8.
36. Le Neve remained in Toronto working as a typist as "Miss Allen" for four years. In 1911, she was granted probate of Crippen's estate, valued at £268. Her application for Cora's estate was turned down, and granted to Cora's sister Mrs. Theresa Hunn. Goodman indicates that in 1914, Le Neve returned to London: Cullen dates her return as 1916. According to

Goodman she used the name Ethel Clara Harvey (95); according to Cullen, she was Ethel Nelson (199). Both agree that she worked as a typist in a London furniture store where she met and married Stanley Smith; they lived in Croydon, and had two children. She died Ethel Clara Smith in 1967 (death certificate reprinted in Goodman, *Crippen File*, 95).

37. In his introduction to the Notable British Trials transcript, Filson Young (wholly confused in his chronology) broadly mistypes the Guild women in attributing their distress to their hopes that Belle would have willed pieces of jewelry to them. *Trial*, p. xxix. However, at the time of the dinner, Belle was to their knowledge only away on business.
38. *Daily Mail*, 18 July 1910.
39. Crippen's son by his first marriage had been adopted by Crippen's parents immediately after Crippen's wife, due within days to deliver their second child, died in Salt Lake City in 1892 of "apoplexy." In July, Crippen moved to New York where he met, and in less than two months, married the 18-year-old Cora. Newspapers gave only a brief flutter of attention to this earlier unexpected death, and did not remark Crippen's remarkably distant, if not nonexistent, interest in his son.
40. In *I Caught Crippen* (1938), Dew does not mention the Guild women's visit that he had ignored four months earlier.
41. Cullen elaborates Young's nastiness about the Guild women with a long flight of fancy characterizing "these demiurges" as avenging Furies who "proceeded to harry Crippen." *Crippen: the Mild Murderer*, 114.
42. *St. Pancras Chronicle*, 15 July 1910; *Daily Mail*, 16 July 1910.
43. Young, for example, gives over two full pages of his essay to reproducing her account: "I cannot do better than quote some notes of Mrs. Harrison's on the life at Hilldrop Crescent," *Trial*, p. xvii.
44. *John Bull*, 10 Dec. 1910, quoted in Young, *Trial*, p. xix.
45. See George R. Sims, "Behind the Blinds," in *Living London*, 1902. Reprinted as *Edwardian London*, 4 vols. (London: Village, 1990), 1: 273–8. See also George Gissing, *In the Year of the Jubilee* (1894), a novel of the suburban world of Mrs. Ada Peachey, a slovenly housewife.
46. Young, *Trial*, 21.
47. Young, *Trial*, 18–19. Occupations among Cora's family were also brought out: her father had been a grocer, her half-sister's husband was a soapmaker. Similar (irrelevant) information about Crippen or Le Neve (her father had worked for the railway) was not introduced in either trial.
48. Ibid., 75–6.
49. Ibid., 88.
50. Crippen implies that what he thought was a miscarriage resulted from prior sexual relations, and is vague about the ovariotomy: "I believe that operation was done . . . shortly before we came to England the first time," he testified (*Trial*, 93) – or, almost five years after her sister's testimony on having seen the scar. For the jury, however, it all signaled sexual promiscuity; for contemporary readers it suggests an appalling medical "solution" to whatever (undetermined) problem she had at that age.
51. Young, *Trial*, 165–7, 174.
52. Ibid., pp. xvi–xxvii.
53. Young, *Trial*, p. xxiii.

12 "The Magistrates are Men"[1]: Working-Class Marital Conflict and Appeals from the Magistrates' Court to the Divorce Court after 1895

Gail Savage

Violent conflicts between husbands and wives present a difficult challenge to those charged with maintaining public order. In domestic matters, defining a boundary between properly accorded privacy and discord which poses a threat sufficient to justify official intervention raises complex issues of both principle and practice. Authorities charged with the responsibility of monitoring this boundary – the police and the courts – must evaluate conflicting stories about the particulars of emotionally-charged situations. They necessarily draw upon widely-shared assumptions about gender and class in order to make judgments. The decisions rendered by judicial institutions in turn enforce and reinforce those assumptions, as well as reveal them to our scrutiny. This essay draws upon new evidence about Magistrates' Court proceedings under the 1895 Judicial Proceedings (Married Women) Act and uses documents that preserve rare transcript testimony as the basis for a more nuanced account of experiences of domestic violence that claimed the attention of legal authorities.

In England during the nineteenth century, the problem of domestic violence, in particular the physical assaults perpetrated by husbands upon wives, entered the province of the civil, secular courts with the passage of the 1857 Divorce Act.[2] This legislation recognized such behavior as cruelty that constituted grounds for a judicial separation, or, in conjunction with the husband's adultery, as a grounds for divorce. The Divorce Court created by this legislation proved very inadequate for dealing with the domestic violence seemingly endemic in English society. Its jurisdiction over such cases, nevertheless, played an important role in developing the rules by which legal authorities treated domestic violence.

Legislators who enacted the 1857 Divorce Act took special care to deny the poorer classes ready access to a legal avenue that would afford them an escape from their family obligations for fear that this would lead to a general dissolution of working-class family life. Accordingly, the newly-created Divorce Court sat only in London. This geographical restriction, combined with the substantial expenses associated with legal practice before the High Court, presumably worked to exclude working-class litigants from both the benefits and the temptations of recourse to divorce necessary to obtain the sanction of the state for the termination of a troubled marriage. In the view of some, however, this left the state without sufficient means to regulate family life among the poor, a gap that became more visible when the issue of domestic violence became a matter of public debate.[3] A series of acts passed in the last three decades of the nineteenth century sought to remedy this oversight by granting Magistrates' Courts broad powers to monitor marital relationships, thus providing the state with outposts in neighborhoods and communities throughout the country.[4]

Public debate about the pervasiveness of domestic violence among the working class generated the political impetus to change the law. Frances Power Cobbe's campaign against wife abuse culminated with the passage of the 1878 Matrimonial Causes Act, which empowered Magistrates' Courts to grant separation orders to wives who had been victims of aggravated assault at the hands of their husbands.[5] Such wives could also obtain a maintenance allowance from their husbands and retain custody of their children. Wives thus might be able to avail themselves of the protection provided by law, which would also serve to discipline the behavior of husbands.[6] The 1886 Married Women (Maintenance in Case of Desertion) Act attempted to offer further protection to working-class wives by granting Magistrates' Courts the power to order husbands who had deserted their families to provide for them. This would also serve to relieve the community of the burden of supporting families left destitute by irresponsible husbands. In 1895 the Summary Jurisdiction (Married Women) Act consolidated the provisions of the two preceding statutes.[7]

The public expression of domestic conflict in civil court, previously restricted to a thin trickle by the stringency of the divorce law, rapidly found a readier outlet before the new public forum offered by the

Magistrates' Courts. The annual number of High Court petitions for divorce had remained very small, standing at only 573 in 1895, increasing to 609 in 1900 and remaining below 1,000 until the First World War. At the same time, however, the number of separation applications submitted to Magistrates' Courts had already grown to over 5,000 by 1895, although magistrates granted only about 1,000 of these in 1894 and 1895. After the passage of the 1895 Act applications to Magistrates' Courts increased even more rapidly – to 7,428 in 1896 and 9,553 in 1900, of which 5,400 and 6,661 were granted in those respective years.[8]

Divorce petitions thus represented only a small proportion of those couples seeking judicial recognition of their marital estrangement. This pattern held even during the interwar decades, despite changes in both statute and legal procedure that eased access to the Divorce Court. The average number of divorce petitions for the first three post-war five-year intervals jumped to 3,180 and then climbed to 3,805 and 4,578. The increase in the average number of Magistrates' Courts applications, while not so dramatic (representing a mere 50 percent increase rather than a 300 percent increase) meant that the number of those seeking separations in the Magistrates' Courts continued to run well ahead of the number of those seeking a divorce. Divorces never constituted more than 23 percent of the combined total of marital proceedings during the interwar years, and the number of divorce petitions did not exceed the number of separation applications until after 1950.[9]

The very small number of divorces under English law thus does not reveal some exceptional harmoniousness in English marital relations; rather it reflected the special restrictiveness of English law.[10] Only a tiny fraction of the married couples whose estrangement led them to seek state intervention could afford the price of admission to the Divorce Court. The rest had to make do with whatever redress the Magistrates' Court could provide. Those who had any expertise in the law of marriage and divorce understood this, and the expositions of the statistical reports of the courts' operation with respect to marriage regularly included some reference to the work of the Magistrates' Courts to give a complete picture of the state of English marital relations.[11] After 1878, the English operated a two-tiered judicial system, roughly bifurcated by social class, providing divorce for the middle class and well-to-do and separation and maintenance for abused and deserted working-class wives.[12]

* * *

The work of the Magistrates' Courts adjudicating marital disputes has attracted scholarly attention for at least two reasons. First, this branch of legal practice, by making special provisions for the protection of working-class wives, necessarily bears the imprint of the interaction of class and gender values in the formulation and administration of the law. Second, this litigation opens a window on the emotional dynamics of working-class family life. The exploration of how Magistrates' Courts' proceedings might illuminate these matters has labored under the handicap of an apparent lack of systematic and official documentation of individual cases. Consequently, research on both Magistrates' Courts and working-class marital life has been carried out by utilizing a range of other sources, such as newspaper reports, memoirs of legal and social welfare professionals, working-class oral histories, and the testimony of interested parties to the 1912 Royal Commission on Divorce and Matrimonial Causes. However, a special category of official transcripts of Magistrates' Courts proceedings, lodged among the records of the Divorce Court, provides an opportunity to fill in this gap in the documentary record.

The 1895 Judicial Proceedings (Married Women) Act that consolidated previous legislation governing the granting of separation orders and maintenance allowances to wives also provided for the appeal of the decisions of Magistrates' Courts to the Divorce Court.[13] Very few of the litigants under the 1895 Act took advantage of this opportunity to pursue their cases before the higher court. In 1896, for example, the Divorce Court reviewed ten such appeals, and, during the first fifteen years of the Act's operation, the number of appeals varied from a low of 5 in 1897 to a high of 24 in 1904. These cases, although few in number, nevertheless have great significance for the study of domestic violence and marital relations among working-class families. In order to monitor the judgments taken by the Magistrates' Courts, the Divorce Court required that the lower courts provide the High Court with a complete record of their proceedings.[14] As Judge Jeune explained: "Unless notes are taken and furnished the [1895] Act would be unworkable, for it would be impossible for us, without the notes, to do justice between the parties upon these appeals."[15]

For the most part, Magistrates' Court clerks carried out their duty in this respect, furnishing transcripts of those cases appealed from the local jurisdiction to the High Court. These records remain in the files of the Divorce Court, providing fascinating and detailed glimpses of the domestic lives revealed to the magistrates. The testimony of embattled spouses, along with that of relatives and neighbors, although mediated by the transcription of a court reporter, captures an authentic echo of the voices of those who brought their domestic difficulties before the purview of the magistrates. An examination of a few of the cases documented in such detail will show how they can aid our study of the ways in which gender and class infused legal practice. Similarly, an exploration of these records will add to our knowledge about married life among the working class. In addition, the analysis below will suggest how a close study of these cases will also contribute to our understanding of the historical dimensions of the experience of domestic violence.

In many respects the case of *Pinfield* v. *Pinfield* conforms to our expectations about the dynamic interaction of the various levels of conflict acted out in the Magistrates' Courts. In January 1903 Sarah Jane Pinfield filed a petition of appeal before the High Court after her petition for a separation order had been refused by the petty sessions of the Magistrates' Court at Bromsgrove, Worcester the previous December. Sarah Jane, who worked as a dressmaker, married Edgar Pinfield, a wagon repairer, in March 1900. At the time of her appeal the young couple, husband and wife both 22 years old, had two children. Sarah Jane told the Magistrates that the two had done fine together for the first six months of their marriage, but that then Edgar began to stay out late. When she spoke up about this, her husband responded angrily. As the records state, he "started cursing and swearing, threatened to smash brains, wished he was not married." He also questioned the paternity of the children and then withheld food in order to starve her into leaving.

Sarah Jane did not tolerate this treatment for long. She had a solicitor prepare a separation deed, but when she presented it to her husband he refused to sign it. When she pressed him, he:

> took his coat off and caught me by throat until I was exhausted. He said he would strangle me ... he then went out and came back locking door & caught me. 2 hands round my throat causing me pain squeezing me. He said if I had not got to swing for it I would do it. Caught me again round throat holding me tight & said "I hate the sight of you." Caught me by arm and dragged me up stairs.

After this incident, Sarah Jane went to see her parents and her solicitor. They unanimously advised her to leave her husband, and she immediately did just that.

The issues generating conflict between the couple became clearer in the course of Sarah Jane's cross-examination. First, Sarah Jane did not think that Edgar was contributing enough money to the household. She testified that he "never gave me enough to keep him going had as low as six and seven shillings" and that, while she paid the rent, "he never bought anything for home." In addition, she told the magistrates: "I object to his playing football & my father does not like it."

The testimony of Sarah Jane's neighbor, Emily Arbour, tended to corroborate Sarah Jane's rendering of these events. She described the relationship between the Pinfields as full of conflict, saying that she:

> Saw Pinfield about every day heard him use very bad language to her in the house. Heard him say he would knock her brains out with a poker. He hoped she would be dead when he came home & he would dance on her chest. Every time he came in he was unpleasant to her. 5th midnight husband woke and heard bumping up Pinfield's stairs & banging of door as though someone had been dragged up.

Although the wording of the questions is not transcribed, Emily Arbour's responses to cross-examination show the questioner establishing the limits of what she had actually witnessed. Emily Arbour did not see an assault, observed no marks on Sarah Jane, and did not hear any call for help. She remained unshaken about her interpretation of events, however, saying that if Pinfield "had not meant it he would not have said it."

The testimony of William Arbour provided an interesting contrast to his wife's version of events. William agreed that Pinfield stayed out late and used bad language to his wife. He recalled Pinfield once denying that he was the father of his children, and he described hearing bumping noises that one night. He did not, however, draw any conclusions about all this. Under cross-examination, William described Pinfield as "a hard working man," who was "civil to me."

Finally, the court heard Edgar Pinfield's testimony. He told the court that he always gave all his wages to his wife, but that they did not always amount to as much as she thought they should. In his view, "football cause of offense," and he was "prepared to take wife back & find home & give up football." He denied that he used bad language, and he admitted that the children were his. Under cross-examination, he declared:

> Do not want to be separated never told her to go. All untrue what she said & Mrs. Arbour. Untrue I wished her dead. She carried pillows upstairs. Always left club 1/2 past or just before. Never said they were not my children. Never threatened her.

The magistrates refused to issue a separation order because of insufficient evidence to establish persistent cruelty. The Divorce Court never made its own ruling, because the Pinfields reconciled before the case came before the judge.

The particulars in the case of *Bonfield* v. *Bonfield* resemble the Pinfields' situation. In this instance the husband instituted appeal proceedings after the wife obtained a separation order and maintenance before the Court of Summary Jurisdiction in Hertford in October 1902. Louisa Sarah married Albert Bonfield in 1901, and, at the time of the separation, they had one child, a daughter born 24 July 1902. Her description of the incident precipitating her departure shows the same pattern of wifely resistance and husband's violence that was exhibited by the conflict between the Pinfields. According to Louisa Sarah's account of events:

> I saw my husband when I put the baby to bed. He had been to his mother's all that day both to dinner and tea. He followed me upstairs and said he wanted cocoa. I told him to go where he had been all day. He said if you don't go out of the room I'll knock you out. I said I was going to stop upstairs. He then took me by the shoulders and pushed me out. I had to take hold of the banister, or I should have fallen down. He then pushed me down into a chair in the front room. He then put me outside I said "Now you have put me out I'll stop out." He then pulled me in again, and stuck me in the mouth and caused my lips to swell. They were very painful. He also struck me with a book across the face, I cried out he put his hand over my mouth to prevent me calling out. My brother came to the back window while I was calling out. I did not leave that night on account of my baby... I left him on the Monday morning, on account of his ill-using me.

Louisa Sarah went on to recount other violent incidents, including his threat that if she applied for a separation order "his first payment would be a pistol and a piece of lead." In her cross-examination Louisa Sarah blamed the couple's problems on the interference of her husband's family and denied ever threatening her husband with a poker or a knife.

The testimony of Mrs. Lilian Woodgate, a neighbor, tends to support the wife's account. According to Mrs. Woodgate, although she never saw Albert Bonfield strike his wife, he did put his fist in her face. With respect to the central incident in the case, she reported to the court:

> I had gone to bed on the 21st September I heard Mr. Bonfield in a violent temper he said if you don't come down I'll knock you down. There was a lot of screaming. It lasted 1/4 of an hour. The next morning Mrs. Bonfield showed me her lips and face, they were very much swollen. I am very glad they have gone.

During cross-examination, Mrs. Woodgate added: "I have never seen him strike her. They lived very unhappily. I think there is next to no fault on the wife's side. Perhaps the incident of the cocoa was not quite the right thing."

Albert Bonfield, for his part, denied everything. He claimed that he never struck or bruised his wife, although he accused his wife of "smacking" his face more than once. He did admit pushing his wife. Obviously, the court did not find this convincing, because they granted his wife a separation order and custody of the child and gave her a maintenance allowance of 14s a week. In addition, they charged Bonfield with 15s costs. Bonfield appealed the court's decision but did not pursue his case, so the legal record does not allow us to see how the Bonfields' story played out.[16] Although the extant record of their marriage does not provide us with as much information about them as does that of the Pinfields, the roles of both family and neighbors and the dynamic of conflict and violence between the spouses exhibit strong similarities.

These two cases manifest many elements of working-class family life that have recently become more familiar to us,[17] both in terms of the issues that generated the conflict between the two sets of spouses and the way each acted out that conflict. Disagreements over Edgar Pinfield's contribution to the household and his involvement with football sparked his violent behavior. The testimony of the Bonfields highlights the incident of the wife's refusal to prepare her husband a cup of cocoa. In both cases, the sharp disjunction between the husband's and wife's roles in the household provided occasions for conflict that escalated to violence. This accords with recent scholarship on English working-class family life, which exhibited both a great precision and a great rigidity in its definition of spousal roles in material situations that made it very difficult to live up to the expectations these roles enjoined on both partners.[18] Low wage levels and uncertain employment could not generate sufficient resources for either the husband or wife to succeed fully in carrying out their responsibilities: his to support the family and hers to keep the house. Such a setting would not only generate conflict; it would define that conflict as zero-sum.[19]

The interventions of neighbors and family in these two cases complicates our understanding of how gender loyalties operated in working-class communities. Emily Arbour evinced concern for Sarah Jane's well-being and indignation at Edgar Pinfield's behavior, but William Arbour avoided addressing that aspect of the situation. He focused instead on the question of Pinfield's respectability in using such bad language not heard "down our part before."[20] Mrs. Woodgate lent her support to Louisa Bonfield at the same time that she expressed her distress at her proximity to the quarreling couple. Neighbors thus reinforced the conflict between the spouses, with female neighbors testifying in support of the wives and men supporting the husbands. This conforms to our understanding of the homosociality of working-class neighborhoods.

The familial solidarity expressed by Sarah Jane's father and Louisa Sarah's brother, both of whom intervened in defense of their daughter/sister against their son-in-law/brother-in-law contrasts with the gender solidarity exhibited by each young couple's neighbors. Indeed, the bad feeling between the two families related through the Bonfields escalated to the point that the wife's mother had been convicted of assaulting the husband's mother before Louisa Sarah Bonfield filed a petition for a separation from her husband. Family loyalties could thus overlay and even supersede gender loyalties. Taken together, however, the cross-cutting connections of gender and familial loyalties served to exacerbate the conflict between the spouses, each of whom found partisans to help them sustain their opposed views of events.[21]

These two cases also illustrate the energy and resilience of working-class wives in the face of their husbands' coercive behavior. Each woman clearly stood up for herself – objecting to behavior she found unacceptable in a husband and demanding that he live up to his responsibilities. They both sought help – from family, neighbors, legal advice, or the court system – when they needed it, and Louisa Sarah won her case before the local magistrates. Sarah Jane did not persuade the magistrates of the merit of her case, and we lose sight of her when a reconciliation takes her out of the legal system. This was a common conclusion to such cases, but Sarah Jane Pinfield's brief appearance in the legal record establishes her resourcefulness. Although we must regard the trajectory of her future life as uncertain – Edgar's temper might worsen and he might eventually wear her down – we can also easily imagine Sarah Jane's continuing resistance and her successfully negotiating a satisfactory married life for herself. Both women showed themselves capable of the vigor and resolve to try to give as good as they got that Ellen Ross thought typical of working-class wives managing their lives in a culture that regarded open conflict between husband and wife as a normal state of affairs.[22]

Recognizing this, however, should not lead us to forget that in at least one crucial way, Louisa Sarah and Sarah Jane did not stand on an equal footing with their husbands. Neither could hope to emerge unscathed from a physical altercation with their husbands, and, when things came to that, each suffered physical injury. The choking and hitting were perpetrated by their husbands, and, in the moment, these wives could do little but wait for a more opportune moment to protect themselves for the future.

The chief elements of the situations that drove both Sarah Jane Pinfield and Louisa Sarah Bonfield to seek protection from their husbands bear a strong resemblance to one another. Nevertheless two different sets of magistrates came to diametrically opposite decisions. The level of violent conflict between the Pinfields revealed by the testimony, although clearly a serious concern for Sarah Jane as well as her family and friends, did not appear to the Bromsgrove court as sufficient to justify separating the couple. The experience of the Pinfields thus did not exceed the boundaries of what some magistrates might regard as "normal" married life among working-class couples. The Bonfields' situation presented a very similar situation to the Hertford magistrates, but they chose to intervene where their Worcester colleagues had not. Clearly, some on the bench thought there existed sufficient evidence to merit taking action where others did not.

Violence among intimates within the home had long enjoyed exemption from judicial intervention – "an area where the force of law meddled little with the law of force."[23] The passage of new laws created the necessary precondition for intervention, but of course the efficacy of the law depended upon the willingness of both police and legal professionals to enforce it. The identification of the law itself with a masculine perspective and its enforcement by institutions staffed exclusively by men, however, raises doubts about whether the justice system might really offer wives effective protection from their husbands.[24] This worry, understandable as it might be, depends upon a too-simple formulation of how gender might actually express itself through the law and its administration.

An evaluation of the law's efficacy must depend on an understanding of the goals sought by enacting new statutes. The laws passed by Parliament in 1878 and 1895 did not govern "domestic violence" in general and did not seek to eliminate all violence in the home. Rather the new statutes sought to curb wife abuse – to protect wives from husbands who took undue advantage of their authority as husbands. In other words, male legislators sought to regulate the behavior of other (presumably working-class) men with respect to their wives. In doing so these laws upheld the authority of some men over other men by defining some male behavior as unacceptable, thus further legitimating the authority of those men who conformed to acceptable standards of husbandly conduct. The law thus offered protections to women as wives that men as husbands did not enjoy – much to the frustration of those who saw the law as the partisan of women rather than of men.[25] Consequently, the magistrates who adjudicated these cases would always uphold male authority, no matter what occurred in a particular case – whether they chose to regard some husband with sympathy because of the provocation they thought he had suffered or whether they chose to offer the protection of the law to his battered wife.

Examples of both perspectives abound. For instance, H.L. Cancellor, who served as a magistrate in the Marlborough Street Police Court after the First World War, recalls a woman who appeared before him "bruised and black," complaining that "her husband had assaulted her with a frying-pan." The husband, under questioning, explained that he had hit his wife when he discovered that she had pawned his best pair of pants. Cancellor cites this as an example of the cases that he heard where "the assault has been trivial and the provocation strong."[26] On the other hand, hearing such cases could also inspire a lifetime career of striving to achieve further reforms to protect wives, as in the case of Justice Claud Mullins.[27]

Undertaking an assessment of which point of view most commonly prevailed presents some difficulties. For instance, although all the petitions filed under the 1878 and 1895 laws would represent wives' appeals for protection, it was very common practice to divert such litigation by referring estranged couples to court missionaries who sought to achieve a reconciliation. It would be very difficult to know how many suits of merit were thus deterred. Once they reached the courts, however, these suits enjoyed a success rate of 67 to 70 percent, which, of course made them much better than a fifty-fifty proposition for the aggrieved wives. This success rate approximated the one enjoyed by wives who filed for divorce, although other evidence suggests that the husband's view of the case might stand a somewhat better chance of receiving a sympathetic hearing from the magistrates than from the judges of the High Court.

The case of *Mellor* v. *Mellor*, one especially well-documented, sheds some light on these questions. The Mellors, who had been married 21 years at the time of Sarah Mellor's 1898 application for a separation, came from a much different social setting than either the Pinfields or the Bonfields. They also had much greater financial resources at their disposal, since Sarah Mellor had inherited considerable property and money from her family. The couple began their life together in 1879 when she came into a legacy of £200, and the couple lived on and worked a farm whose lease had long been held by Sarah's father. Both husband and wife had several hundred pounds in savings, as well as income derived from bonds and rentals.

In her testimony, Sarah Mellor detailed a long history of abusive and drunken behavior on the part of her husband, Ben Mellor. In 1896, Sarah had dropped proceedings for a separation when her husband had signed a memorandum promising to treat her and their children "properly" and to refrain from assaulting or ill-treating them. This turned out to be a promise he could not keep. Sarah's testimony depicted a home life in constant turmoil as a consequence of Ben's propensity for violence. Wife and children did their best to protect one another from his outbursts. Sarah often sought shelter in her daughter's room, and sometimes they all fled to a neighbor's house. In another instance, Sarah reported: "On the 10th March the def. was striking my daug[hter] Lizzy and I pulled him away from her and he struck me up the arm & on the shoulder and he put me out of the house & told me to go."

Both daughters, an employee, and a local friend all corroborated Sarah Mellor's testimony. In a poignant twist to the story, Ben Mellor's chief complaint turns out to be that his family hated him and did not want him, which might well have been so – understandably so in light of his behavior. Despite this range of evidence, the magistrates who heard the case for the Petty Sessions Division of Upper Agbrigg in the West Riding of Yorkshire, remained unmoved by Sarah Mellor's plight. They concluded: "We have considered this case and we think it a pity the parties have not come to terms, they ought to have arranged to live amicably together and in our opinion the case should never have been brought before the Court. It is dismissed."

The local magistrates dismissed Sarah Mellor's case on May 24, 1898. On June 14 we find her filing a notice of appeal in the Divorce Court. The judges heard her appeal on July 5. (This is very fast work for the Divorce Court. A typical divorce case took at least 18 months to reach a conclusion.) Mrs. Mellor's legal counsel, John Herbert Turner, explained to the High Court that her case had been assigned to temporary magistrates pressed into service because of a heavy case load and that they had not allowed him to present all the evidence relevant to the case. Sir Francis Henry Jeune, the President of the Divorce Court, and Sir Gorell Barnes, recognized the force of this argument and allowed the appeal. They "ordered that the said refusal of the Justices be set aside and further ordered that the said Sarah Mellor be no longer bound to cohabit with the husband the said Ben Mellor on the ground that he has been guilty of persistent cruelty to her."[28] In this judgment, Judge Jeune disciplined not only Mr. Mellor, but also the magistrates who had acted improperly by failing to recognize the validity of Mrs. Mellor's claim for protection.

The Mellor case suggests that Magistrates' Courts might have served a somewhat socially more varied clientele than generally assumed. Sarah Mellor clearly could afford to go to the Divorce Court – indeed, she immediately did just that with her appeal. Her original case against her husband rested solely on the cruelty charges, however, which would have been insufficient to obtain a divorce in any case. Other lower-middle and middle-class wives might well have chosen to pursue this much less expensive legal avenue to a separation.

The level of violence authorities could accept before perceiving a threat to public order must have varied from one jurisdiction to another. In the three cases above, only the magistrates of Hertford responded favorably to a wife's application for a separation, even though the description of the successful plaintiff's situation, that of Louisa Sarah Bonfield, does not appear to have been more dangerous than that of Sarah Pinfield. Indeed, from the record it seems that Sarah Mellor lived in a much more dire and continuously threatening situation; nevertheless she encountered a totally unsympathetic response from local magistrates. An examination of a sufficiently large number of these cases might help to define the parameters of both these somewhat different categories of variability. The cases at hand do suggest, however, that Magistrates' Courts accepted a higher level of violence before acting to protect the wife than the Divorce Court, which, as James Hammerton has shown, exhibited much less toleration for such behavior on the part of middle-class husbands.[29] The possibility of an appeal to the High Court, although not often exercised by litigants, must have served to uphold High Court standards of litigation among magistrates.

The transcript testimony before the Magistrates' Courts in these three cases thus illuminates the degree to which the High Court monitored the lower courts' performance of its duties. These records also reveal much about the dynamic of social interaction between spouses and among neighbors as well as the nature of the interaction between local courts and the larger community. These documents encompass three distinguishable hierarchical layers – husband/wife, local courts/family–community, higher court/lower court.

The examples at hand illustrate the ready and direct expression of conflict that so often seemed to characterize working-class marriage.[30] The transcripts of testimony combined with a record of the outcome of such cases augments our understanding of the position of local courts in the larger community. Magistrates' Courts have been seen as a civilizing force for the working class, bringing a middle-class vision of law and order to bear on everyday life. The responsibility for the administration of the laws governing separation certainly fell under this rubric. The research of Jennifer Davis has shown how the working class and the poor would utilize the courts' offices and resources to resolve disputes and to air grievances.[31] Even these few cases show how spouses, locked in a power struggle, could turn to the court in an attempt to tip the balance one way or the other. In order to achieve success the wife had to establish a claim for protection. In his defense, a husband had to justify his claim to authority. The remarks family members and neighbors offered in testimony often had the air of grievances previously-rehearsed in private. Such a dynamic suggests that the boundary between the public forum provided by these courts and the realm of private life was not hard and fast, or rigid, but rather more like a permeable membrane.

Records such as these give us the raw material with which to grapple with the conundrum of experience understood as part of history.[32] In particular, the transcript testimony of the original cases tried by the magistrates gives us access to the way in which husbands envisioned conflicts and confrontations with their wives. Since under statute these cases began with a wife's charges against her husband, we would expect that his first line of defense would be a denial of their validity. The form of the denials recorded by Bonfield, Pinfield, and Mellor exhibit some telling similarities.

First, each husband offered an uncategorical denial of having subjected his wife to brutal treatment. Pinfield protested to the magistrates: " . . . all untrue what she said & Mrs. Arbour." Bonfield began his testimony by declaring: "I have never struck my wife." Mellor concluded his testimony by claiming: "I did not treat my wife badly altho these two men swear so." Each man then admitted to conflict that included some physical altercation that they described as mutual. Bonfield and Mellor went further with this tack than Pinfield, both claiming that they had been the victim of their wife's violent aggression. Pinfield described an occasion when his "wife had a paper which I wanted out of my pocket. She told me she had it & I caught hold of it & pulled it out." Bonfield, after strenuously denying having ever struck his wife, claimed that his wife had threatened him with a knife and had "smacked my face on several occasions." In spite of this provocation he had "used no force on her," although he did admit: "I have pushed her." Mellor, who faced the unanimity of several witnesses attesting to his violent treatment of his wife, accused her of hitting him with a Bible and accused all the rest of lying.

All three men thus began with their denial of the charges, a logical recourse for them in an adversarial system of justice. They then attributed violent behavior to their wives. By recasting the violence as mutual rather than perpetrated by one (guilty) spouse upon another (innocent) spouse, they undermined one of the key assumptions of an adversarial legal proceeding. In the case of spousal assault, a victim who participates in the crime ceases to be a victim in the eyes of the law. They also sought to redefine what might be understood as violent. The "pulling" admitted to by Pinfield and the "pushing" admitted to by Bondfield fall into this category.[33] These accused husbands thus described situations characterized by mutual, non-violent conflict. Such situations would not come within the purview of the Magistrates' Court but would more properly remain within the realm of private life. This strategy appears to have found an appreciative audience among the magistrates in two out of the three cases at hand. The rebuttals offered by Louisa Sarah's swollen lips or by the sound of Sarah Jane's body thumping on the steps and her vivid memories of near-strangulation lost their efficacy in light of shifting definitions of violent behavior, understood without respect to the injuries inflicted.

The testimony recorded in these transcripts allows us to investigate further the political nature of family life itself.[34] The legal record clearly establishes the political nature of the definition of cruelty, especially when we compare the way in which the Divorce Court handled that charge with respect to middle-class couples to the way in which the magistrates responded to cruel and abusive behavior among working-class couples.[35] Although the separation and maintenance legislation left magistrates responsible for protecting working-class wives from their husbands, magistrates endeavored to accomplish this without either disrupting the marital bond or challenging the more fundamental authority of husbands over wives. These different goals obviously conflicted with one another – and in grappling with that conflict the courts often did not give their protective responsibilities top priority. In contrast, the Divorce Court, under the leadership of a small judicial elite who upheld a very high standard of masculine conjugal behavior, established a clearer mandate to penalize abusive behavior. Violent conflict between spouses thus clearly carried different constructions in different social settings, and in different judicial venues.

These transcripts and the results of the legal proceedings that they record underline the salience and power of the social construction of experience in social processes. In particular, they reveal the complex and uncertain action of concepts of gender and class as jurists and litigants deployed them in particular cases. This evidence also illuminates further the nature of marital conflict in working-class households. Finally, the power of the testimony of embattled husbands and wives resonates with the material impact of violent and abusive behavior on the bodies of the wives who sought the protection of the magistrates. The import of the stories told before the magistrates' bench thus points in two different directions. At the same time that the testimonies of husbands and wives enact conflicting and contending definitions of violent behavior, they also confront us with the experiential core, by itself inchoate but nevertheless intractably present, of social construction.

NOTES

1. Ada Nield Chew, "Assault and Battery" reprinted in *The Life and Writings of Ada Nield Chew*, ed. Doris Nield Chew (London: Virago Press, 1982), 183.
2. Discussions of the passage of the Divorce Act include Margaret K. Woodhouse, "The Marriage and Divorce Bill of 1857," *American Journal of Legal History* 3 (1959): 260–75; Mary Lyndon Shanley, "'One Must Ride Behind': Married Women's Rights and the Divorce Act of 1857," *Victorian Studies* 25 (Spring 1982): 355–76; Dorothy Stetson, *A Woman's Issue: the Politics of Family Law Reform in England* (Westport: Greenwood Press, 1982), 28–50; Lee Holcombe, *Wives and Property: Reform of the Married Women's Property Law in Nineteenth-Century England* (Toronto and Buffalo: University of Toronto Press, 1983), 88–110; Allen Horstman, *Victorian Divorce* (New York: St. Martin's Press, 1985), 56–84; and Gail L. Savage, "'Intended Only for the Husband': Gender, Class, and the Provision for Divorce in England, 1858–1868," in *Victorian Scandals: Representations of Gender and Class*, ed. Kristine Ottesen Garrigan (Athens: Ohio University Press, 1992), 11–42. In addition Keith Thomas, in his classic analysis, "The Double Standard," *Journal of the History of Ideas* 20 (April 1959): 195–216, draws upon the divorce debates as an important source. Shanley and Mary Poovey have each placed their analyses of the divorce debates in a larger context. See Mary Lyndon Shanley, *Feminism, Marriage, and the Law in Victorian England, 1850–1895* (Princeton: Princeton University Press, 1989); and Mary Poovey, *Uneven Developments: the Ideological Work of Gender in Mid-Victorian England* (Chicago: University of Chicago Press, 1988). Lawrence Stone has recently provided an extremely lucid narrative of the passage of the 1857

Divorce Act in *Road to Divorce: England, 1530–1987* (Oxford: Oxford University Press, 1990), 368–82. The role of the Divorce Act in laying the groundwork for the reform of the law of women's property has attracted much attention, but the role of this legislation in the development of civil protections for wives subjected to physical abuse has not been explored.

3. Savage, "Intended Only for the Husband," 12–14.
4. For discussions of the history of the Magistrates' Courts and their role in English class relations see Jennifer Davis, "A Poor Man's System of Justice: the London Police Courts in the Second Half of the Nineteenth Century," *Historical Journal* 27 (1984): 309–35; Paul Johnson, "Class Law in Victorian England," *Past & Present* 141 (Nov. 1993): 147–69; and George Behlmer, "A 'Wiff of Stale Debauch': Summary Justice and Working-Class Marriage," *Law and History Review*.
5. Cobbe's justly famous essay "Wife-Torture in England," *Contemporary Review* 32 (April 1878): 55–87 set the tone of this debate. For Cobbe's career as a feminist see Barbara Caine, *Victorian Feminists* (New York: Oxford University Press, 1992). For Cobbe's role in this episode see C. Bauer and L. Ritt, "'A Husband is a Beating Animal': Frances Power Cobbe Confronts the Wife-abuse Problem in Victorian England," *International Journal of Women's Studies* 6 (1983): 99–118 and "Wife Abuse, Late-Victorian English Feminism and the Legacy of Frances Power Cobbe," *International Journal of Women's Studies* 6 (1983): 195–207.
6. The discussion of how best to treat the problem of wife-abuse included proposals to subject transgressing husbands to physical punishment, in the form of public whipping, as well as the proposals supported by Cobbe, ultimately implemented, to protect victimized wives by allowing them to live apart from their abusive husbands. Laws that provided for such punishment of husbands actually passed into law in some American states. See Elizabeth Pleck, "The Whipping Post for Wife Beaters, 1876–1906," in *Essays on the Family and Historical Change*, eds. Leslie Page Moch and Gary D. Stark (College Station: Texas A & M Press, 1983), 127–49 and David Peterson del Mar, *What Trouble I Have Seen: a History of Violence Against Wives* (Cambridge: Harvard University Press, 1996), 72–96.
7. See Mary Lyndon Shanley, *Feminism, Marriage, and the Law in Victorian England, 1850–1895* (Princeton: Princeton University Press, 1989), 159–76; Maeve E. Doggett, *Marriage, Wife-Beating and the Law in Victorian England* (Columbia: University of South Carolina Press, 1993), 105–34 for accounts of the passage of this legislation.
8. Great Britain, *Judicial Statistics* (Part II – Civil), 1908, 17.
9. Giselda Rowntree and Norman H. Carrier, "The Resort to Divorce in England and Wales, 1858–1937," *Population Studies* 11 (1957–8): table 1, 190.
10. See Gail L. Savage, "Divorce and the Law in England and France Prior to the First World War," *Journal of Social History* 22 (Spring 1988): 499–513.
11. The Introduction to the annual report of Judicial Statistics, Part II (Civil) would often combine the separation orders granted by magistrates with the divorces and judicial separations granted by the Divorce Court in order to arrive at some summary figure of marital breakdown in England. See, for example, "Introduction," *Judicial Statistics*, Part II (Civil), 1908, 17.

12. In practice, this bifurcation was by no means absolute, in that many more working-class litigants managed to find some means to avail themselves of the auspices of the Divorce Court than one might expect given the obstacles thrown in their path. (Savage, "Intended Only for the Husband," 20–3, 35–6; Gail Savage, "The Operation of the 1857 Divorce Act, 1860–1910: a Research Note," *Journal of Social History* 15 (Summer 1983): 103–10.) Conversely, middle-class wives may have taken advantage of what help the Magistrates' Courts offered in numbers greater than we might expect to find. (See below)
13. "Appeals Under the Summary Jurisdiction (Married Women) Act 1895, and Notes of Evidence," *The Law Times* 108 (10 Feb. 1900): 339.
14. *Robinson* v. *Robinson*, L.R. (P), 1898, 153–4.
15. *Cobb* v. *Cobb*, L.R. (P) (1900), 146.
16. PRO, J77/769/3411, *Bonfield* v. *Bonfield*, 1902.
17. See especially Elizabeth Roberts, *A Woman's Place: an Oral History of Working-Class Women 1890–1940* (Oxford: Blackwell, 1984), and Ellen Ross, *Love and Toil: Motherhood in Outcast London, 1870–1918* (Oxford: Oxford University Press, 1993).
18. Ellen Ross, "'Fierce Questions and Taunts': Married Life in Working-Class London, 1870–1914," *Feminist Studies* 8 (Fall 1982): 575–602; idem, *Love and Toil*, 56–90; Roberts, *A Woman's Place*, 110–21; Pat Ayers and Jan Lambertz, "Marriage Relations, Money and Domestic Violence in Working-Class Liverpool, 1919–39," in *Labour and Love: Women's Experience of Home and Family, 1850–1940*, ed. Jane Lewis (New York: Blackwell, 1986): 195–219.
19. The analysis of Ayers and Lambertz in "Marriage Relations, Money and Domestic Violence" makes this dynamic clear. See also the discussion of the wife's and husband's financial roles in Ross, *Love and Toil*, 72–8. You can also see this dynamic in the tensions generated by the role of pawning in working-class family finances. See, for an especially vivid example of this, Ross, "Fierce Questions and Taunts," 590–1.
20. Public Records Office, J77/773/3532, *Pinfield* v. *Pinfield*, 1903.
21. M.P. Baumgartner, "Violent Networks: The Origins and Management of Domestic Conflict," in Richard B. Felson and James Tedeschi eds., *Violence and Aggression: the Social Interactionist Approach* (Washington, DC: American Psychological Association, 1993): 209–31.
22. Ross, "Fierce Questions and Taunts," 592.
23. Deborah L. Rhode, *Justice and Gender: Sex Discrimination and the Law* (Cambridge: Harvard University Press, 1989), 237.
24. See Catherine A. MacKinnon, "Sex and Violence: a Perspective," in *Feminism Unmodified: Discourses on Life and Law* (Cambridge: Harvard University Press, 1987), 85–92 for an eloquent expression of this suspicion.
25. Masculine resentment at the supposed advantages that women enjoyed over men became acute in the 1920s. See, Gail Savage, "'Equality From the Masculine Point of View': the Second Earl Russell and Divorce Law Reform in England," *russell: The Journal of the Bertrand Russell Archives* (Summer 1996): 14–15.
26. H.L. Cancellor, *The Life of a London Beak* (London: Hurst & Blackett, Ltd., 1930), 138–9.

27. Claud Mullins, *Fifteen Year's Hard Labour* (London: Victor Gollancz Ltd., 1948), 125–45. See also George Behlmer's discussion of Mullins' career in his "Wiff of Stale Debauch."
28. PRO, J77/643/9613, *Mellor* v. *Mellor*, 1898.
29. A. James Hammerton, *Cruelty and Companionship: Conflict in Nineteenth-Century Married Life* (London: Routledge, 1992), 132–3.
30. Roberts, *A Woman's Place*; Ross, *Love and Toil*, 56–90; Lambertz and Ayers, "Marriage Relations, Money and Domestic Violence," 195–219.
31. Davis, "A Poor Man's System of Justice," 309–35.
32. I have in mind here the questions raised by Joan Scott in "Experience," *Feminists Theorize the Political*, eds. Judith Butler and Joan W. Scott (New York: Routledge, 1992): 22–40.
33. This continues to be am important question in the discussion of domestic violence. Whether or not one considers behavior such as "pushing" and "shoving" as violent has an enormous impact on an assessment of the scale of domestic violence. See Armin A. Brott, "Battered-Truth Syndrome: Hyped Stats on Wife Abuse Only Worsen the Problem," *Washington Post*, 31 July 1994 and the reply by Karen Davis in Letters to the Editor, *Washington Post*, 19 Aug. 1994. Including the "shoving" category of behavior increases the incidence of domestic violence by 300 percent.
34. Linda Gordon's discussion of the political nature of abusive behavior is most helpful. See her introduction to *Heroes of Their Own Lives: the Politics and History of Family Violence* (London: Penguin Books, 1988).
35. James Hammerton does the best job to date bringing together evidence bearing on both middle-class and working-class marriage in his recent work, *Cruelty and Companionship*.

Index